DATE DUE

4- 28 - 10			

Demco

DISASTER RESPONSE

LIBRARY IN A BOOK

DISASTER RESPONSE

Fred C. Pampel

Facts On File
An imprint of Infobase Publishing

Disaster Response

Facts On File, Inc.
An imprint of Infobase Publishing
132 West 31st Street
New York NY 10001

Library of Congress Cataloging-in-Publication Data
Pampel, Fred C.
    Disaster response / Fred C. Pampel.
        p. cm.—(Library in a book)
    Includes bibliographical references and index.
    ISBN-13: 978-0-8160-7023-7 (alk. paper) 1. Disaster relief.
    2. Emergency management. I. Title.
    HV553.P35 2007
    363.34'8—dc22   2007003666

Facts On File books are available at special discounts when purchased in bulk quantities for businesses, associations, institutions, or sales promotions. Please call our Special Sales Department in New York at (212) 967-8800 or (800) 322-8755.

You can find Facts On File on the World Wide Web at http://www.factsonfile.com

Text design by Ron Montoleone
Illustrations by Accurate Art, Inc.

Printed in the United States of America

MP Hermitage 10 9 8 7 6 5 4 3 2 1

This book is printed on acid-free paper.

CONTENTS

PART III
APPENDICES

PART I

OVERVIEW OF THE TOPIC

CHAPTER 1

INTRODUCTION TO
DISASTER RESPONSE

The images of the disaster brought by Hurricane Katrina in August and September 2005 remain fresh today. They showed water pouring through broken levees and floodwalls, putting most of the city of New Orleans under five to 20 feet of water. As the water rose above their heads, some residents who had stayed at home climbed into their attic, chopped a hole in their roof, sat on top of the house, and waited for someone to pick them up. Tens of thousands in shelters waited for someone to deliver food and water, treat the sick and injured, clear out the dead bodies, and rescue them from the filthy conditions they endured. Hundreds (including well-known reporters) waited for days on a highway overpass above the floodwaters without food and water and in the burning sun, hoping for someone to come and get them.

The victims as well as those watching the images on television wondered: Where is the government? How long will this misery go on? How could this happen? The disaster involved more than the hurricane and flooding of the city. It also involved the feeble response of the government. When thousands died; tens of thousands lacked water, food, and medical supplies; and hundreds of thousands lost their homes, help from the government should have come quickly. Critics called the failure in response a national disgrace.

Today billions of dollars raised through taxes and private donations go to disasters. A large bureaucracy exists solely to prepare for disasters and help victims. And disaster officials are guided by a National Response Plan that promises to create "a cohesive, coordinated, and seamless national framework" to deal with all types of major hazards. The response to Katrina should have been better.

Problems in disaster response in fact predate Katrina. For more than a century, a puzzling tendency to underprepare for disasters has persisted.

3

Some believe that the government bureaucracy inevitably responds clumsily and slowly to sudden events. Others recognize the potential for effective government action but see the need for complete restructuring of the agencies that handle disaster response and for better leadership from elected officials. Still others blame the human tendency to focus on immediate problems and minimize the importance of uncertain future events like disasters.

In any case, with the growing threats of disasters from hurricanes, tornadoes, earthquakes, floods, wildfires, landslides, droughts, blizzards, ice storms, nuclear accidents, terrorist attacks, and chemical spills, helping victims of disasters would seem to be one of the key tasks of the government. As such, it raises several questions. Can the government provide the leadership in disaster response that the public expects and the victims demand? How well have government agencies with responsibility for disaster response done in the past? Will future disasters lead to the kind of death, destruction, and failed relief as Katrina, or will the lessons learned lead to better, more efficient, and timely performance?

WHAT IS A DISASTER?

To evaluate the effectiveness of disaster response, one must first answer the question. What is a disaster? Perhaps surprisingly, experts disagree on an exact definition. In the 1990s, scholars prepared several papers to address this question. The 1998 book based on the papers, *What Is a Disaster*, devotes 22 chapters and 300 pages to describing and debating the disagreements.[1] Another book by the same name followed in 2005 to consider, among other things, how terrorist events fit into definitions of disasters.[2] The disagreements suggest that any brief definition will either include too few or too many types of events. Even so, some common elements appear in most definitions.

A WORKING DEFINITION

A disaster can be defined as an unusual and dramatic event that, in a relatively short time span, causes enough death and destruction as to disrupt normal patterns of living in a community, region, or society. Most often, disasters come from natural hazards relating to the weather—hurricanes, tornadoes, heat waves, droughts, winter storms, and floods—or to geological changes—earthquakes, volcanic eruptions, landslides, and avalanches. Disasters also come from technological hazards, such as the accidental release of radiation from a nuclear power plant, and from willful or intentional events, such as the destruction of cities or landmarks by a terrorist bombing.

These disasters have similarities to natural disasters—they all cause great harm or damage.

Disasters most always have limited durations. Some natural disasters such as a tornado or earthquake and willful disasters such as a terrorist bombing start and end quickly, while others such as hurricanes and floods give more warning and last anywhere from a few days to a few months. However, they all require urgent or immediate action. Other problems such as war, poverty, pollution, and cigarette smoking cause damage but differ from disasters. These problems emerge more slowly, last years and decades, and belong to a different category of harmful occurrences.

Along with causing death and destruction and occurring over a relatively short time span, disasters disrupt the normal functioning and routines of a community, region, or society. A hurricane, for example, closes off streets, communication, regular business, and routine travel. By disrupting normal life, the supply of food and water, and the safety of most homes, a hurricane puts strain on the entire community. Some other kinds of events, although terrible tragedies, do not have the same impact. The deaths of hundreds in a nightclub fire, the sinking of a ship filled with passengers, or the damage to a factory from an explosion do not disrupt the normal functioning of the larger community. These tragedies do not require the same kind of response and recovery as a disaster.

Although useful, this definition blurs along the edges. People differ in the meaning they give to terms such as *damage, duration,* and *disruption.* Debates continue over why one event comes to be called a disaster but another event does not, or why one event gets special disaster funds from the government and another does not. Although imperfect, this definition nonetheless helps distinguish disasters from many other types of negative events.

One other point follows from this definition: All disasters have a social component. On the surface, natural disasters appear to differ from technological or willful disasters in the involvement of humans. Those related to the weather, earth, and water—those stemming from the natural environment—are in one sense uncontrollable by humans. Society cannot stop powerful atmospheric forces and underground shifting of the Earth. In contrast, technological and willful disasters are human-caused, and human action can stop toxic dumping or terrorism. In another sense, however, all disasters are to some extent human-caused. Hurricanes in south Florida, earthquakes in California, and floods in the Midwest have occurred for ages. However, they caused disasters only when human settlements developed in areas of high risk. The growth of population in south Florida, along the coast of California, and on the major rivers of the Midwest, for example, have turned natural events into natural disasters.

Natural, technological, and willful disasters may vary from one another in important ways. Scholars are working to identify similarities and differences in the magnitude of damage, duration of the danger, and amount of disruption caused by different types of disasters.[3] However, all disasters have a social impact on community life as well as a physical impact on people and property.

DISTRIBUTION OF RISK

Partly because of social factors, some areas of the country suffer more from hazards than other areas. California, Texas, and Florida rank highest on an index of hazardousness developed by experts for each state.[4] The South (North Carolina, South Carolina, Georgia, Alabama, Mississippi, Tennessee, Arkansas, Louisiana), Midwest (Oklahoma, Kansas, Missouri, Illinois), and Northeast (Ohio, Pennsylvania, New Jersey, New York) have medium hazardousness. All other states face low hazardousness. Texas and Florida rank high because of their proximity to the Atlantic and Gulf Coasts and the hurricanes spawned there. In addition, their large and densely concentrated populations make hurricanes more damaging than in the rural areas of Mississippi and Louisiana. California is similarly at high risk not only because of earthquakes, wildfires, and mudslides but also because the dense population of the state makes it vulnerable. Far from rare events, disasters occur regularly and repetitively in heavily populated areas.

What disasters most threaten the U.S. population? From 1940 to 2003 (the latest year with comprehensive data on disaster deaths), floods killed the most people (6,836), followed by tornadoes (6,409), hurricanes (2,246), and earthquakes (434).[5] Compared to decades of the late 19th and early 20th centuries, deaths from most disasters have declined.[6] The drop likely indicates the benefits of early warning and mitigation. However, the most recent deaths from the 9/11 terrorist attacks and Hurricane Katrina have moderated the downward trend.

Unlike deaths, economic damage caused by disasters has increased dramatically. Floods cause the most damage to property and crops, followed by hurricanes and tornadoes. The costs have grown exponentially. The average annual losses per 1 million people rose from $20 million in 1974 to more than $1 billion in 1994. In 2005, Hurricane Katrina caused $125 billion in property damage, the most expensive disaster in human history according to the United Nations. The next most expensive natural disaster in the United States, Hurricane Andrew, caused $30 billion in 1992 ($44 billion adjusted for inflation, or in 2007 dollars). The September 11 terrorist attacks cost nearly $80 billion. Disasters to come will certainly break the current records.

How have the nation and the government responded to the death and destruction of disasters? The response has evolved slowly and steadily over time.

EARLY AMERICAN
DISASTERS AND RESPONSE

Compared to Europe, North America has been particularly prone to natural disasters. The continent serves as the meeting place of warm, moist air from the Caribbean and Gulf of Mexico and the dry, cold air from the Arctic. When these air masses collide, severe weather follows. In the words of a historian of natural disasters: "The United States is a prisoner of its own geography ... No nation on earth has more extreme weather phenomena than the United States."[7]

Although Native Americans knew of the danger of severe weather, the ferocity of the storms surprised and scared the new settlers. Europeans had experienced strong storms and flooding on occasion, but nothing compared to the intensity of hurricanes that lashed the eastern coast of the New World. As early as 1495, Christopher Columbus wrote of terrible winds that pulled up trees by their roots. In 1635, only 15 years after the Pilgrims of the *Mayflower* landed at Plymouth Rock, the Great Colonial Hurricane swept through southern New England. Massachusetts governor William Bradford said, "Such a mighty storm of wind and rain as none living in these parts, either English or Indian ever saw."[8]

In 1686, residents of Charles Town (later Charleston), South Carolina, saw a hurricane send ships ashore, blow houses down, and ruin settlements. One resident wrote, "Your Lordships cannot imagine the distracting horror that these united evils plunged us into."[9] The area became a map of devastation, scattered with heaps of trees, fences, and the remains of houses. Having lost their crops and livelihoods, those who survived dreaded the next major storm. At least in the southern part of the United States, hurricanes became the settlers' most fearsome enemy.

Even more than 300 years ago, settlers in South Carolina planned a response to coming storms.[10] They learned to evacuate houses, find caves or pits in which to hide, and, in some extreme cases, tie themselves to trees to keep from being blown away. After the storm, colonists could not count on crop insurance or organized public relief to help deal with their losses, so they found ways to protect themselves. They shipped goods before and after the hurricane season to shield ships and their cargo from destruction. They stopped building three- or four-story houses common in England and replaced them with one-story, wide-framed houses that could better withstand the winds. Landowners with the wealth to cover short-term losses bought out smaller farmers, which led to large plantations in the South. Because of the severe weather, some owners left the country and ran their farms as absentee owners.

The early experiences of American settlers set a pattern in disaster response for most of the history of the country. Along with hurricanes, Americans had to deal with floods, tornadoes, blizzards, and, less commonly, volcanic eruptions, tsunamis, and earthquakes. Communities facing one or more of these disasters largely had to fend for themselves. The response was informal, as no official policies existed. Congress might pass makeshift legislation on some occasions that gave cities or states victimized by a disaster some direct financial assistance or relief from tariffs. No formal policy emerged, however. Fortunately, damage from disasters remained modest because of the small population of the country and its dispersion in small towns and rural areas.

By the late 19th century, however, the dangers of disasters and the need for a response system began to change. The growth of the population and the dense settlement in cities made more people vulnerable to natural hazards. Further, the development of new technology and the growth of industry gave Americans a false sense of protection. City dwellers felt secure against the forces of nature that so worried residents of rural areas. In fact, the worst disasters in the United States occurred at a time of growing cities and new industry. According to one historian, natural disasters killed more people during the period from 1880 to 1930 than in any other period in U.S. history.[11]

A review of these early disasters reveals several themes. First, the disasters combined forces of nature with unwise human action: Fires, winds, floods, and earthquakes led directly to the disasters, but humans (often foolishly) put themselves in harm's way. They created conditions for the spread of fires, left dams in poor repair, located cities in areas prone to natural hazards, and maximized the risks of a disaster. Second, the disaster response relied largely on the volunteer efforts of the local community and on private contributions. Organizations such as the Red Cross helped greatly, but the government played only a small role in disaster management and relief. Third, relief efforts favored more advantaged groups over poor, minority, and immigrant groups. Scandalous treatment of the most vulnerable was the norm rather than the exception. Fourth, for better or worse, citizens pulled together to rebuild and recover. Towns and economic activity arose from the destruction, but the potential for new disasters remained. A brief history of some of the most famous and important U.S. disasters illustrates these themes.

THE FIRES OF 1871

Two deadly fires—one urban and one rural—both occurred on October 8, 1871, in areas near the western shore of Lake Michigan. The more famous of the two, the Great Chicago Fire, killed hundreds, destroyed the city center, and did millions of dollars in damage. The less famous Peshtigo fire in northeastern Wisconsin did more damage. It started as a forest fire but consumed several villages and killed thousands—the deadliest fire in U.S. history. Although unrelated (other than by unusually dry weather in the region), the two fires alerted the country to the risks of this natural hazard and the need for more effective response.

The Great Chicago Fire

In Chicago, legend has it that a cow owned by Mrs. O'Leary, who ran a local dairy business, kicked over a lantern that started the fire. The fire certainly started near her barn in the evening of October 8, but no one truly knows the real cause. The fire spread quickly from one closely built wooden house to another. Aided by strong winds, it moved with surprising speed north and east toward the downtown. There the fire destroyed famous hotels, department stores, government buildings, churches, and theaters. The force of the fire was so strong that it even jumped the Chicago River to burn buildings on the other side. Residents who saw the fire coming moved to parks and beaches, but not all could escape.

After burning all night and most of the next day, the fire was extinguished when the winds slowed and some light rain started. It had destroyed an area about one mile wide and four miles long. The estimated property damage reached $222 million ($3.8 billion today) and left 100,000 of the 300,000 residents homeless. For a fire that size, the death of 200 to 300 people seemed small, but much of the city remained in ruins. The dense concentration of buildings made it hard to stop the fire and overwhelmed the primitive firefighting methods.

The mayor and the city council met afterward in a church outside the burned area. They proclaimed that they would preserve order, relieve suffering, and protect property. According to the Chicago Historical Society, executive orders "established the price of bread, banned smoking, limited the hours of saloons, and forbade wagon drivers from charging more than their normal rates."[12] The mayor also launched a relief committee to organize the distribution of food, supplies, and money. Word of the fire brought contributions from across the country.

With the support of city leaders, the mayor appointed civil war hero Lieutenant-General Philip Sheridan to preserve order in the city. Sheridan, who lived in Chicago at the time, assembled a mix of militia, police, and volunteers to patrol the city. For two weeks after the fire, the city stayed under a form of martial law. To organize relief efforts, the mayor turned to the Chicago Relief and Aid Society. The society organized offices in each district to provide food, clothing, housing, supplies, and vaccinations to those in need. Although some criticized the effort for ignoring immigrant workers, the relief efforts generally received praise.

The destruction of the city center allowed business leaders to start anew in creating a modern city. After three months, the city had constructed many new buildings. Within a year, the most obvious signs of the fire were gone. New buildings used fire-resistant materials, and the system of fire alarms and firefighting improved. The fire was a turning point in the history of the city, allowing it to become one of the most modern, planned, and industrious cities in the country. It was also a turning point for other cities that came to see the need for better fire protection.

The Peshtigo Fire

By 1871, ways of clearing the land in northeast Wisconsin near Green Bay had made it ripe for a forest fire.[13] The logging industry had left piles of unusable brush near its operations, new railroads had left cleared brush by the side, and sawmills had stacked logs, wood, and waste materials nearby. To clear debris, these piles were often set afire and left unattended. Farmers also used burning to make areas usable for farming. The small towns supported by these activities used wood for buildings, boardwalks, and homes.

A dry fall made this material tinder for a fire. Much as they did in the Chicago fire, strong winds on October 8 fanned the flames from small fires in the area. Southwest of the logging and farming town of Peshtigo, a large fire began to spread quickly through the woods. Lighting piles of dry wood and trees, it moved toward the farms on the outskirts of Peshtigo and then into the town itself. The fire became so intense that it created its own winds of up to 80 miles per hour. Families could do nothing but run, trying to reach the nearby Peshtigo River before dying of burns or smoke inhalation. Most did not make it, and the fire moved through the town to burn other areas and towns in the region.

Rain would come the night after the fire but too late to prevent the enormous damage. The fire ended up burning 1,875 square miles, an area twice the size of the state of Rhode Island. Besides Peshtigo, it destroyed 11 other towns. The total number of deaths ranged between 1,200 and 2,500. A newspaper story the next week called the fire a "holocaust of destruction," noting the annihilation of whole towns and the burning to death of whole families.[14] It was the largest natural fire in the history of the United States.

Word of the disaster soon reached the Wisconsin capital of Madison, but the governor and other state officials had left to help with the relief efforts in Chicago. The governor's wife took the initiative to redirect a boxcar of blankets and other supplies from Chicago to Peshtigo. Once word of the tragedy got out, telegrams of support and monetary contributions came from around the country. A committee from Cincinnati visited the area and brought supplies and support. One observer from Cincinnati wrote that too many people were in charge of relief, which slowed rather than aided the efforts.

The Peshtigo fire never got the attention that the Chicago fire did. People sending supplies knew little about the state of Wisconsin and sometimes sent goods to other places in the state unaffected by the fire. In the end, the town of Peshtigo was not rebuilt, and only a small memorial now stands at the location of the town. The fire did lead, however, to changes in forest management. New fire-control policies required logging and railroad companies to follow fire-safety procedures.

THE 1889 JOHNSTOWN FLOOD

The 1889 flood in Johnstown, Pennsylvania, located to the east of Pittsburgh, illustrates the combination of natural forces and human action that lead to the worst of disasters. By 1889, the city had become something of a boomtown, with a population of 30,000. Its location near iron-ore deposits made it a logical place for iron and steel factories. The expanding business attracted laborers and service workers, and the needs of the growing population led to new housing, roads, and stores. Along with its growing prosperity, residents also enjoyed the beautiful mountains that surrounded the town.

The location of the city brought some problems, however. Johnstown was centered on a floodplain between two rivers. During heavy rains, the rivers would overflow and flood the city. Largely an inconvenience, this flooding did not damage the city permanently. Yet another risk lay 14 miles away in the mountains. Between 1835 and 1853, engineers built a dam some 450 feet high in the mountains. An impressive feat of engineering, the dam created Lake Conemaugh, a reservoir of 20 million tons of water sitting above Johnstown.

The builders of the dam intended to use the lake as a source of water for a canal between Johnstown and Pittsburgh. By the time builders finished the dam, however, new railroads had replaced canals as the main way to move raw materials and products. Making use of the natural beauty of the area, private investors then bought the lake from the state, built cottages around it, and promoted its use for recreation, hunting, and fishing. It became a popular resort for newly rich steel millionaires. Yet the owners did little to repair small breaks in the dam that held back the lake water. Despite warnings of weaknesses in the dam, those responsible assured residents of Johnstown of their safety.

Disaster Response

In May 1889, record rains drenched the area. On May 30, eight more inches fell and filled Lake Conemaugh. By the next day, the pressure of the lake caused new cracks in the dam, which broke at 3:30 P.M. A thunderous roar signaled the break as a 40-foot wall of water and debris began moving at 40 miles per hour toward Johnstown. It crushed houses, carried locomotives in its path, and killed those living in small towns closest to the lake. It took only 10 minutes for the wall of water to reach Johnstown.

Many tried to escape the waters and ended up on a high railroad bridge that withstood the floodwaters. However, the bridge also trapped debris from houses, trees, telephone poles, brush, and oil tanks. The debris then caught fire and killed hundreds more city residents before it could be extinguished three days later. In the end, 2,209 people died, including 396 children. A four-square-mile section of the downtown and 1,600 houses were destroyed, costing an estimated $17 million in property damage—the equivalent of $387 million today.

Word of the disaster spread quickly to the outside world. A train came from Pittsburgh on the morning of June 1, less than 48 hours later, with goods and volunteers. Locals organizing the relief effort put out a call for undertakers and coffins to recover and bury the dead. Residents of nearby cities sent food, supplies, and money for the relief effort. Standard Oil and other companies contributed, as did millionaires Henry Frick and Andrew Carnegie, who belonged to a club on Lake Conemaugh. Even Buffalo Bill Cody organized a benefit in Paris to help the survivors. Citizens of the United States and 18 other countries contributed more than $3.7 million for the relief effort.

Beyond these informal volunteer efforts, Pennsylvania governor James A. Beaver organized government relief. He appointed the Pennsylvania Relief Committee to take over leadership from local residents and called out the militia to assist in the recovery. With up to 10,000 people helping, the effort managed to replace 20 miles of destroyed railroad tracks and opened the city to trains from all directions. He further persuaded President Benjamin Harrison to order army engineers to help with the cleanup. Within six weeks, cleanup efforts had removed all the debris, and by July 9, officials announced that they would rebuild the ironworks mill that the flood had destroyed. By the end of the summer, new prefabricated houses built for the residents who lost their own homes were ready for occupancy.

The American Red Cross began its permanent disaster relief mission in Johnstown. Just five days after the flood, Clara Barton, founder of the American Red Cross and 67 years old at the time, came to the city with five Red Cross workers. Established initially to aid the battlefield wounded during wars, the American Red Cross took a new step with this peacetime relief effort. It handed out supplies to survivors and built hotels for those left homeless by the flood. Barton stayed in Johnstown until October. With this effort, the American Red Cross became the primary private disaster relief organization in the country.

THE 1900 GALVESTON HURRICANE

Over a decade after the Johnstown flood, the nation's most deadly natural disaster occurred. On September 8, an unexpectedly powerful hurricane moved from the Gulf of Mexico through Galveston, Texas. Near a busy port in Galveston Bay, Galveston had become the largest (population 42,000) and most prosperous city in Texas. Yet the town had few defenses to withstand a storm. It was located on a low, flat island—merely 8.7 feet above sea level at its highest point—on the Gulf of Mexico. Only a two-mile-long, raised roadway connected the island to mainland Texas. The city had flooded many times since its founding in 1839, but citizens survived without too much trouble.

Hurricane forecasting at the end of the 19th century was primitive at best, and no one, including Galveston Weather Bureau section director Isaac Cline, expected what would come. Cline had some nine years earlier dismissed the worry that a hurricane could devastate Galveston as an absurd delusion. On September 3, the U.S. Weather Bureau reported a tropical storm over Cuba but expected it to travel toward Florida. It instead moved toward Galveston and strengthened into a full-blown hurricane (based on the Saffir-Simpson scale of 1 to 5, it reached category 4). The captain of a ship that went through the storm estimated winds of 150 miles per hour. Residents of Galveston, however, received little warning.

Early on the morning of September 8, Galveston residents near the gulf shore noticed a rise in the tide that flooded their yards. A storm was blowing in. Rather than evacuating, however, most residents decided to ride out the storm. Many even went down to the beach to watch the storm advance. By evening, gale winds reached such a force as to blow down houses, trees, and buildings, while a storm surge sent waves of water flowing through the city. As the storm worsened, winds of around 130 miles per hour and flooding 15 feet high knocked buildings off their foundation and washed residents away to their death.

By the time the sun came out the next day, this one hurricane killed more than the next 300 hurricanes to strike the United States. More than 6,000 Galveston residents died, most drowned or crushed by debris. Some 4,000–6,000 others located along the Texas coast died as well. So many bodies were scattered throughout the city that residents had to burn rather than bury them. Much of the beach washed away, the causeway to the mainland disappeared, and 3,600 homes and three-quarters of the city were gone.

Relief efforts came slowly. With communication between the island and the rest of Texas lost during the hurricane, others in the state did not hear of the destruction for a day or two. Survivors who reached Houston on a ship telegraphed the Texas governor and President William McKinley to say that Galveston lay in ruins. Houston residents responded most quickly with help. They sent supplies, 100,000 gallons of water, and 250 volunteers by train and boat to Galveston. A few days later, the Galveston mayor had the Texas militia brought in to prevent looting and to set up tents on the beach for the homeless.

Continuing the disaster relief efforts of the Red Cross, 78-year-old Clara Barton arrived a few days later to help. Her fame led people from across the country to donate to the relief and recovery. Besides raising money, she organized local women to help in the relief effort, established an orphanage for children who lost their parents, and helped set up tents and rebuild housing.

Most relief efforts came from local residents, however. By 10:00 A.M. the day after the hurricane, the mayor called an emergency city council meeting and by the end of the day appointed a relief committee. Residents gathered the dead, cleaned the debris from buildings and streets, and built crude houses from scattered lumber. In the next few days, workers restored water service and rebuilt telegraph lines. By the end of three weeks, emergency relief ended and the task of rebuilding began.

City leaders decided to rebuild rather than abandon the city but to make drastic changes. They built a 17-foot seawall to protect the city from storm surges. The initial section was in place by 1904, and more sections followed over the next decades. The city also raised the island by 17 feet in some places. Engineers managed to raise existing buildings and place sand dredged from nearby Galveston Bay under the buildings. A new all-weather bridge that connected the island to the mainland made for quick evacuation of residents and delivery of emergency supplies. Because of these efforts, a storm in 1915 of similar strength killed 275 people—a tragedy but not nearly as terrible as the 1900 hurricane.

THE SAN FRANCISCO EARTHQUAKE AND FIRE OF 1906

At the turn of the 20th century, a population of 410,000 made San Francisco the nation's ninth-largest city and the largest on the west coast. It enjoyed a reputation as the financial center of the West, a busy port, and a place of entry for Asian immigrants. The natural beauty of the city—its steep hills, location on the Pacific Ocean and San Francisco Bay, and wonderful vistas of surrounding water and hills—hid a problem. The San Andreas Fault—a fracture in the underlying rock formation caused by shifting in the Earth's crust—passed to the south of the city on the peninsula and to the west under the ocean. The fault made the area around San Francisco (and indeed, much of California) prone to earthquakes.

On April 18, 1906, at 5:12 A.M., a major earthquake occurred. The quake reached at least 7.7 on the Richter scale, making it one of the strongest ever recorded in the United States. With its epicenter near San Francisco, the city shook terribly. Pictures taken after the earthquake show houses toppled, roads split in half, and buildings missing walls and floors. One hotel night clerk described the force of the earthquake: "The hotel lurched forward as if the foundation were dragged backward from under it, and crumpled down over Valencia Street. It did not fall to pieces and spray itself all over the place, but telescoped down on itself like a concertina."[15]

On its own, the earthquake would have caused plenty of damage but the aftereffects made things worse. Fires ignited throughout the city and ended up causing 90 percent of the final damage. Breaks in natural gas pipes caused by the earthquake spread the fires, as did many arsonists. Thinking that insurance would not cover earthquake damage but would cover fire damage, some residents set their homes on fire. Likely causing more fires, the military tried to stop the spread of fires by clearing out buildings with dynamite. Whatever the causes, the fires burned out of control for four days and destroyed 500 blocks of the city center. With water mains broken by the earthquake, the fire department could do little to battle the blaze.

The damage proved enormous. Despite early claims that only 478 deaths occurred, the toll in San Francisco and surrounding towns likely fell between 3,000 and 6,000 people. Worried about the bad publicity for their growing city, government officials and business leaders tried to minimize the harm of the disaster by understating the deaths (and ignoring deaths among the poor and immigrant Chinese). With about 80 percent of the city destroyed by the earthquake and fire, and up to 300,000 residents left homeless, it was hard to hide the devastation brought by the disaster. Unlike other disasters up to that time, photographers captured this one with many still photos and some films. The pictures, easily accessible on the Web today, reveal the destruction.

Unlike previous disasters, the U.S. Army led the relief efforts. About 2,000 troops came from the nearby Presidio base to help with the fire and keep order. Under the command of Brigadier-General Frederick Funston, the military took an active role, sometimes without official approval from the federal government or the city leaders. The mayor issued a shoot-to-kill order to stop looting, for example, but vigorous enforcement of the order killed hundreds. Some claimed that San Francisco had become a military dictatorship.

More positively, the military issued tents, clothes, and blankets to civilians, offered shelter on its base grounds, and eventually took over the food distribution. Thanks to the army, tent cities sprouted in Golden Gate Park, the Presidio, and elsewhere in the city; there were 21 official army refugee camps in all. The army made special efforts to ensure sanitation and eliminate the spread of disease—always a major problem after a disaster. However, some groups benefited more from the efforts than others. Tens of thousands of Chinese immigrants lost their homes after fires destroyed Chinatown, but they had to go to camps separate from the white citizens or fend for themselves.

The federal government offered relief funds. On April 20, Congress passed its first appropriation, $500,000. President Theodore Roosevelt gave responsibility to Secretary of War (and future president) William Howard Taft to deliver supplies from army bases across the country. In all, Congress provided $2.5 million for emergency relief, the equivalent today of $56.9 million. These funds, as well as those donated by private citizens and organizations, helped feed the quake victims.

Rebuilding began quickly. Four days after the earthquake, work to fix pipes and sewers began. Soldiers forced able-bodied citizens to help clear rubble and later paid workers to use horses and heavy equipment to finish the job. Dropped into the bay, the cleared rubble left the city looking cleaner and more modern. New, steel-framed buildings replaced slums, cable cars started running, newspapers began publishing, and Chinatown restarted in its original location. Within a year, residents of the tent cities in the parks had moved into permanent housing. The city lost some of its population and wealth after the earthquake, but it recovered surprisingly quickly.

THE TRISTATE TORNADO OF 1925

The deadliest and longest-lasting tornado in U.S. history moved through Missouri, southern Illinois, and southern Indiana in 1925. Because tornadoes cover a narrow area and emerge in open spaces, their winds often cause less damage than hurricanes. In this case, however, the force and persistence of the tornado made it particularly damaging. It covered a 219-mile track, lasted three-and-a-half hours, killed 695 people (more than twice as many as the next deadliest), injured 2,027 people, destroyed 15,000 homes, and caused $16.5 million in damage ($193.3 million in today's dollars). The weather conditions also spawned many other tornadoes in Kentucky and Tennessee.

The tornado began in Missouri around 1:00 P.M. on March 18, 1925, moving northeast at around 60 to 70 miles per hour. It crossed the Mississippi River and into Illinois, the state that suffered the most damage. It later reached Indiana before dissipating around 4:30 P.M. The afternoon event caught many unprepared. The tornado did not have the normal appearance of a funnel cloud but resembled a rolling mass of dark clouds and blowing dust. It occurred while children attended school, destroying nine buildings and killing 69 students. It passed through small towns rather than major cities. In one town, Murphysboro, Illinois, 234 people died.

The response to the tornado began locally. The small and isolated towns with the worst damage did not get the attention that large cities did when a disaster occurred. At least initially, their major resource came from the time and effort of the survivors. For example, one lawyer, Isaac Levy, who was 20 miles away from his hometown of Murphysboro during the tornado, returned to organize locals.[16] A search for injured or trapped survivors came first, followed by gathering the dead bodies and then checking lists of residents to account for missing persons. Those in nearby towns that the tornado missed came by to help with these tasks.

Several private organizations also assisted. Over the decades, the Red Cross and the Salvation Army had set up procedures for quick response. They provided milk, food, and basics to help victims right away but also did much to help rebuild the towns. The Red Cross, for example, gave money to many victims to repair houses, purchase furnishings, and pay for medical care. To use its resources carefully, the organization conducted a census of families, the damage the tornado did to their property, and the resources they had to rebuild. It then directed their funds to those most in need. In interviews decades later, many who survived the tornado had appreciative memories of the Salvation Army and the Red Cross.

The state helped with the relief effort by calling out the National Guard. The guard kept outsiders who came to see the damage from getting in the way of relief work. More important, the state provided tents to the homeless. At the urging of local townspeople, the Illinois state legislature set aside special funds to rebuild and insure the schools destroyed by the tornado.

Along with government and relief organizations, citizens and businesses across the country contributed to the recovery. Chambers of Commerce, American Legions, the American Farm Bureau Federation, schools, churches, and radio stations all raised funds for the victims. Chicago organizations offered $500,000, and St. Louis residents raised about the same for the Red Cross. Engineers from St. Louis came to restore public services, doctors and nurses provided medical care, and fruit and vegetable producers sent truckloads of food. Other contributions came in the form of clothing, shelter, and caskets.

THE GREAT MISSISSIPPI FLOOD OF 1927

During summer 1926 and through winter 1927, the Midwest experienced record-high rainfall. The rain raised rivers in states as distant as Colorado in the west, Minnesota in the north, Ohio in the east, and Tennessee in the south. More worrisome, rivers in these states and many others fed into the Mississippi River. Always prone to flooding, the Mississippi was growing higher throughout the period. Low-lying areas had built levees—high embankments or reinforced earthen walls—to protect themselves from the river. Yet the rising level of the Mississippi threatened to overflow some levees, and the force of the water flowing downstream threatened to break through others.

By April 1927, residents of Mississippi River towns south of St. Louis worried about the rising river. The Army Corps of Engineers—a unit of the military that provides engineering services to the nation—had built the levees and assured the public that they would withstand the rising water. In the state of Mississippi, however, African-American workers from nearby plantations had been put to the task of raising the height of the levees with sandbag walls. Then a storm came on April 15, 1927, that added six to 15 inches of rain in less than a day. The rising river water would cause the levees to break in 145 places but would do the most damage to the Mississippi Delta, an area of low-lying ground east of the river used for cotton growing.[17]

On April 21, the levee protecting the delta town of Greenville, Mississippi, broke. A channel more than a half-mile wide allowed river water to pour into the low-lying land. The water passing through the channel had a force greater than Niagara Falls. In the city of Greenville, more than 10,000 people ended up on the only piece of high ground—the eight-foot-wide crown of a levee left standing. After flowing through breaks in the levees for 10 days, water covered 1 million acres at a height of 10 feet. In rural areas, rescue boats traveled as best they could to nearby farms to get survivors.

Overall, the flood covered 16.5 million acres in seven states. It killed 250 to 500 people, dislocated 637,000 people, caused $102 million in crop losses, flooded 162,000 homes, and destroyed 41,000 buildings.[18] One historian describes the enormity of the disaster: "Twenty-seven thousand square miles were inundated. This was about equal to the combined size of Massachusetts, Connecticut, New Hampshire, and Vermont. By July 1, even as the flood began to recede, 1.5 million acres were under water. The river was 70 miles wide."[19]

Unlike in the past, the federal government played an active role in relief—it in fact acted with surprising speed and efficiency. Given the vast region of the country affected by the flooding, President Calvin Coolidge believed that only the federal government had the resources to handle the problem. Moreover, the failure of the levees was in part the responsibility of the U.S. Army Corps of Engineers, which had designed and built them. Secretary of Commerce (and future president) Herbert Hoover, an engineer by training, took charge of coordinating the response of eight federal agencies, the Red Cross, and other private agencies. No federal insurance program existed, but Congress passed several relief bills to help. President Coolidge also asked the public to contribute $5 million to the Red Cross for the relief effort and later asked for another $5 million. Beyond that, the relief groups could rely on the existing resources of federal government agencies to help.

The response quickly brought goods and services to the victims. Hoover had complete authority to take action—there was no power struggle between federal, state, local, and private agencies or confusion over responsibility. Hoover set policy, the Red Cross led the implementation, and state directors worked with locals to do the work. The strategy did much good according to a congressional report: "The public donated and the Red Cross delivered over $21 million [$234.9 million] in aid. The federal government provided, perhaps, $10 million [$111.8 million] in resources and manpower."[20] The Red Cross used army cots and tents to set up 154 refugee camps. Later it helped to rebuild homes, restart farms, and purchase furnishings. The federal government contributed by sponsoring loans from local banks to disaster victims trying to rebuild.

Hoover's action brought him much celebrity and contributed to his victory in the 1928 presidential election. That success in turn led other presidents to take a more active role in disaster response. Congress also got more involved than it had in the past. It passed the Flood Control Act of 1928, which funded flood control improvements on the Mississippi. Some complained that the government did not do enough—only more extensive and expensive engineering could contain the river—but locals appreciated the government help.

One failure stained the otherwise successful government response to the flood. Relief efforts favored whites and in some cases illegally abused African Americans. The parts of the Mississippi Delta flooded by breaks in the levees were largely populated by poor blacks who worked as sharecroppers on land owned by whites. Sharecroppers rented land by paying owners a share of the crop, leaving them barely enough to survive on and often in debt to the landowners. This arrangement, nearly a form of slavery, favored the wealthy landowners. After the flood, blacks complained that planters and the National Guard forced them at gunpoint to stay in the relief camps and do repair work. James Gooden, a black resident of Greenville, was shot in the back after refusing to work a second cleanup shift. Planters worried that if their black workers left the area, they would not return to work on the plantations.

Other instances of racism marred the relief efforts. In Greenville, African Americans who had been building sandbag walls were trapped without food, water, or facilities when the levee broke. Some boats came to remove whites but refused to take African Americans. Only many days later, after the Red Cross chose Greenville as a supply distribution center, did those left on the levee get help. Even after relief came, locals directed funds and supplies to plantation owners for distribution rather than directly to the African Americans who most needed them. Such actions typified disaster relief throughout the country: Advantaged groups received the most attention, and minorities and the poor suffered most.

FEDERAL INVOLVEMENT IN DISASTER RESPONSE

The largely successful relief action during the 1927 Mississippi flood marked the start of a more active role of the federal government. Up until then, the federal government viewed disaster response as a state and local responsibility. Congress would often provide funds—between 1860 and 1930, 90 separate disaster relief measures passed—yet each disaster had to get its own bill before funds could be committed, a process that stalled speedy relief. When Herbert Hoover became president in 1929, his disaster work spurred more active federal disaster policies.

Shifts in Disaster Policy From 1930 to 1960

In 1929, another event underscored the need for relief legislation. The stock market crash signaled the start of the Great Depression, which would last through the 1930s. Financially strapped voters prodded Congress to provide work for the unemployed with federal spending. Toward that end, President Herbert Hoover established the Reconstruction Finance Corporation (RFC) just before his term ended in 1932. Although primarily aimed at helping banks, the RFC received authority to make loans for the repair and reconstruction of facilities harmed by earthquakes and, later, other disasters. In 1934, during the administration of President Franklin Delano Roosevelt, the Bureau of Public Roads received funding to repair roads and bridges damaged by disasters. These steps toward disaster assistance were modest—most new relief programs during the Great Depression went to help those harmed by the poor economy rather than those harmed by disasters. Even so, they represented a shift in federal philosophy about disasters.

During the 1930s, the federal government and the Red Cross extended relief efforts to include another sort of disaster—one that developed more slowly and lasted longer than fires, earthquakes, tornadoes, hurricanes, and floods. A series of droughts during the years from 1930 to 1937 dried up farmland in dozens of states but chiefly hurt the southern prairie states of

Kansas, Oklahoma, Texas, New Mexico, and Colorado. The droughts made farming useless, and winds blew the dusty soil into storms that made it hard to breathe.

Responding to the plight of many farmers, the Red Cross gave food, clothing, medical aid, shelter, crop seeds, or other assistance worth millions to 2.7 million people. By March 1931, more than 150,000 children were receiving hot lunches in 3,600 rural schools.[21] As described in John Steinbeck's famous novel *The Grapes of Wrath*, the federal government helped by setting up camps for families relocating from their farms to new land in California. The long-lasting droughts did not occur suddenly as other disasters did, but they still devastated communities in the Great Plains. The help from the federal government would lead to future help for other kinds of disasters.

In the meantime, disasters occurred on a regular basis—although none killed as many as the Galveston hurricane, the San Francisco earthquake, or the tristate tornado. On April 5, 1936, a strong tornado moved through Tupelo, Mississippi, killing at least 233 people (but missing the home of one-year-old Elvis Presley). The next day, another tornado moved through Gainesville, Georgia, killing at least 203 persons. Most of the victims lived in trailer parks, places notoriously defenseless against tornadoes. That same year, spring flooding devastated much of New England. With the still-frozen ground in Connecticut, Massachusetts, New Hampshire, and Vermont unable to absorb the runoff from melting snow and heavy rain, floods killed at least 150 people.

On September 21, 1938, a hurricane reached New England, destroying much of the shore along Long Island and Rhode Island. Given the primitive storm-tracking technology of the time, residents did not expect the storm, which had moved unexpectedly up the Atlantic Coast from the Caribbean. The storm killed 682, felled 275 million trees, and caused $600 million in damage ($8.7 billion today). In response, President Roosevelt sent 100,000 relief workers from the Works Progress Administration (WPA), the Civilian Conservation Corps (CCC), the U.S. Army, and the U.S. Coast Guard.[22] The WPA and the CCC created jobs for the unemployed to work on repair projects and sent some of its employees to the disaster area. The Red Cross also came to New England to help with the relief.

The federal government did little more to address disaster response in the 1940s and the 1950s. Instead, attention went first to supporting the U.S. military in Europe and the Pacific Ocean during World War II (1941–45). Beginning in 1949, when the Soviet Union tested its first nuclear bomb, the federal government shifted attention to preparing for a nuclear attack. An arms race developed between the United States and the Soviet Union that many expected to lead to nuclear war. At the urging of the federal government, communities appointed civil-defense directors to manage emergency response. The Department of Defense stockpiled supplies to distribute in case of nuclear war and planned ways to get the supplies to those in need. The world avoided nuclear war, while the cold war brought both gains and losses for disaster response. Civil defense created warning plans that natural disaster response programs could adopt, but at the same time, it directed government funds away from natural disasters.

One small step toward new kinds of government involvement in disaster relief came with the Federal Disaster Relief Act of 1950. This legislation created the first formal role for federal agencies in disaster response. It authorized the federal government to grant relief funds to states harmed by disaster without Congress having to pass a relief bill first. A few large-scale disasters occurred during the 1950s that invoked the new federal relief law. However, the effects of the law were modest. After hurricanes damaged parts of Virginia and North Carolina, the northeastern states, and Louisiana and North Texas, Congress did much as it had done in the past. It reacted to each disaster with specially legislated disaster assistance. This piecemeal approach to disaster response, however, was about to change.

HURRICANES CAMILLE AND AGNES AND THE SUPER TORNADO OUTBREAK

The 1960s brought new legislation for disaster relief. During the decade of civil rights protests, the war on poverty, and the space program, the federal government became more active in social issues. This approach spilled over into disaster response. Congress did not yet give the federal government a major role in responding to disasters, but it moved in that direction. In 1964, Congress passed the National Plan for Emergency Preparedness. By focusing on preparation for disasters from both nuclear war and natural hazards, this legislation gave new federal attention to natural disasters.

In 1968, Congress passed flood relief legislation. The National Flood Insurance Act created the National Flood Insurance Program (NFIP). When several hurricanes brought extensive damage to homeowners along the Atlantic and Gulf coasts, private insurers could not cover the damage (or charged rates too high for most homeowners to pay). Congress aimed to rectify this problem with the legislation. For communities that joined the NFIP, residents could obtain low-cost government flood insurance. However, communities participating in the insurance program had to restrict future development on floodplains—Congress did not want to pay for insuring new buildings almost certain to be flooded in the future. At least initially, few communities joined the voluntary program, and some that joined imposed few limits on development.

Still greater involvement of the federal government came with two major hurricanes. In 1969, Hurricane Camille, the strongest hurricane to strike the United States in the 20th century, killed 256 people and caused $1.4 billion (the equivalent of $7.8 billion today) in property damage. Early warning of the power of the coming storm prevented more deaths. About 200,000 residents evacuated and 50 civil defense shelters opened just before Camille reached the Mississippi coast on April 17. However, the evacuation could not prevent damage to property. Having reached category 5 (the highest level of force), Camille flattened towns near the shore. It left only slabs of concrete where hotels and brick apartment buildings once stood. The tidal surge raised the water level 22.6 feet higher than normal and washed away much of the coastal property.

Although weakened, the storm later brought rain and flooding to the Appalachian Mountains, Virginia, and West Virginia. As one expert said, "All told, Camille caused more than 200 deaths and billions of dollars in damage. In its aftermath, the storm was called the greatest catastrophe ever to strike the United States and perhaps the most significant economic weather event in the world's history."[23]

President Richard M. Nixon sent 1,000 federal troops to the area, the governor of Mississippi declared martial law, and the local authorities imposed a curfew. Along with burying humans who died during the hurricane, volunteers and relief workers had to dispose of dead animals scattered throughout the area. The carcasses attracted insects and spread disease. The state and federal government brought in bulldozers and dump trucks to carry away the wreckage. Public and private relief groups worked to find shelter, water, and food for the 15,000 homeless.

On August 19, President Nixon declared parts of Mississippi and Louisiana as major disaster areas. The Office of Emergency Preparedness coordinated the activities of government agencies and groups involved in the relief effort. It had only 15 people staffed to help but relied on the actions of others.[24] The Department of Housing and Urban Development, after some difficulties in delivery and setup, brought in 5,000 mobile homes for victims. The Department of the Treasury sponsored loans of $25 million (the equivalent of $140 million today), and the Internal Revenue Service helped victims get special tax deductions for victims. Still other federal government departments, such as Commerce, Health, and Agriculture, gave time, goods, and services to the victims. The Red Cross helped with 913 volunteers, 805 professional staffers, and $15 million in spending. One author described the changes in federal policy that resulted:

At the time of Hurricane Camille, the federal government viewed its responsibility in natural disasters as limited to issuing regional alerts to populations that were in projected paths of storms and, after disaster struck, assisting in emergency recovery efforts for people exposed to health hazards and other threats to personal safety. Hurricane Camille marked the beginning of an era when the U.S. federal government recognized that its responsibility ran deeper than the traditional emergency food kitchens and temporary shelters it had previously provided.[25]

Spurred by Hurricane Camille, President Nixon signed the Disaster Relief Act of 1969 on October 1. It aimed to improve response to disasters such as Camille by creating a new position called the federal coordinating officer. Acting under the authority of the president, the officer had responsibility for coordinating and managing disasters. The act also allowed the federal government to grant modest disaster benefits for housing, education, unemployment, and small-business recovery. For example, the Small Business Administration could now make special loans to businesses harmed by a disaster and forgive repayment of up to $1,800 of the loan. The act also offered funds for temporary housing, the cost of clearing debris, and food coupons for low-income people.

Soon after, the Disaster Relief Act of 1970 created a comprehensive response plan for the federal government. The new law incorporated many of the efforts that had been authorized in previous legislation but added more assistance for temporary housing, legal services, unemployment insurance, and individual needs.

In 1972, Hurricane Agnes highlighted the need for still more legislation. In June, Agnes made landfall in Florida and eventually moved through the Mid-Atlantic states to Pennsylvania and New York State. As it moved north, the winds did little harm, but drenching rains led to severe flooding. Agnes ended up killing 129 and causing $3.1 billion in damage ($15.2 billion today). Although the storm hit many states, Pennsylvania suffered the worst damage. About 250,000 residents of the state had to leave their homes. With the damage it brought, Agnes replaced Camille, as the costliest disaster ever to hit the United States. Federal assistance covered little of the costs.

Still another disaster followed in 1974 that prodded Congress to pass new disaster relief legislation. On April 3 and 4, a huge storm moved through 13 states that spawned 148 separate tornadoes. Six of the tornadoes reached the maximum of F5 on the Fujita-Pearson tornado intensity scale, which means they had winds of 261 to 318 miles per hour. Overall, the tornadoes covered 2,500 miles, killed 330, and injured 5,484, justifying the name of the super (or jumbo) outbreak of 1974. Like Agnes, this disaster affected a large region of the country. Relief groups had trouble coordinating resources and activities across so many states, counties, and cities.

In response to the recent disasters, the Disaster Relief Act of 1974 made a crucial change in federal policy. It made assistance from the federal government available to individuals and families as part of the Individual and

Family Grant Program. Rather than giving all funds to states and communities to distribute, the program gave some funds directly to victims. The president first had to make an official disaster declaration, however. According to the legislation, the president could declare either a major disaster or an emergency. A major disaster brought in federal assistance needed for areas to recover from the damage; emergencies involved more limited and specific relief goals and received less federal support. For major disasters, the Federal Disaster Assistance Administration, established in the 1960s as part of the Department of Housing and Urban Development, would lead relief efforts.

FEDERAL EMERGENCY MANAGEMENT AGENCY (FEMA)

Despite the legislation of the 1970s, problems in disaster response remained. Laws from Congress, executive orders from the president, and decisions from several federal agencies fragmented government efforts. All told, more than 100 federal agencies took part in risk protection and disaster response. The Departments of Commerce, Housing, Treasury, and Defense had major roles, and dozens of other agencies such as the Federal Insurance Administration, the National Fire Prevention and Control Administration, the National Weather Service Community Preparedness Program, the Federal Preparedness Agency of the General Services Administration, and the Federal Disaster Assistance Administration made it hard to coordinate disaster response.

The National Governors Association took the lead in recommending changes. Having worked with the federal government in disaster relief, the states knew firsthand of the organizational problems. The governors sponsored an Emergency Preparedness Project, which made recommendations for streamlining disaster response at the federal level and getting cooperation across federal, state, and local governments. The project report stressed the need for a comprehensive national emergency policy to guide disaster response. It further recommended that the federal government take the lead in setting up the policy.

In the late 1970s, the federal government acted on the recommendations. To consolidate the disaster activities of all the separate agencies, President Jimmy Carter created the Federal Emergency Management Agency (FEMA) in 1979. FEMA had four primary responsibilities:

- To establish federal disaster policies;
- To mobilize federal resources in response to a disaster;

- To coordinate federal activities with those of states and local governments; and
- Manage federal disaster response.

Authority once shared among agencies now fell under one federal agency. FEMA would also handle civil-defense tasks, which were transferred to the agency from the Defense Civil Preparedness Agency in the Department of Defense.

Soon after its creation, FEMA faced two new kinds of disasters—one stemming from nuclear technology and one from chemical technology. The first one involved the Three Mile Island Nuclear Generating System near Harrisburg, Pennsylvania. On March 28, 1979, problems with the nuclear reactor led to the release of deadly radiation into the atmosphere. Conflicting and confusing information about the seriousness of the problem created fear among nearby residents, but no clear evacuation plans existed. FEMA worked to make sure in the future that areas surrounding nuclear power plants had such plans in place. Second, a neighborhood in Niagara Falls, New York, called Love Canal had been a dump for toxic chemical waste many decades before the building of roads and homes. With growing evidence that the buried chemicals had increased the risk of cancer and genetic damage among the residents, President Carter declared a state of emergency at Love Canal on May 21, 1980. Acting as it would for a natural disaster, FEMA helped evacuate families. Neither of these events, though serious threats, caused immediate deaths. They did, however, give FEMA some experience in dealing with technological disasters.

In responding to these and other disasters, the new agency faced a daunting problem: How could it integrate the many agencies that had once been separate? To give order to FEMA's diverse units, the first permanent director, John Macy, set up an Integrated Emergency Management System. This system defined procedures to handle all sorts of disasters, including weather-related events, technological breakdowns, and nuclear war. It also defined specific roles for the various parts of FEMA and for organizations that would cooperate with FEMA.

Even so, the agency faced troubles. FEMA offices remained scattered in different buildings across Washington, D.C. Authority remained scattered as well. Different types of disasters still fell under the oversight of different congressional committees. FEMA had the tricky job of answering to 23 committees and subcommittees in Congress.[26] As a result, FEMA lacked the tightly linked organization it needed to be effective. For at least the next decade, however, no major disaster exposed the flaws of the organization.

During the 1980s, the administration of President Ronald Reagan contributed to problems at FEMA. By emphasizing the role of FEMA in preparing for a nuclear war, the government directed resources away from the response to natural disasters. Between 1982 and 1991, FEMA spent 12 times as much money preparing for a nuclear attack as it did for a natural calamity.[27] By many accounts, the agency also became a place for political appointees with little or no experience in emergency management. Ties between federal and state administrators weakened, and Congress accused FEMA of misusing funds. According to two experts, "As the 1980s closed, FEMA was an agency in trouble. It suffered from severe moral problems, disparate leadership, and conflicts with its partners at the state and local level over agency spending and priorities."[28]

During these years, Congress worked to improve the process of disaster response. In 1988, it passed the Stafford Act, which amended the 1974 Disaster Relief Act to create a more orderly system. The law specified that FEMA would take responsibility for coordinating relief when the president declared a major disaster. FEMA would enlist help from many other agencies—Commerce, Transportation, Health and Human Services, for example—and work closely with state and local governments and private relief agencies. However, the law also directed state governors to first make a formal request to the president before FEMA took the lead.

Despite giving FEMA more authority, the legislation did nothing to deal with the problems at the agency. According to a report on FEMA, "The disaster agency that President George H. W. Bush inherited [in 1989] was under-funded, loosely structured, poorly integrated, overly specialized in national security preparedness, and weakly led by a succession of political appointees with little emergency management experience."[29] Because no major disasters had occurred recently, the weaknesses worried few. Indeed, President Bush did not even appoint a director until 19 months after his inauguration. The problems would soon become all too obvious, however.

FEMA FAILS ITS FIRST MAJOR TESTS

The inability of FEMA to meet the demands placed on it—and to get the support it deserved—became apparent in the years from 1989 to 1992, when three major disasters occurred. By nearly all accounts, FEMA and the George H. W. Bush administration performed badly in responding.

Hurricane Hugo and the Loma Prieta Earthquake

On September 21, 1989, Hurricane Hugo struck the South Carolina coast near Charleston and moved through the state to North Carolina. Millions of people along the coasts of Georgia and South Carolina evacuated in anticipation of the storm, causing a good deal of confusion and gridlock.

However, the effort saved lives. Hugo caused $7 billion in damage on the U.S. mainland but killed relatively few—estimates range from 32 to 56.

Both during and after the storm, FEMA acted slowly. For example, it took six days for sufficient quantities of food and clothing to reach Charleston and 10 days for FEMA to set up a disaster center in a heavily damaged rural area outside Charleston. Some 1,200 families had not received help after nine months. Despite the time pressure of a disaster, bureaucratic delay was the norm. One story tells of a request for aid sent to FEMA by the governor of Puerto Rico as Hurricane Hugo approached. A FEMA employee sent the request back via U.S. mail because one section was not completed. By the time the governor received and corrected the form, the hurricane had already hit Puerto Rico.[30]

The slow response led to harsh criticism. Reflecting his frustration working with FEMA. Fritz Hollings, a democratic senator from South Carolina, called the agency a "bunch of bureaucratic jackasses."[31] Senator Hollings had personally called the FEMA director to get help but felt that his call did little good. Some time later, Congress investigated FEMA's poor performance and proposed reforms to overhaul the agency.

The next month, an altogether different disaster drew more attention to the problems at FEMA. The Loma Prieta earthquake occurred on October 17, 1989, just before the start of a World Series baseball game between the San Francisco Giants and Oakland Athletics. Centered in the Santa Cruz Mountains in California, it damaged San Francisco, Oakland, Santa Cruz, and other cities around the San Francisco Bay. At least 63 died (most when a double-decked highway collapsed), 3,757 were injured, and 12,000 were left homeless. President Bush declared seven counties as major disaster areas. Emergency responders in the state and cities acted quickly and kept casualties to a minimum.

According to California senator Barbara Boxer, however, FEMA did not perform as well. She called FEMA's response chaotic, overly bureaucratic, and even arrogant.[32] After six weeks, some 50,000 people, many homeless, had not received assistance. Even after two years, some were still waiting. A 1993 report from the General Accounting Office noted that FEMA lacked staff and clear guidance on how to respond. Congressman Norman Mineta of California summed up his view of FEMA by saying, "it could screw up a two-car parade."[33]

Part of the problem in response came from a tendency common among emergency response organizations at the time. It is easy to develop a written response plan but difficult to carry it out. Experts refer to this as the "Paper Plan Syndrome," a tendency to create a response document that then sits on the shelf without undergoing adequate testing and practice.[34] All such plans make unwarranted assumptions, miss pertinent information, and do not account for apathy among the public. They need to be checked, rehearsed, and improved. By its response, FEMA demonstrated that it had not learned this lesson.

Hurricane Andrew

Another mishandled response followed a few years later. Despite criticisms leveled in 1989 and some reforms at FEMA, the agency failed miserably in its next challenge. On August 24, 1992, Hurricane Andrew, which had become a category 5 storm, moved through a 50-mile swath in south Florida. Having just missed heavily populated Miami, Andrew severely damaged the town of Homestead and surrounding areas. Its high winds and storm surge left nearly 200,000 residents homeless and 1.3 million without electricity. Andrew destroyed 97 percent of the 10,000 mobile homes in the area. It was at the time the third-strongest hurricane in U.S. history. It killed only 25 but caused $30 billion in damage ($44 billion today). The damage was so extensive that claims for reimbursement bankrupted several insurance companies.

Food, shelter, clean water, and medical assistance were scarce. For the first three days of the disaster, however, FEMA did not appear. Once there, FEMA acted slowly in bringing in water, food, and medical supplies to the victims—most federal aid did not reach victims until six days after the storm. Those in need relied on army troops and private organizations for relief rather than the federal agency in charge.

What happened this time? According to some critics, part of the problem came from sheer incompetence. At the time, FEMA had more political appointees than most federal agencies, and some agency leaders had little experience in emergency management. More important, FEMA responded slowly because it waited for an aid request from the state government. Yet the damage to the area was so severe, even destroying the homes and offices of emergency workers and police, that local officials hardly knew what to request. The search for food, water, and shelter kept everyone so busy that they could not survey the damage and make a formal application. Florida state officials likewise did not realize the extent of the damage. Worried about predictions that the storm would hit Miami, they were relieved when it went south of the city to less densely populated areas. They concluded that the state had avoided the worst damage. In fact, Homestead and surrounding areas suffered terrible damage. In the meantime, FEMA took a wait-and-see approach, doing little to move the relief process forward.

Responding to criticism of the slow response, President Bush appointed a special hurricane task force to deal with the disaster.[35] Headed by Andrew Card, the secretary of transportation (rather than a FEMA official), the task force immediately flew over the damaged area to see the devastation firsthand.

The airborne view made clear the extent of the disaster. Card then met with the Florida governor, offering massive aid and insisting that the state could not handle the relief. After President Bush signed an aid order, army troops moved quickly into the area to treat injuries, build shelters, and distribute food. Eventually, FEMA gave out more than $1.8 billion in relief funds. The Red Cross, which performed well in the disaster, spent $81.5 million. Though late in coming, the federal effort cheered the victims, who had been waiting for help.

Afterward, Congress debated eliminating FEMA because of its poor performance. It instead amended the Stafford Act in 1993 to extend federal relief and requested a report from the General Accounting Office (GAO) to describe the response problems revealed by Hurricane Andrew and suggest solutions. The GAO report emphasized one major problem: In a catastrophic disaster like Hurricane Andrew, it made no sense for FEMA to wait for state and local authorities to make a formal request and for the president to declare a major disaster. By the time everyone followed proper procedures, victims of the disaster would have gone days without much help.[36]

FEMA needed to plan more before a disaster so that it could respond immediately—within hours—with food, water, and temporary shelter. The GAO report recommended that for hurricanes and rising floodwaters, when the weather service could give several days' warning, FEMA should mobilize its resources as a storm approaches. Then it could quickly assess the damage and provide relief to those most in need. For sudden and unexpected events such as flash floods, tornadoes, and earthquakes, FEMA could not foresee the disaster, but it should be prepared to act immediately.

To do so, FEMA had to end its organizational rivalries. Since the beginning, conflict and tension between the major divisions had persisted. Only a united effort could meet the demands created by major disasters such as Hurricane Andrew, when FEMA had to call on the resources of multiple departments of the federal government, the Red Cross, state and local agencies, and other relief organizations. Yet problems in coordinating all the activities often led to paralysis rather than action. The president sometimes worsened the problems by turning to other cabinet agencies and leaders for help. FEMA needed a clear administrative structure and support from outside agencies to act effectively.

The GAO report also recommended a more active role for White House staff in the disaster response. The demands of other issues naturally occupy the president during periods between major disasters. Only when a disaster occurred did the president devote time and attention to the problem. By then it was too late to guide a quick response. The report suggested that the president appoint a disaster official to work with FEMA and other relief agencies. That would ensure continued attention to disasters at the White

House. Easy contact with the White House disaster official would also give FEMA representatives more authority to act quickly and sidestep bureaucratic rules. Disasters require strong leadership, and leadership close to the president would improve the effectiveness of government response.

Another recommendation came from the experience with Hurricane Andrew: FEMA needed to do more to help prepare state and local agencies for a disaster response. According to the GAO report, state and local responders lacked training and funds to handle a major disaster. FEMA did not have authority over state and local disaster relief organizations, but it could establish performance standards for other agencies to follow. It could also develop training and exercise programs to help meet those standards. With all levels of government similarly prepared, a unified and vigorous response could follow a disaster.

While agreeing with most of the criticisms, defenders of FEMA pointed out that the agency often took the blame for problems not of its own making. Legislation had not designated FEMA as an agency that delivered relief. It remained too small and had too few funds to do that. Rather, it served as a single point of contact in relief efforts and coordinated the activities of other agencies. Yet the poor performance of any of the cooperating state governments, local groups, federal agencies, military units, and private organizations led back to FEMA. In some ways, FEMA faced expectations that it did not have the resources to meet.

Even with unrealistic expectations, however, FEMA could do better. The agency would prove that over the eight years following Hurricane Andrew.

FEMA SUCCESS UNDER JAMES WITT

Beginning in 1993 with the presidency of Bill Clinton, FEMA improved so much that it gained modest fame. Scholars studied the turnaround as an example of how government agencies could move forward and thrive. The credit for the improvement goes to James Witt, appointed to head FEMA by President Clinton. Unlike previous directors, Witt had experience in emergency management. He had previously served as the Arkansas state director of the Office of Emergency Services, where he managed the state response to major floods in 1990 and 1991.

As director of FEMA, Witt had an advantage other directors lacked—the confidence and support of the president. President Clinton knew Witt from his time as the governor of Arkansas. As president, he followed Witt's recommendation to fill other top positions in FEMA with experienced emergency managers. Rather than using high-level appointments to reward political supporters, Clinton and Witt made the agency more professional. Showing even more support for the agency, President Clinton elevated

FEMA to cabinet status in 1996. The elevation raised the profile and authority of the agency. FEMA could work as an equal with other federal departments such as Transportation, Justice, and Health and Human Services.

Witt brought several changes to FEMA. He strengthened ties to other federal agencies, state and local governments, charitable organizations, and the private sector. With stronger ties, all could cooperate more smoothly in responding to a disaster. He improved training for state and local officials in emergency response. He reorganized FEMA to streamline its mission and eliminate regulations that blocked quick action. For example, he moved the division on response to nuclear war out of FEMA so that the agency could focus on natural disasters.

Perhaps most important, FEMA adopted a strategy of responding to disasters before rather than after they occurred. Witt broadened the interpretation of the 1988 Stafford Act that guided the agency. Under the new interpretation, FEMA sent staff and resources to locations where there was adequate warning of a disaster rather than wait until the disaster happened. Since relationships with state and local governments had improved, FEMA worked informally with officials before they submitted a formal request for assistance. The goal was to send in emergency response teams within four hours of a disaster. The new philosophy and organization of FEMA would pay off soon in dealing with several major disasters.

The Great Midwest Flood of 1993 and Northridge Earthquake

From April to September 1993, the nation's worst flood since 1927 occurred along the Mississippi and Missouri Rivers. A wet autumn in 1992 followed by heavy snow in the winter and then extensive rains in summer 1993 raised rivers across the upper Midwest. In Des Moines, Iowa, for example, the Raccoon River overflowed into the city's water-treatment plant. As a result, the city had no running water from July 11 to July 29. More widespread flooding occurred in the Midwest's two largest rivers—the Missouri and Mississippi. The Missouri overflowed hundreds of levees, while the Mississippi crested at 49.6 feet above sea level at St. Louis.

President Clinton declared all of Iowa and parts of eight other states as disaster areas. Some towns on the Missouri lived with flooded streets for 100 days, and some on the Mississippi lived for 200 days under the same conditions. Not until October 7, several months after the start, did the Mississippi fall below flood stage in St. Louis. The flooding killed 50, caused $15 billion in damage, and destroyed 10,000 homes. The rivers flowed too quickly and wildly to allow boat traffic during most of the summer and left more than 15 million acres of farmland covered with water. As is often the case, human actions made things worse. Levees built to stop flooding prevented the rivers from overflowing into low-lying areas that in the past created a natural form of flood control. That change led to more flooding of cities downstream. Worse, many of the levees failed, thus flooding cities and farms allowed to develop on floodplains.

By moving quickly with help during the disaster, FEMA earned unfamiliar praise. Norman Mineta, a congressional representative once highly critical of FEMA now said, "FEMA has delivered finally on its promise to stand with the American people when floods or hurricanes or earthquakes devastate their communities."[37] The key to success came from speed and close ties to state and local emergency offices. For example, Iowa officials called FEMA just after midnight when it looked as if the Raccoon River would flood the city's water plant and contaminate the water supply. By 11:30 A.M. that same day, FEMA had set up a plan to distribute freshwater at 29 locations throughout the city.

After the flood, FEMA devised a new strategy to deal with the costly destruction. Rather than providing relief funds only after a flood, it started a program to prevent or mitigate the damage from natural disasters. The buyout and relocation program for flood-prone communities on the Mississippi and Missouri paid property owners to move from flooded areas and turned the areas into parks and natural landscapes.[38] The parks and open space could then serve as flood-control areas. Building on this mitigation strategy, FEMA started Project Impact in 1997. The project funded other community mitigation activities such as adding a reinforced safe room to homes damaged by tornadoes in Ohio and installing hurricane shutters to homes in Key West, Florida. FEMA reasoned that spending money before a disaster would save money afterward.

The next year, California experienced a disaster that would again challenge FEMA. At 4:30 A.M. on January 17, 1994, an earthquake centered in the community of Northridge in the San Fernando Valley of Los Angeles reached 6.7 on the Richter scale. Although not a strong earthquake, its center in metropolitan Los Angeles brought considerable damage. Some apartment buildings collapsed from the shaking, a few hospitals suffered major damage, numerous fires started, and several busy highways split. It killed 51 people and seriously injured 9,000. The damage of $25 billion made it the most expensive earthquake since 1906.

City and federal emergency services responded quickly. Within five minutes, the Los Angeles City and County Emergency Operations Center activated a response; within 15 minutes, FEMA began to act; and within one hour and 15 minutes, the Los Angeles mayor declared a state of emergency. By that afternoon, President Clinton declared a national disaster for Los Angeles County. FEMA organized two urban search-and-rescue teams to look for injured and trapped victims. The Red Cross set up 26 shelters, and the Salvation Army set up five shelters. Of special importance, emergency personnel staffed highways to direct traffic away from dangerous splits in the pavement, while the media's reports on the earthquake calmed residents.

A report from the Department of Transportation on the earthquake summarized the performance of FEMA:

FEMA coordinated the response of the 27 federal agencies involved in the Northridge earthquake using the FEMA Incident Command System (ICS). With the coordination of agencies, services were provided quickly, decisions were made on need and without the usual formal process, and financial challenges were overcome. FEMA positioned emergency equipment and supplies for the state's use at a nearby air force base and opened an Earthquake Service Center with representatives of all disaster assistance agencies to aid victims.[39]

Unlike in the past, FEMA worked closely and effectively with local agencies and avoided the slow bureaucratic formalities.

The Oklahoma City Bombing and Hurricane Floyd

A year following the Northridge quake, FEMA distinguished itself in dealing with one more terrible disaster—the Oklahoma City bombing. At 9:02 A.M. on April 19, 1995, a bomb contained in a rented truck exploded in front of the nine-story Alfred P. Murrah Federal Building in Oklahoma City. The partial collapse of the building killed 168 people, including 19 children in a day-care center in the building. The bomb injured 800 others, damaged 300 nearby buildings, and shut down offices downtown. As later discovered, the disaster came from domestic terrorism: Two men convicted of the bombing, Timothy McVeigh and Terry Nichols, apparently planned the bombing to avenge the deaths of cult members in Waco, Texas, during a raid by federal agents.

Oklahoma City firefighters sped to the site of the explosion. They entered the damaged building to find survivors but worried that the rest of the building would collapse. In the meantime, FEMA sent staff to Oklahoma City, and President Clinton declared an emergency for the city. By 6:00 P.M. FEMA and local agencies organized search-and-rescue operations. Teams moved through dangerous sections of the damaged building looking for victims. Cooperation with charitable agencies likewise worked smoothly. The Red Cross and Salvation Army, for example, provided food and supplies for injured persons and family members of those killed.

The response to the disaster worked so smoothly that it became a standard for future action. Disaster responders in other places hoped to live up to the "Oklahoma standard." Some special features of the Oklahoma City disaster aided the successful response. Unlike most weather disasters, the damage covered only a few blocks. Moreover, anger about the bombing brought citizens together in ways that anger about the weather cannot. All levels of government exhibited unusually strong leadership, public and private groups cooperated smoothly, and volunteers concerned about the victims and the damage to the city gave critical help.

One other major test for FEMA came under the watch of director Witt. In September 1999, Hurricane Floyd, one of the largest Atlantic hurricanes on record, moved along the eastern coast of the United States. It finally made landfall in North Carolina on September 15. Although the winds had weakened before it hit land, torrential rains caused severe flooding. Floyd then moved up through Virginia to the mid-Atlantic states, where it did more damage. In all, the hurricane killed 57 people and caused $4.5 billion in damage.

FEMA took a different approach to preparing for Floyd than it did for Andrew. It activated emergency response teams even before landfall. First responders were in place to supply water, food, and medical care almost immediately. FEMA also offered financial assistance to victims within days of the hurricane. Some heavily flooded rural areas proved difficult to reach, however, and led to complaints over a slow response. Jesse Jackson, for example, accused FEMA of not doing enough to help the primarily African-American population in rural parts of North Carolina and Virginia. This accusation of racism in disaster response echoed those following many other disasters in the South (and foretold criticism to come after Katrina in 2005). Otherwise, those involved in the relief said that early action by FEMA saved lives and reduced damage.[40]

TERRORISM AND A
NEW DISASTER FOCUS

The September 11, 2001, terrorist attacks on the New York City World Trade Center and the Pentagon in Arlington, Virginia, dramatically changed the focus of disaster response. President George W. Bush, in office for less than nine months, faced an unprecedented disaster. The terrorist attacks ended up shifting disaster response away from its past emphasis on natural disasters and gave new power to military and law enforcement agencies. Many also say the concern with terrorism that followed the attacks ended the improvements made in FEMA during the 1990s and weakened its ability to respond to natural disasters.

The change in disaster response stemmed from the hijacking of four commercial passenger jets by 19 men affiliated with an alliance of militant and radical Islamic groups called al-Qaeda. The hijackers crashed two of the jets into the Twin Towers of the World Trade Center, one into the Pentagon, and a fourth into a field in Pennsylvania (after passengers tried to retake control). The worst damage occurred at the site of the World Trade Center in New York City, now known as Ground Zero. About 2,819 died there, 403 of them police, paramedics, and firefighters helping the rescue operations.[41] In addition, 189 died in the Pentagon crash and 45 in the Pennsylvania crash.

NEW YORK CITY RESPONSE

In New York City, the first hijacked plane crashed into the north tower of the World Trade Center at 8:45 A.M., and the second plane crashed into the south tower at 9:03 A.M.. The World Trade Center contained as many as 40,000 people at the time of the crashes. Evacuation of the buildings, spurred by many acts of heroism, prevented a much higher death toll. Firefighters and police arrived quickly to the towers to help evacuate the buildings. The task was a difficult one. It took up to an hour of maneuvering through narrow, smoky, and dark stairways for people located on the highest floors to get out. Sadly, the south tower collapsed at 9:59 A.M., only 56 minutes after the crash. Many employees and rescue workers still in the building or standing nearby died. Those on surrounding streets had to hide from a massive storm of wind, dust, and debris from the collapsed tower. The north tower then collapsed at 10:28 A.M. (later that day, at 5:20 P.M., a smaller, 47-story building, 7 World Trade Center, also collapsed).

Units from the Fire Department of New York City, the New York City Police Department, and the Port Authority of New York and New Jersey Police Department rushed to the scene of the first explosion. Fire safety officials located at the World Trade Center began evacuation of the north tower immediately but briefly delayed doing the same for the south tower. Because no one expected a second plane, it seemed safe at first for those in the south tower to remain in the building and stay out of the way of evacuation of the north tower. In the north tower, most of the workers below the impact floors got out using the stairways.

Two problems emerged, however. The different agencies involved in the initial response largely worked separately, without a unified command. One unit did not know what other units were doing or planned to do. The responders also lacked effective communication. The high-rise buildings and the overwhelming traffic blocked radio communication.

Under the leadership of Mayor Rudolph Giuliani, the New York City Office of Emergency Management coordinated the response. Acting quickly, the mayor ordered evacuation of lower Manhattan at 10:45 A.M. In the meantime, first responders had to keep bystanders away, find hospitals to treat the injured, and organize search-and-rescue efforts. The search-and-rescue efforts proved daunting. The unstable and enormously heavy mass of rubble made it impossible to look for survivors without the use of heavy equipment. Even then, moving parts of the pile risked further collapse and threatened rescue workers.

As in many other disasters, volunteers gave their time and effort to the response. Soon after the towers collapsed, New York City residents came by to see if they could help, and those with needed skills were soon put to work. By 10:00 P.M., Mayor Giuliani announced that the relief effort no longer needed volunteers. People still came from places across the country and the world to help (only to be turned away). Although not without mishap, the informal rescue and relief work helped considerably in dealing with the masses of injured.

Perhaps more than other disasters, the brave and selfless actions of volunteers in New York City contradicted the myth that people panic after a disaster. Studies show quite the opposite: People typically organize themselves sensibly and unselfishly. After the first plane crashed into the north tower, workers started to evacuate on their own. They helped one another stay calm, find their way out, and adapt to difficult and confusing conditions. Rather than giving into chaos, responders devised solutions to unforeseen problems. When it became hard to pass through the narrow streets of lower Manhattan, a small flotilla of Coast Guard vessels, tour ships, passenger ferries, and recreation boats came along the shore to the Hudson River to help. Some 500,000 people left the island by boat, including many injured persons brought to New Jersey for treatment. Although unplanned and without formal supervision, the boat rescue worked well.

The more formal disaster leadership also had to devise solutions to unexpected problems. The New York City Emergency Operations Center was located in 7 World Trade Center, right next to the towers. Having to leave its state-of-the-art technology and equipment behind, the center moved elsewhere before the building collapsed later in the day. The center managed to relocate at the same time it coordinated emergency action. In addition, the city lacked a comprehensive disaster plan that addressed special issues of terrorism and defined clear leadership responsibilities and channels of communication. Such a plan might have prevented the death of so many police and firefighters. Overall, however, the city did well given the unexpected severity of the disaster.

Part of the success of the response came from the leadership of Mayor Giuliani. Avoiding a turf battle with state and federal agencies, the mayor and the city took the lead role, calling on others to help them. Although some bureaucratic wrangling among rescue agencies occurred, the shared grief and outrage over the attack helped diminish rivalries. Problems came more from physical limitations rather than organizational ones. Excessive radio traffic, the lack of functioning elevators, and difficulty in keeping track of all the responding units did the most to slow response.

To aid New Yorkers, President Bush ordered the release of federal disaster resources and funds to the city. He first signed a major disaster declaration for the five New York counties most affected by the attacks. Federal funds then could be used to purchase and deliver food, water, heavy machines, medical supplies, and lifesaving equipment. The president also promised assistance for stricken individuals, families, and businesses. Typically, federal funds pay 75 percent of the cost for emergency services, debris removal, and building repair—the state covers the other 25 percent. On September 18, however, President Bush said that the federal government would cover 100 percent of the costs to the New York counties most affected by the terrorist attacks.

Government aid could not begin to cover the full costs. Economic losses went well beyond the destruction of the buildings. The terrorist attacks led to a shutdown of the airline industry for several days and drastic loss of travelers when planes began flying again. Tourism across the country suffered, unemployment rose, the stock market fell, government budgets were strained, and the insurance industry was hurt. It may be impossible to determine the full costs, but the Institute for Analysis of Global Security offered the following assessment: "Counting the value of lives lost as well as property damage and lost production of goods and services, losses already exceed $100 billion. Including the loss in stock market wealth—the market's own estimate arising from expectations of lower corporate profits and higher discount rates for economic volatility—the price tag approaches $2 trillion."[42]

WASHINGTON, D.C., RESPONSE

Police, firefighters, and emergency responders in Washington, D.C., and Arlington, Virginia, moved quickly after the plane crash at the Pentagon. They put out the fire caused by the plane explosion, searched for and treated survivors, and moved workers and nearby residents away from the danger. The more limited area of damage to the Pentagon made rescue work easier than in New York City. Some problems did emerge, however. Emergency workers did not have special phone lines and could not communicate on overloaded cellular phone lines. They also lacked an ample supply of critical emergency equipment and a secure command center from which to run operations. Overall, the National Commission on Terrorist Attacks upon the United States (also known as the 9/11 Commission) lauded the response for dealing well with the complexities of working across federal, state, county, and city divisions.

The emergency response in the larger Washington, D.C., area did not go as well. Although no damage occurred outside the Pentagon, the possibility of other attacks heading toward the White House put the city on alert. In response, the mayor's office gave conflicting orders. One e-mail told city workers to evacuate, and then another followed shortly to say they should stay and keep the government functioning. Not until 1:27 P.M. did Mayor Anthony Williams declare a state of emergency and deploy National Guard troops. Even then, the mayor's office could not coordinate the emergency response by phone because callers overloaded the city's system. Satellite phones for an emergency stayed locked in storage because emergency operation leaders did not know about them. More generally, the D.C. police lacked an antiterrorism plan, and the Emergency Management Agency in the city lacked staff and funding.

Orders to evacuate federal office buildings in Washington, D.C., for all but essential federal workers came earlier, at 10:45 A.M. When federal workers left to go home, it caused massive traffic jams. The city had no plan in place to keep the streets clear, and local police and emergency vehicles could move only slowly through the gridlock. Fortunately, no other attacks came besides the one at the Pentagon, and the failures in response did not lead to loss of life.

According to an editorial in the *Washington Post*, "A review of last Tuesday's events suggests that the District was unprepared for the emergency and therefore unable to react and assist the public in a timely and effective fashion."[43] Mayor Williams later admitted the city responded slowly to the crisis, and Congress threatened to hold back funding for the city until it overhauled its emergency response plan.

THE FEDERAL GOVERNMENT RESPONSE

After an earlier 1993 bombing of the World Trade Center by Islamic terrorists and the 1995 Oklahoma City bombing, FEMA had started preparing for future terrorist attacks. In March 2001, less than six months before the September 11 attacks, the General Accounting Office submitted a report to Congress entitled *Combating Terrorism: FEMA Continues to Make Progress in Coordinating Preparedness and Response*.[44] The largely positive report noted that FEMA had taken several steps to deal with terrorist events. It first updated the Federal Response Plan to include terrorist events and established new emergency response teams to deal with mass casualties from terrorist attacks. It then worked with state and local agencies to make sure their plans mirrored federal plans. To help local responders, FEMA revised its training courses and drills for a terrorist attack. Despite the good efforts, however, the agency was unprepared for the special problems created by the events of

September 11. For example, the shutdown of the airports and airlines after the hijackings made it impossible for FEMA to fly its people and supplies to New York City quickly.

Still, FEMA implemented its terrorism response plan. It first sent urban search-and-rescue teams with specialized training to New York City and Washington, D.C. It set up field offices near the disasters and publicized a toll-free hotline to help disaster victims get assistance. It put medical care and mortuary teams on standby in New Jersey and Washington, D.C., to help when needed. And it helped local efforts to remove the millions of tons of debris. According to a White House memo, 3,571 federal personnel, including 1,596 from FEMA, worked directly on the response to the terrorist events.[45]

Besides using its own workers, FEMA coordinated the actions of 11 other federal agencies. Consider a few examples:

- The Department of Labor helped dislocated workers find jobs and checked the health and safety conditions at the site of the collapsed buildings.
- The Department of Health and Human Services brought health-care personnel to the sites to treat injuries of victims and workers.
- The Small Business Administration set up field offices to make low-interest loans to small businesses harmed by the attacks.
- The Environmental Protection Agency monitored air quality to lessen the environmental risks faced by disaster workers.
- The Army Corps of Engineers helped guide the safe removal and disposal of debris from the buildings.
- The Department of Justice offered victim assistance to individuals and families harmed by the attacks.

The Departments of Education, Interior, and Treasury contributed as well.

Two days after the disaster, on September 13, FEMA reported on response activities. Engineers had reopened roads, tunnels, and train tracks to and from Manhattan, more than 1.5 million people had donated blood, and utility companies had worked overtime to restore full power and other services to lower Manhattan. Soon after, FEMA requested special help from veterinarians and volunteers to deal with pets—a population often ignored in the effort to help people.

Perhaps the major source of federal support was financial. Within one month of the attacks, Congress and the president had approved a $40 billion emergency response package. About $2 billion went to FEMA for rescue and clearing operations and for individual and family assistance. Other federal departments and agencies joining the response also received a share, and much went directly to help state and local relief activities.

FEMA advertised the benefits it offered to victims of the terrorist attacks. According to a press release:

Federal disaster aid for victims and their families may include: reimbursement of temporary housing costs; low-interest loans for homeowners, renters and business owners to help with repair and replacement expenses not covered by insurance; financial assistance for those unemployed as a result of the disaster, including self-employed persons and others not normally eligible for unemployment; and grants for medical, funeral and other serious disaster-related expenses not covered by other assistance programs or insurance. In addition, free crisis counseling, disaster-related legal consultation, and information and referral services are offered.[46]

The official partner in federal relief efforts—the Red Cross—also assisted with people and money. It immediately called up 6,000 volunteers to help with the rescue and relief operations. The organization and its volunteers then opened 13 shelters for victims; counseled survivors, family members, and others; and organized drives for blood donations. The Red Cross also helped travelers stranded in airports after the attacks shut down all air traffic. For long-term assistance, the Red Cross created the Liberty Disaster Relief Fund to collect contributions for victims of the September 11 attacks. Within a year, it had distributed $643 million in assistance and planned to distribute another $200 million. As part of the Family Gift Program, the funds went largely to families of victims of the tragedy.

A MOVE FOR FEMA

In February 2001, seven months before the terrorist attacks, President George W. Bush appointed Joe Allbaugh as the director of FEMA. The former national campaign manager for the Bush 2000 Election Campaign planned to trim the agency and concentrate more on its primary goals. As the new director, Allbaugh expressed concern that FEMA had become bloated and wanted to reorganize and streamline the agency. One step in that direction came with the creation of a new office to manage attacks from weapons of mass destruction. After the 9/11 terrorist attacks, a more drastic reorganization of FEMA followed.

The Department of Homeland Security

Within a month of the September 11 attacks, President Bush created the Office of Homeland Security (OHS). Until a new Department of Homeland Security (DHS) could be established, the office would work from the White House. According to his executive order, "The mission of the Office shall be to develop and coordinate the implementation of a comprehensive national strategy to secure the United States from terrorist threats or attacks."[47] Tom Ridge, former congressional representative and then-governor of Pennsylvania, agreed to head the office as the special assistant to the president for homeland security.

As part of its mission, the new office took on duties that overlapped with those of FEMA. The duties included coordinating national efforts to prepare for and mitigate the consequences of terrorist attacks within the United States. Since terrorist attacks were one form of emergency or disaster, FEMA previously had some of these responsibilities. Another agency would now review and assess emergency response plans, coordinate exercises to respond to terrorist attacks, and ensure the readiness of federal response teams. It seemed logical to make FEMA part of the larger homeland security effort, and plans to move FEMA to DHS went forward.

The creation of DHS from OHS involved the largest government reorganization to occur in 50 years. The authority for the change came from the Homeland Security Act passed by Congress on November 22, 2002. Tom Ridge became secretary of the new department, which would have cabinet status like the Departments of Defense, Justice, and Transportation. Although the department officially began operating on January 24, 2003, bringing the varied parts of the department together took longer. DHS had the difficult task of merging agencies as diverse as FEMA, the Coast Guard, and the Immigration and Naturalization Service.

Not everyone favored shifting FEMA to DHS. Critics believed that the change would impair FEMA's effectiveness. They worried that DHS would concentrate almost exclusively on terrorism and select personnel from the military and law enforcement. FEMA, in contrast, had broader goals and a civilian tradition. Worse, in becoming part of DHS, FEMA would lose its cabinet rank. It no longer would have the prestige and access to the president that it had during the Clinton years. It seemed as if FEMA had been demoted to second-string. Defenders of the change pointed to some positives: FEMA would gain new responsibilities in dealing with the terrorist threat and receive billions in new funding to help communities face the threat. Secretary Ridge, for example, believed that FEMA would become more effective when it belonged to an organization devoted more generally to security.

FEMA employees took the more negative view. Worried about the loss of independence and feeling low morale, scores of lifelong employees left.[48] The director of FEMA, Joseph Allbaugh, joined the private sector in 2003 and was replaced by Michael Brown, the FEMA counsel. The former director, James Witt, believed that downgrading the cabinet status of FEMA badly hurt the agency. In testifying before Congress about his concerns, he predicted that loss of morale, resources, and experienced people in FEMA would weaken the nation's ability to respond to a major disaster. Witt's predictions proved true. As part of DHS, FEMA could no longer appeal to the president for funds. It instead had to compete with other divisions for a share of the money going to DHS. In comments several years later, Michael Brown, the new director of FEMA, said that funds meant for FEMA ended up going to other parts of DHS. With concerns over terrorism heightened by the September 11 attacks, preparations for natural disasters lost out in the bureaucratic infighting.

Other problems created by the reorganization did not appear until several years later, during the next major disaster. Placing FEMA within DHS confused the responsibility for primary leadership in disaster response—both the secretary of DHS and the director of FEMA had major roles. The move added another layer of bureaucracy to work through in responding to a disaster.

Echoing these concerns, the General Accounting Office published a January 2003 review of FEMA and the special challenges it faced in joining DHS.[49] The report complimented FEMA for the progress it made in working with state and local governments to prepare and respond to disasters. However, it also expressed concerns about shifting resources from natural disasters to human-caused disasters. With its lean staff, the agency had to respond to 49 disasters in 2002. Adding new homeland security demands, the report noted, could overwhelm FEMA. Indeed, Director Brown complained that FEMA budget cuts and loss of personnel would keep it from responding properly to a major disaster.

One other change that split traditional duties of FEMA would not come for many years. In June 2005, a formal proposal circulated to move emergency training and planning from FEMA to another part of DHS. Historically, FEMA focused on four components of disasters: preparedness, response, recovery, and mitigation. DHS now developed plans to move the preparedness and mitigation goals to another DHS unit. In principle, it made sense to combine sections with the similar goals of preventing terrorism and preparing for natural disasters into one division. However, the two goals required different approaches: preventing terrorism worked through security and law enforcement, while preparing for disasters worked through planning and evaluation of risk. According to the defenders of FEMA, a new and separate preparedness division would lack the critical knowledge of disaster response and recovery duties that remained part of FEMA.

National Response Plan

In November 2004, DHS announced a new framework for disaster response. Called the National Response Plan (NRP), it presented an all-hazards approach for responding to both natural and terrorist disasters.[50] By adding goals of preventing and responding to terrorism, the plan extended the Federal Response Plan used previously to deal with natural disasters. It laid out a framework to combine the activities of all the partners in disaster response into a unified structure. Implementing the framework would be no small task given the variety of partners—homeland security, emergency managers, police and law enforcement, firefighters, public workers, public health experts, first responders, recovery workers, health and safety specialists, medical services, volunteer organizations, the private sector, and elected officials at all levels of government. The plan described how the federal government would coordinate and work with these partners.

Reaffirming previous practice, the NRP designated that all incidents would be handled first at the lowest level. The response would begin with police, firefighters, public health and medical workers, emergency managers, and other personnel located closest to the event. Federal support would come only when the incident exceeded local or state capabilities. In the words of a DHS document, the plan then "ensures the seamless integration of the federal government" and "provides the means to swiftly deliver federal support."[51]

The NRP proposed three general strategies to reach these laudable goals. First, it advised setting up a procedure to declare that an Incident of National Significance occurred. An Incident of National Significance is an event that threatens such extraordinary casualties, damage, and disruption as to require a coordinated response from all levels of government, the private sector, and nongovernmental organizations. The incidents affect not only the immediate location but, like the September 11 terrorist attacks, also affect the national economy. A declaration gives the secretary of Homeland Security authority to manage the multiagency response to the incident.

Second, the declaration of an Incident of National Significance would trigger a response based on the National Incident Management System (NIMS). The system lays out duties, procedures, and guidelines for each partner in the response to follow. Ideally, consistent procedures and guidelines allow different types of organizations located in diverse parts of the country to share common understandings and communicate easily. Setting up a unified command based on the procedures and guidelines ideally minimizes confusion across towns, counties, states, and levels of government. At the same time, the management system should remain flexible enough that partners can adjust to the circumstances of a particular incident.

Third, the NRP recommended that there be several centers to coordinate the varied response activities. The Homeland Security Operations Center in Washington, D.C., "serves as the primary national-level multiagency situational awareness and operational coordination center." [52] This center includes a national response coordination center and a regional response coordination center. In turn, these two centers are aided by an interagency incident management group, a joint field office, and a designated principal federal official.

Given its ambitious goals, the NRP is filled with complex and daunting details. Figuring out how it works requires careful study and substantial experience with incident response. Even one long-term FEMA employee, Leo Bosner, called the plan difficult to understand.[53] He said that the administration could have revised the more familiar and effective Federal Response Plan to include terrorism but, for political reasons and publicity, started from scratch in developing the NRP. The plan ultimately included 32 separate agencies as partners, making it politically popular but also expansive and complex.

Whatever the strengths and weaknesses of the NRP, its adoption was accompanied by new funding from the federal government. Success of the plan depended on preparation by state and local organizations, which required financial support. First responders, so important in the attacks on New York City and the Pentagon, received funds for new training and equipment. Local emergency management organizations received funds to develop plans and go through exercises. And communities across the country received funds to simulate a terrorist attack and response. However, a real test of the NRP would come in less than a year after its publication.

HURRICANE KATRINA: FAILURE IN DISASTER RESPONSE

In August 2005, Hurricane Katrina grew into one of the most destructive natural disasters in U.S. history. Katrina caused at least 1,863 confirmed deaths and 1,840 missing persons now presumed dead. With winds reaching 130 miles per hour, covering 93,000 square miles, and causing a storm surge to reach 27 feet, the hurricane displaced 770,000 people, destroyed the homes of tens of thousands, and did $96 billion in damage. Taking the brunt of the hurricane's force, the Gulf Coast states will take years to recover, and the city of New Orleans will never be the same.

In the face of this challenge, the disaster response failed at all levels of government. The changes made in FEMA after the September 11 terrorist attacks and the new National Response Plan hurt rather than helped in the federal response to Hurricane Katrina. State and local officials, also unprepared for the magnitude of the disaster, performed poorly. With this failure, questions once more arose about the government's ability to deal with catastrophic disasters.

Ironically, government officials knew of the risk for such a catastrophe. Experts had said for years that New Orleans could not survive a direct hit from a major hurricane. About 70 to 80 percent of the city lies below sea level, and the system of levees (reinforced earthen banks) and floodwalls (cement walls built on top of the levees) that stopped the flooding under normal circumstances could not contain the surge from a strong hurricane. FEMA had known these facts when in 2004 it performed an exercise called Hurricane Pam based on a scenario for a hurricane to hit New Orleans and flood the city. As the events of August 25 to September 7, 2005, showed, however, the knowledge helped little in the response.

BEFORE, DURING, AND AFTER KATRINA: A DAY-BY-DAY ACCOUNT

On Thursday, August 25, 2005, a Category 1 hurricane named Katrina moved through southern Florida. Although not a severe storm—its winds reached only 80 miles per hour—it killed 11 state residents and left millions without electricity. As it moved into the Gulf of Mexico, however, the hurricane strengthened.

On Friday, August 26, the storm became a Category 2 hurricane with winds of 100 miles per hour. Experts predicted that it would get even stronger. Anticipating that the storm would move up through the Gulf Coast, Louisiana governor Kathleen Blanco and Mississippi governor Haley Barbour declared states of emergency.

On Saturday, August 27, Katrina became a Category 3 hurricane with winds of 115 miles per hour. The National Hurricane Center issued a hurricane watch early in the day and upgraded it to a hurricane warning later in the day. More worrisome than the strong winds was the potential for severe flooding. If the hurricane struck New Orleans directly, as computer models suggested, then massive flooding would result. The storm surge might well exceed the height of the levees and flood areas of the city below sea level. Before the storm reached land, President Bush declared a state of emergency for Alabama, Mississippi, and Louisiana. Residents began to evacuate coastal areas, clogging all lanes of the highways out of town. Mississippi governor Haley Barbour ordered mandatory evacuation from Hancock County on the coast near New Orleans. FEMA Director Michael Brown and hurricane experts urged New Orleans to do the same for its residents. Still, the weather service could say only that there was a 45 percent chance that a Category 4 or 5 hurricane would strike New Orleans directly.

On Sunday, August 28, Katrina reached the most powerful stage of a hurricane—Category 5. With winds of 160 miles per hour, the storm worried experts, who predicted dire consequences for the Gulf Coast. At 9:30

Introduction to Disaster Response

A.M., New Orleans mayor Ray Nagin announced mandatory evacuation of the city. Those people remaining in the city and surrounding areas who could drive started to leave, but more than 100,000 people did not have access to a car. The New Orleans Comprehensive Emergency Management Plan called for buses to take residents without cars out of the city, but city leaders decided to move them to shelters in town. Some 10,000 residents went to the New Orleans Superdome, a large football stadium on high ground. A last-minute decision sent many others staying in the city to the Ernest Morial Convention Center. Although a large and sturdy building, the center had not been formally designated as a shelter and had no stored water, food, or supplies.

On Monday, August 29, Katrina made landfall at 6:10 A.M. as a Category 4 storm with winds of 145 miles per hour. The winds left much damage—downed trees and power lines, roofs torn off (including part of the Superdome), and shattered windows. In Mississippi, 30 confirmed deaths occurred among residents of an apartment complex near the casino resort town of Biloxi. Evacuated buildings along the coast were obliterated by the winds and water. The worst damage did not become apparent immediately, however. Some of the levees in New Orleans that surrounded canals gave way, letting water from Lake Pontchartrain flow into city streets. President Bush released funds for the city by declaring a major disaster, and Governor Blanco called in the National Guard. Surprisingly, however, little action occurred. According to a memo from Michael Brown, the 1,000 rescue workers ordered to New Orleans had 48 hours to get there; another 2,000 had seven days to arrive. Governor Blanco called President Bush for help and got assurance that it was on the way. In the meantime, looting broke out in the city.

On Tuesday, August 30, the city continued to flood, and efforts to plug the levees failed. Water eventually covered 80 percent of the city and reached the rooftops of homes in the lowest areas. Rescue workers traveled in boats and helicopters to pick up those stranded by the water. In gruesome images of the damage, dead bodies floated through the water. Looting became more widespread, sometimes from people desperate for food, water, and supplies, sometimes from theft of nonessential goods. The looting received much attention in the media, but officials seemed unaware of the seriousness of the ongoing flooding. FEMA activated the National Response Plan but asked rescuers coming into the city to wait until the National Guard had secured the area and could guarantee safety. In the meantime, some 50,000 to 100,000 people remaining in the city, most concentrated in the Superdome or the convention center, had no way to get out. At the convention center, dead bodies were stacked on the side of the building, a dead man was left sitting in a lawn chair in the sun, bathrooms overflowed with feces, blood stained the stairways, and people shrieked in pain.[54] Although not in as desperate shape as New Orleans, Mississippi reported 100 dead from the hurricane and a shortage of shelter, food, and water.

On Wednesday, August 31, evacuation of some trapped New Orleans residents began. After Governor Blanco ordered evacuation of the city, the Texas governor offered use of the Houston Astrodome for those currently in the Superdome (where conditions had become intolerable). That morning, buses began arriving to take survivors out of the city. However, Mayor Nagin responded to looting by declaring martial law and shifting police from search-and-rescue operations to crime duties. Other federal agencies began to help. The Department of Defense dispatched four navy ships with supplies, the Department of Health and Human Services trucked in medical supplies, and FEMA sent 39 medical teams and 1,700 trucks. These efforts did little to deal with the massive problems, however.

On Thursday, September 1, problems mounted in New Orleans. Despite the presence of 30,000 National Guard troops in the area, crime and violence continued. National Guard troops arrived from Iraq with orders to shoot-to-kill if needed to restore order. Reports of shots fired at rescue helicopters led FEMA to suspend water rescue operations. Other rescue efforts slowed too. A shortage of buses made it hard to remove the tens of thousands of people still in the Superdome and convention center. People without food and water spilled out onto the sidewalks. Doctors in hospitals, where many patients remained, said they had no food, water, or power. Residents trapped on an overpass above the water wrote the word *HELP* in large block letters on the pavement for media helicopters to see. Mayor Nagin called the situation critical and called for more buses (hundreds of buses in a flooded lot remained unusable). As the city appeared to descend into anarchy, FEMA leaders said they did not know about all the people trapped in the convention center.

On Friday, September 2, President Bush, who had flown into the New Orleans airport, admitted to the failed relief effort and promised to correct the problems. He said earlier in the day that Michael Brown, the FEMA director, had done a heck of a job. More convoys of National Guard troops entered the town along with truckloads of supplies. At noon, military trucks delivered food and water to the Superdome. However, officials turned down a request from the Red Cross to bring in supplies; they said more time was needed to prepare an escort, and the aid never got to the city. While many appreciated the decisive action of the military in bringing supplies, those still trapped in the city shouted with anger about the lack of help. A situation update from FEMA described the response:

In what looked like a scene from a Third World country, some people threw their arms heavenward and others nearly fainted with joy as the trucks and hundreds of soldiers arrived in the punishing midday heat. But there were also profane jeers from many in the crowd of nearly 20,000 outside the Convention Center, which a day earlier seemed on the verge of a riot, with desperate people seething with anger over the lack of anything to eat or drink.[55]

Fox news reporter Geraldo Rivera, reporting live from New Orleans, expressed the dismay and anger he and others felt over not getting rescued or even knowing when the rescue would come.

On Saturday, September 3, still more active duty forces went to the Gulf Coast, with National Guard troops now numbering 40,000. However, the strain on police had taken a toll: Reports said that 200 walked off the job, and two committed suicide. Progress continued in evacuating people from New Orleans, with planes flying many residents to other cities. Workers began removing corpses that had been floating in the water for several days. The Superdome finally was cleared, but those trapped inside for many days told stories of filth, rape, violence, and even murder during their stay. The U.S. Department of Labor announced a grant of $62 million to provide work for dislocated workers. In a national address, President Bush said, "Many of our citizens simply are not getting the help they need, especially in New Orleans. And that is unacceptable."[56]

On Sunday, September 4, evacuation efforts concentrated on those centered in and near the convention center and on patients still in hospitals. Some armed gangs still roamed the city, but the presence of the National Guard limited violence and looting. States across the country took in evacuees from New Orleans, and Carnival Cruises sent several ships to house hurricane victims. As rescue efforts proceeded, concern grew about the deaths, which numbered in the thousands. Criticisms that the federal government failed to act because of racism and unconcern with the largely African-American residents of New Orleans grew, though federal officials denied the charge.

On Monday, September 5, one week after the hurricane hit, workers closed a major gap in one of the levees and began to pump water out of the city. Rescuers on boats continued a house-to-house search for survivors, while a curfew remained in force at night. Former presidents George H. W. Bush and Bill Clinton announced they would lead a fund-raising effort for victims of Katrina.

On Tuesday, September 6, an estimated 10,000 people remained in the city, many still waiting for rescue. Given the threat of disease from the contaminated water, Mayor Nagin called for total evacuation, but some residents wanted to stay with their homes. By this time, the streets were safe and some power and utilities started working. To speed financial help, FEMA planned to give victims debit cards to use for expenses. President Bush and congressional leaders announced they intended to investigate the botched response to Katrina.

On Wednesday, September 7, with the worst of the crisis over, President Bush called for $52 billion in aid to supplement the $10.5 billion already provided by Congress. Congress passed the supplement the next day. Police and soldiers continued to go house to house to evacuate stragglers and minimize the dangers of the bacteria-infested water. By this time, disaster efforts began to focus on recovery rather than relief. However, one other tragedy of the disaster received new attention: Some 600,000 animals either died or were left without shelter because of the hurricane.

BLAME AND MORE HURRICANES FOLLOW

With the death, suffering, and destruction caused by Hurricane Katrina and the obvious problems of response, criticism came from many sources: the victims, the media, Congress, and the public. Even the United Nations Human Rights Committee weighed in, saying that the U.S. government needed to do more to protect the rights of the poor and disadvantaged.

Charges and Countercharges

Blame for the failed response centered on FEMA. Director Michael Brown, accused of bungling the operation, was removed from control and sent back to Washington on September 9. Critics say Brown had a padded résumé and few qualifications to lead FEMA. He resigned on September 12 as FEMA director. David Paulison, a career firefighter with experience in emergency preparedness, later took his place. President Bush also accepted responsibility for the failed response. According to polls, the public agreed that the government did not do enough to deal with the damage caused by Katrina.

State and local officials claimed that the federal bureaucracy sometimes blocked efforts to get aid to the city. Aaron Broussard, president of Jefferson Parish south of New Orleans, complained on *Meet the Press* that the federal government turned back trucks with water sent by Wal-Mart. Others in the state government said FEMA interfered with the delivery of aid from the governors of Illinois and New Mexico. Federal officials, worried about the dangers to outsiders, even kept the Red Cross from entering the city. Worse according to critics, FEMA kept promising supplies and help that it did not deliver. They simply could not handle the problems brought on by the hurricane.

It seems that paralysis set in as high-level officials debated who was in charge. DHS officials operated out of a communications center in Washington, D.C., but could not get accurate information to make decisions from so far away. Tensions between FEMA Director Michael Brown and DHS Secretary Michael Chertoff weakened their leadership. The secretary of the Department of Defense did not want to overstep the authority of FEMA or replace local law enforcement with troops. And neither the mayor nor the governor took charge as Rudolph Giuliani had in New York City after the September 11 attacks.

Critics see the failure as ultimately a problem with leadership of the president. On vacation when the storm came, President Bush did not cut short his time off until several days later. His delayed recognition of the seriousness of the disaster reinforced the slowness of the FEMA bureaucracy. More important according to critics, the government had redirected resources toward prevention of terrorism and threats such as biochemical weapons. In a report on its sluggish response, DHS admitted that it deserved criticism: "DHS's prevention and preparedness for terrorism have overshadowed that for natural hazards."[57] Similarly, government resources, military equipment, and the National Guard troops deployed for the war in Iraq could not help. Because of administration priorities, FEMA lacked staff, funding, and the ability to respond adequately to a major natural disaster.

Black activists such as Jesse Jackson saw the problem as coming from elsewhere—racism. Jackson claimed that disregard for poor African Americans in New Orleans led government agencies to downplay the seriousness of the disaster until it was too late. The media exaggerated the negative impression of disaster victims by showing pictures and films of black residents they labeled as looters. If the city was largely white and affluent, Jackson implied, FEMA would have responded quickly, efficiently, and generously. Other celebrities echoed these criticisms. During a hurricane relief telethon on NBC, rapper Kanye West caused controversy by saying, "George Bush doesn't care about black people."[58]

There was in fact plenty of blame to go around. Mayor Nagin and the city of New Orleans also performed poorly. Despite knowing that at least 100,000 people in the city did not have cars, city officials did not help to evacuate them. The decision to send tens of thousands to the sturdy structures of the Superdome and convention center made some sense. However, neither building could house large numbers of people over several days. These shelters ran out of water, lacked police to keep order, needed medical supplies to treat the sick, and could not dispose of all the waste. With gangs, criminals, and drug users mixed in with families, the Superdome in particular became dangerous. The term *Nagin's folly* described his decision to delay mandatory evacuation and concentrate so many people in small areas.

State and local officials failed in other ways. According to DHS Secretary Michael Chertoff, his agency had trouble working with the state and city governments. FEMA typically acts on requests made by state and local governments. Without clear direction from state and local officials, however, federal officials said they lacked authority to act. Communication channels across levels of government certainly worked badly. Further, the state and city failed in its law enforcement goals. The New Orleans police, although understandably overwhelmed by the demands it faced, could not keep order. Despite this problem, the governor was slow in sending the National Guard and state police to help.

Many New Orleans residents added to the response problems. For example, owners of one nursing home left the city without evacuating the residents. After 34 died, the owner was later arrested and charged with negligent homicide. Gangs and criminals also disrupted rescue operations. Concerns about crime led authorities to concentrate on stopping looting rather than aiding disaster victims. Keeping bus drivers, truck drivers, and volunteers from entering the city until the National Guard made the streets safe delayed the rescue.

Rita, Wilma, and the Worst Hurricane Season on Record

While still assigning blame and trying to deal with the devastation in New Orleans, another hurricane called for more emergency preparations. On September 24, less than a month after Katrina, Hurricane Rita made landfall near the Louisiana-Texas border. Rita forced re-evacuation of New Orleans and postponed reopening the city. Residents in several Louisiana parishes evacuated as well. In Texas, Governor Rick Perry, having seen the damage of Katrina to Louisiana and Mississippi, ordered mandatory evacuations of coastal areas in his state and mobilized the National Guard.

The federal government aimed to prepare better for this hurricane than it did for Katrina. To monitor preparations for Hurricane Rita, President Bush visited FEMA headquarters in Washington, D.C., and the Northern Command headquarters in Colorado. DHS Secretary Chertoff declared Rita an Incident of National Significance before the hurricane reached land. The federal government moved truckloads of supplies near the Gulf Coast to allow for quick delivery to damaged areas. Coast Guard ships stayed near the coast so that, if needed, they could evacuate residents. The National Guard went on early alert, and medical personnel stood by to help. Utility companies drew up special plans to restore power and phones quickly.

In the end, Hurricane Rita killed 120 and caused $10 billion in damage. Texas avoided major destruction, but some towns in southwest Louisiana suffered heavy damage. Many residents stranded in these towns had to be rescued. The storm fortunately did not hit New Orleans directly, but water broke through the levees and re-flooded some parts of the city. The rest of the country felt the impact as well: Drivers endured rising gas prices as the storm closed many oil refineries.

Still another storm, the strongest of the season and indeed the strongest Atlantic hurricane ever recorded, came several weeks later. Hurricane Wilma first hit Mexico and Cuba before making landfall in Florida on October 24. Officials in Florida ordered mandatory evacuation of areas in the Florida Keys in preparation for the hurricane. At least 35 residents of south Florida died in the storm.

Wanting to avoid the communication problems apparent in dealing with Katrina, FEMA did more to cooperate with state and local authorities this time. According to a FEMA press release, "The State Emergency Response Team (SERT) and FEMA officials' joint Wilma Command at the State Emergency Operations Center in Tallahassee immediately put response measures into place to support the efforts of local emergency responders following the landfall of Hurricane Wilma."[59] FEMA had teams in place close to the projected path of the hurricane on Florida's west coast. The teams planned to move in as quickly as possible once the storm passed. Federal Coordinating Officer Justin DeMello said, "We've equipped our teams with satellite phones so that as they assess the situation, they can report the needs of the community to the command center and we can immediately help our local partners meet residents' needs."[60]

Overall, Katrina, Rita, Wilma, and other hurricanes made the 2005 hurricane season the most active in recorded Atlantic history. During the period from June 1 to November 30, 2005, a record 28 tropical and subtropical storms formed, and 15 became hurricanes. Florida suffered through eight hurricanes over a period of 14 months. State residents could barely settle back from one evacuation before they had to leave again. Across all states, the deaths and damages, most prominently from Katrina, topped all previous records. The severe weather also overwhelmed emergency relief organizations.

Predictions that the 2006 hurricane season would be just as severe as the previous year put Gulf Coast residents on edge. Forecasters called for eight to 10 hurricanes, leading to fear, stockpiling, and millions spent on preparation in hurricane-prone areas. The forecasts thankfully turned out wrong. To the relief of nearly everyone, the 2006 hurricane season was a mild one.

WHAT WENT WRONG

Three reports, all released in February 2006, investigated the relief problems after Katrina and recommended improvements.[61] Reports from the General Accounting Office (GAO), the House Select Committee, and the White House agreed that Katrina brought catastrophic problems that would challenge even the best response system. The sheer size of the storm, the millions of people affected by it, and the flooding of New Orleans that followed made the disaster more severe than normal. The reports further agreed that the breakdown in response involved all levels of government. Despite many heroic actions of individuals and groups, Katrina exposed flaws in the national capacity to respond to a catastrophic event.

First, the reports concluded that the disaster response lacked clear and decisive leadership. No one seemed willing to take the initiative to get the job done. FEMA said it waited for state and local officials to make requests, while state and local officials waited for FEMA to take action. The GAO report recommended that one person needed to be in charge, and this person needed to have access to the president. Just as after the poor response to Hurricane Andrew, the reports called for placing a disaster head in the White House who could act on behalf of the president. Although the FEMA director became part of the cabinet in the 1990s, the arrangement was dismantled in 2003. The reorganization that came with the creation of DHS led to confusion and infighting among government agencies. It left many in DHS unfamiliar with disaster procedures. And though the NRP called for a unified command structure, this never emerged.

With the lack of clear leadership came inaction rather than action, passivity rather than initiative. Mayor Nagin delayed the mandatory evacuation, while federal officials delayed declaring Katrina an Incident of National Significance and implementing the NRP. Not knowing what to do, some officials hoped to avoid making a mistake by doing little or nothing at all. Some of the reports attributed such problems at least in part to poor leadership in the White House. More than anyone else, the president can stop the infighting and order action.

Second, the reports concluded that poor advance planning made effective response nearly impossible. The planning failed to include ways to evacuate persons without cars in New Orleans, get supplies and trucks ready to go immediately after the hurricane passed through, and find communication channels when normal channels went out. Officials should have foreseen these problems. It seems obvious that many residents would need public transportation, supplies would need to be organized for delivery ahead of time, and phone lines would become unusable after the storm. Although plans somewhere no doubt listed these needs, those in charge appeared unfamiliar with them.

The reports argued that responders need practice and training to follow the plans effectively. Some pointed out that FEMA had not completed the Hurricane Pam exercise begun earlier in 2004. Even the incomplete exercise offered lessons for the real thing, but these lessons did not guide preparations for Katrina. If they had, those in charge would have foreseen some of the problems. For example, government officials would have known to work more closely with the military and private companies. About 20,000 active-duty troops and 50,000 National Guard troops ended up helping but had little guidance. Similarly, private companies helped deliver supplies but could not overcome the confusion among emergency leaders.

Third, emergency planning should focus on severe disasters, not just normal disasters. The reports noted that FEMA did well responding to smaller disasters but did not prepare for something as overpowering as Katrina. Business-as-usual approaches do not work in extraordinary circumstances. As the House Select Committee says, "Category 5 needs elicited a Category 1 response."[62] For severe disasters, special efforts must help police keep law and order, medical personnel deal with injuries, and officials assess the damage and determine areas of greatest need. Most of all, leaders need to act quickly—delay in recognizing the seriousness of a disaster makes the response all the more difficult.

Plans for Change

The White House report listed many other more specific recommendations—125 in total. Given the president's sponsorship of the report, DHS and disaster agencies will adopt most of them. To summarize, changes to come will include the following:

- outlining a clear command structure that involves the White House and the military;
- developing advanced technology for communication during the breakdown of normal channels;
- stockpiling supplies and planning to deliver them quickly to areas in need;
- planning evacuations from large cities, including for those people unable to leave on their own;
- supporting law enforcement agencies undergoing the excess strain of dealing with disorder after a disaster;
- delivering medical support and supplies during a crisis;
- finding temporary housing for evacuees;
- restoring critical utilities, roads, bridges, and levees after a disaster; and
- taking advantage of charitable groups and volunteers ready to help.

The list could go on—failures occurred in almost every aspect of the response to Katrina. Even a short list of improvements could do much to save lives and property in the next catastrophe.

Congress passed legislation to handle one other problem not addressed by FEMA—the death and suffering of pets left on their own during a disaster. The legislation requires local emergency organizations to include pets in their preparedness plans. Such plans might involve building emergency pet shelters or finding ways to transport pets out of danger. Along with helping the pets, animal protection efforts might prevent owners from risking their lives to save their pets.

One last point deserves mention. Despite the many things that went wrong in the Katrina response, many things also went right. Charitable and volunteer organizations showed remarkable commitment to helping. Mississippi governor Barbour received praise for his handling of the disaster. People running hotels, hospitals, local neighborhood groups, and search-and-rescue teams dealt creatively with the problems they faced and did much to limit the suffering of those trapped in New Orleans. Despite the stress they faced, victims of Katrina generally acted responsibly and rationally.

Government officials aim to use these lessons in planning for the next catastrophic disaster. FEMA has increased the number of contractors to provide supplies and purchased new Global Positioning System devices to attach to delivery trucks. Authorities can then keep track of movement of supplies and direct them to areas most in need. FEMA also bought thousands of satellite phones and handheld radios to help responders keep in touch and coordinate their actions. For New Orleans in particular, sound evacuation plans are in place. FEMA director David Paulison says of the evacuation plans, "We've gone through those, we've rehearsed them, we're very comfortable that those are going to work."[63] Even DHS Secretary Michael Chertoff came to town to join one evacuation exercise. Of course, the success of these changes can be tested fully only with a real disaster.

Longer-Term Problems of Recovery

Controversy involving FEMA did not end with the response—it has continued steadily since September 2005. With most housing destroyed in New Orleans and many parts of Mississippi, many victims of the disaster still needed new places to live as of 2007. Many residents moved to other parts of the country but hoped to return to their homes or find new ones in New Orleans. FEMA wanted to supply trailers to replace tents, shelters, and homes of friends. By the end of 2005, however, locals again blamed FEMA for slow action. In a repeat of the confusion between federal and local authorities, FEMA said that it had 125,000 trailers ready but could not deliver them until parish officials told them where the trailers should go. Around the same time, a New Orleans judge ordered FEMA to postpone its plan to evict disaster victims from hotels in which they had been staying.

Months later, FEMA announced it would end or cut benefits for 55,000 families receiving housing vouchers. Many Katrina victims who lost their homes had moved to other cities such as Houston and relied on vouchers to pay rent. By their accounts, FEMA promised them a full year of free housing. Eight months later, however, FEMA determined that many were no longer eligible for the vouchers and wanted others to move to less costly trailers. The victims and mayors of the cities they lived in objected, accusing FEMA of reneging on its promises. In this case, efforts to control costs conflicted with the lack of alternative housing and resources of some victims.

Scandal also has occurred in recovery operations. GAO criticized the federal agencies in charge of the cleanup—FEMA and the Army Corps of Engineers—for lax oversight.[64] According to reports, costs grew because four to six contractors ended up doing cleanup work. The first contractor often hired a subcontractor, which hired another, and so on. As summarized in a newspaper story, after accounting for all costs, "the prime contractor bills the government 15 times as much for the same job."[65] Complaining about the abuse, Representative Henry Waxman (D. Calif.) said the Katrina cleanup showed "widespread mismanagement, waste and fraud."[66]

Still another report from the GAO in 2006 highlighted one more failure in recovery efforts: FEMA lacked proper controls for abuse and fraud in dispersing relief funds. The Individuals and Households Program gives money to victims soon after a disaster. These funds are meant for repairs and living expenses until recipients get back on their feet. After Katrina, FEMA got the funds out quickly by giving debit cards to victims, which made it hard to prevent misuse of the funds. The GAO report gave examples of people registering falsely for relief, getting duplicate payments for damage, and improperly spending the funds. FEMA funds paid for bail, weapons, adult entertainment, and football tickets. Calls followed for FEMA to do more to prevent such abuse and to prosecute those cheating the government.

Progress So Far

A year after Katrina, New Orleans has seen mixed progress toward recovery. On the plus side, a vibrant nightlife has returned to the French Quarter, and many restaurants have reopened. Convention business and tourism have returned (often mixed with side trips to damaged areas). According to a story in the *New York Times*, "Census estimates suggest that the city is repopulating at a much faster pace than predicted a few months ago."[67] On the minus side, the population is only half of its pre-Katrina size of 455,000, and only one of 10 businesses has reopened. Most small businesses do not have cash to make repairs or even repay disaster loans available from the federal government. Chain stores such as McDonald's and Toys "R" Us have not reopened because they lack customers and housing for employees.

Disputes in New Orleans between the city council and homeowners in less affluent neighborhoods flooded by Katrina have slowed plans for rebuilding. The homeowners believe the council's plan for redevelopment emphasizes projects for tourists and business, such as a new light-rail system, rather than housing for former residents displaced by the flood. A moratorium on building recommended for some neighborhoods angered many residents, especially African Americans. They worry that buying up land with damaged homes for redevelopment will price them out of the housing market.

In Mississippi, legalized casinos on the coast near Biloxi started to reopen in summer 2006. Katrina demolished many of the casinos and nearby resorts, but demand for gambling has created a small boom. The main problem in the area comes from lack of housing. Little remains for casino workers, and rents have skyrocketed. One area attorney summarized the major recovery problem: "Affordable housing is the number one, two, and three priority down here."[68]

Private charities continue to help the damaged areas. In just the first two months after Katrina, Americans gave well over $1 billion in donations. Former presidents George H. W. Bush and Bill Clinton raised about $119 million for relief. Damaged colleges and universities received $30 million, while damaged churches, temples, mosques, and other places of worship received $20 million. The remaining funds went for recovery needs in Louisiana, Mississippi, and Alabama that other assistance did not cover. The Salvation Army maintained a center in New Orleans that helped 75–100 people a day by counseling victims and handing out vouchers for beds, refrigerators, and furniture. Catholic Charities likewise continues to help those in need. During a visit in April 2006, President Bush joined Governor Blanco and Mayor Nagin in visiting a house being built by volunteers for Habitat for Humanity. The president encouraged other volunteers to come to New Orleans.

President Bush continued to offer support for recovery. In addition to $60 billion in federal funds already allocated, the president proposed spending another $4.2 billion in grants for places damaged by Katrina and $2.2 billion for levee repairs in Louisiana. A spending bill passed in July 2006 did not grant all the president's requests but was generous: It set aside $3.7 billion for Louisiana flood-control projects and $5.2 billion for direct grants to states. Louisiana plans to use its share to repair and rebuild damaged housing.

Despite billions in aid, homeowners in New Orleans complain they have received little money for rebuilding. Funds went to the Army Corp of Engineers and cleanup contractors, and private insurers started to pay those who purchased an expensive flood policy. Otherwise, those most in need struggle with the bureaucracy to get even a small share of the public funding. The funds also have done little to rebuild the institutions needed for families to return to New Orleans. Public schools, hospitals, and electrical utilities remain badly damaged. Like the response to Katrina, the recovery in New Orleans has been slow.

Any meaningful recovery for New Orleans and areas close by must include ways to prevent another disaster. Most experts knew the levees in New Orleans and towns along the Mississippi Gulf Coast could not withstand a severe hurricane. The billions going toward rebuilding the levees and damaged towns will return them more-or-less to the state before Katrina. Without doing more, another strong hurricane will do the same damage as Katrina. At one extreme, some suggest rebuilding New Orleans on higher ground that lies farther upstream on the Mississippi. Less extreme changes might include razing rather than rebuilding some low-lying parts of New Orleans, though residents of those areas angrily reject such a plan. Along with funds for recovery, improved protection against future hurricanes is needed.

THE FOUR STEPS OF EFFECTIVE DISASTER RESPONSE

Experience with disaster response over the last several decades has increased the knowledge needed for response. Experts today treat effective disaster response as part of a four-step cycle: preparedness, response, recovery, and mitigation. *Preparedness* (or the state of being prepared) refers to actions taken before the disaster to allow effective response. *Response* refers to emergency actions taken just before, during, and just after the disaster to reduce casualties, damage, and disruption. *Recovery* refers to actions taken after the disaster to repair, rebuild, and restore community life to normal. *Mitigation* refers to actions taken both after one disaster and before another to reduce the physical impacts of hazards on a community.

PREPAREDNESS

Preparing for a disaster involves more than the actions of FEMA, the government, emergency managers, and disaster relief organizations. Individuals, families, and businesses also must do their part to get ready. Disaster experts give guidance, but community members must follow that guidance. All too often this point gets lost in discussing disasters. So much attention goes to what the government does that citizens appear as helpless victims.

In fact, people and private organizations should be prepared to rely first on their own actions during an emergency.

Citizen Preparedness

The first thing citizens should do in preparing for a disaster is to learn about what could happen. What type of natural hazard is most likely to strike? What kinds of dangers are they most likely to face? Most residents of areas prone to hurricanes, tornadoes, and earthquakes vaguely know about the risks but tend to minimize their importance. The more knowledge people have about a potential disaster, the better they prepare. Ideally, they know to stay attuned to warning systems, sirens, and alarms and to act on recommendations made in television alerts and radio announcements.

The second thing citizens should do in preparing for a disaster is protect themselves against financial loss. Homeowners and renters need insurance to replace lost and damaged property. When private policies exclude damage from earthquakes and floods, or they are not available at a reasonable price, government-sponsored insurance may fill the gap. With insurance in hand, the next step is to protect buildings against damage. Move valuables out of flood-prone basements, secure heavy items in earthquake-prone homes, and install special windows and roofs in hurricane-prone areas. These investments, even if costly before a disaster, will save money and prevent injury during a disaster.

The third thing citizens should do is have a plan to evacuate or stay safe in the home. It helps to write down the plan, discuss it with family members, and practice it before a disaster. The evacuation plan should include ways to get out of town, belongings to take, and places to stay during an emergency. With mass evacuations clogging the roadways and filling nearby hotels, evacuation may not be as simple as it seems. Those living in hazard-prone areas should prepare to load essentials and leave quickly; those with disabilities or without transportation should have contacts to help.

Sometimes a sudden disaster makes it impossible to leave. Then people should know where to find safety in their home. Families should practice moving to a safe area—basements during tornadoes, high ground during flash floods, under sturdy furniture during earthquakes, and outside during fires. If family members get separated, they should select a place to reunite. Beforehand, they should set aside water, food, change of clothing, blankets, a first-aid kit, cash, medicines, a battery-powered radio, and other supplies to last several days (those affected by Hurricanes Andrew and Katrina, for example, did not get help for several days). This takes some effort, as water, food, and batteries set aside for a disaster need regular changing.

Pet owners have responsibility for the needs of their animals. Owners should evacuate their pets or bring them into the same area of protection as the family. In the worst circumstances, such as occurred with Hurricane Katrina, pets left behind should not be caged, chained, or kept from moving. They do best when left inside to move about so they can get water from the toilet and eat food left out. Much as zoos make special efforts to protect animals during a disaster, families should do the same.

Most of these disaster recommendations sound like common sense. Obviously, those living in places prone to earthquakes, hurricanes, floods, or tornadoes should prepare for disaster. Yet understanding the importance of preparation does not always lead people to follow recommendations. Most underestimate their risk and overestimate their ability to respond at the last moment. A major disaster may seem too distant or rare to devote substantial resources to preparing—if the disaster does not occur, then the effort to prepare is wasted. Many wait to do something until a disaster is fast approaching or has actually occurred.

Since people need convincing, the media and the government can do more to communicate the risks of a disaster and the benefits of preparation. Media messages about the importance of preparation and evacuation help, particularly when they include frightening and vivid stories about what happened in previous disasters to those who failed to prepare. Conversations with family, neighbors, and friends can reinforce media messages to encourage preparedness. Anyone who suffered through an earthquake or hurricane will know the dangers and prepare for the next one. Stories of their experiences can convince others to prepare as well.

Some social groups tend to do more to get ready for disasters than others do. Homeowners, married couples with children, and well-educated persons with high incomes are best prepared, as are longtime residents of a neighborhood. An example can illustrate this point. In July 1995, more than 700 people died in Chicago during an eight-day heat wave. A study of the heat wave found that most who died—largely elderly persons—lived in neighborhoods with high poverty and crime where they were afraid to go outside or even open their windows.[69] Neighborhoods with closer social ties between the elderly and neighbors had fewer deaths. There, networks led community residents to look after those most in danger from the heat. In July 2006, more than 120 people died from the heat in California—more than in the most recent California earthquakes. The victims again were often poor and elderly persons isolated from family and community.

In general, poor communities have fewer resources than wealthier ones to use in protecting themselves from disasters. They often cannot afford insurance, live in poorly constructed housing (including mobile homes), and are located in less expensive land prone to flooding. Communities with large minority populations and a high proportion of non-English speakers likewise have special problems in preparedness. The social distance between races and ethnic groups leads to distrust and makes cooperation with the authorities more difficult. For example, low-income African Americans in New Orleans had more trouble evacuating before Hurricane Katrina than high-income whites.

Even recognizing that some groups do better than others, the problem remains widespread. One journalist summarizes the problem nicely: "Americans are particularly, mysteriously bad at protecting themselves from guaranteed threats. We know more than we ever did about the dangers we face. But it turns out that in times of crisis, our greatest enemy is rarely the storm, the quake or the surge itself. More often, it is ourselves."[70]

Businesses

Businesses and nonprofit private organizations must prepare for disasters much as households and families do. In some ways, they have the most to lose. They have large investments in facilities and employees to protect. They suffer financially when forced to close down and stop sales. And they have responsibilities to the community and stockholders to protect the business. More than a short-term inconvenience, a disaster can bankrupt private companies. Emergency planning done beforehand can help get a business going again after a disaster. Yet most businesses procrastinate in preparing for a disaster—even those in high risks areas such as California, Florida, or the Gulf Coast.

Preparedness for businesses involves both physical and social aspects. The physical aspects relate to protecting buildings, equipment, inventories, business records, and supplies. Protecting these assets requires investment of money. It is expensive to pay for insurance, reinforce buildings to withstand hurricanes and earthquakes, have emergency generators on hand to supply power, and install emergency warning and fire-sprinkler systems. It helps to view these costs as an investment in future profit, a way to save money in the long term by minimizing the damage of a disaster. Modest costs ahead of time can prevent major costs later.

The social aspects of business and organization preparedness relate to protecting employees and customers. This goal also requires investment of time and effort. Managers need to do all they can to reduce injuries and save the lives of employees during a disaster. Both employees and customers deserve safety and quick action during an emergency. Assigning employees responsibility for managing a disaster and for practicing drills gives them a stake in disaster response. Businesses should likewise have a plan to inform customers, suppliers, and partners about what they will do before, during, and after an emergency.

How many private organizations follow these recommendations? Research shows all too few. A study of companies in San Francisco in 1993, only a few years after the 1989 Loma Prieta earthquake, found that less than half had developed disaster plans, trained employees, and practiced drills.[71] Companies in areas less prone to disaster performed worse, doing little if anything to prepare. Larger firms do more to prepare than smaller firms, in part because large firms can afford to assign staff to the tasks. Those firms that have already suffered damage from a disaster also do more in the way of preparation—they have learned from experience. Otherwise, disaster preparedness gets low priority among private organizations.

Why not do more? The major impediment comes from the lack of time and money to make the needed investments. On top of other worries about employee morale, customer demands, legal requirements, and, most of all, profits, preparedness for a low-probability event gets set aside. Businesses, like households and families, prefer to put off preparations until a disaster seems near.

Some recent progress has occurred, however. Firms such as Hewlett-Packard and IBM have created disaster recovery centers for its corporate clients. The centers include buildings, offices, and computers that executives can use to get their business restarted after a disaster. One reporter sees this innovation as "part of the rapidly growing disaster-recovery industry that specializes in keeping businesses afloat even when their buildings are under water."[72] Large firms can set up their own disaster plans, but smaller firms can contract with Hewlett-Packard, IBM, and other companies to help prepare for disasters.

Local Governments and Emergency Personnel

If households and businesses are to follow, local governments must take the lead in preparedness. By most accounts, they have improved their performance over the past decades but can do better.[73] Emergency preparedness still has low priority and relatively few funds in most communities because infrequent events lose out to more immediate demands for government services. Communities may optimistically think that because they handle small emergencies, they are prepared to deal with big ones. Many examples prove this thinking wrong.

To improve community preparedness, local government officials can sponsor emergency education, training, and exercises for city workers and residents. Cities should have written plans for action to guide these efforts—planning at the last minute will fail badly. The plans should assign duties to city workers and volunteers who will help speed evacuation, notify residents of risks, and assist vulnerable and special needs groups. However, reports and documents alone are not enough. They tend to sit on the shelf until the disaster occurs. Instead, putting emergency workers and volunteers through exercises and simulations will prepare them better for a real crisis.

Disaster Response

Local governments that are most ready for disasters have designated a position or unit with responsibility for preparedness and response. Professionals with training in emergency response can best fill these positions and units. With professional leadership, communities can forge close ties among government departments and establish an emergency operations center. Larger cities can do more to professionalize disaster operations than smaller ones, but even towns with few funds can get grants from the federal government. Pacific Grove, California, a town close to the 1989 Loma Prieta earthquake, obtained funds from FEMA, the fire department budget, and the city budget to hire a disaster coordinator.[74] With an emergency planner and regular earthquake drills, the city later won awards for emergency preparedness.

To help community professionals and volunteers, FEMA has set up the Emergency Management Institute to sponsor courses in emergency management. Dozens of courses on topics such as disaster operations, emergency program management, hazardous materials, floodplain development, and working with voluntary agencies help train and update disaster leaders. These courses allow independent study and sometimes give college credit. Other courses allow managers to get certification in the National Incident Management System.

Police, firefighters, and emergency medical personnel also require training and practice to deal well with disasters. These first responders understand the important role they have in disaster response. They also have the advantage of undergoing emergency training as a routine part of their jobs. However, first responders sometimes mistakenly think that dealing with normal emergencies will prepare them for major disasters. In fact, major disasters present altogether new and different challenges. They require more detailed planning and cooperation with other organizations than routine emergencies. For example, the Arlington, Virginia, emergency responders came quickly to the terrorist airplane crash at the Pentagon but did not have a center of operations to help organize the search and rescue. The heroic and quick action of first responders after the New York City attacks also demonstrated their readiness to respond, but problems of communication hampered their efforts. Even emergency workers used to acting under crisis can improve their skills for disaster response.

Consider an example of how one city prepares first responders, emergency organizations, and the public for a disaster. Boulder, Colorado, went through a flash-flood exercise in April 2006. City workers simulated what they would do in case Boulder Creek flooded to a level four times as high as predicted to occur in 100 years. The flood would wash debris, sewage, and uprooted trees through the center of town, leaving up to eight feet of water in some places. During the exercise, sirens went off around the city, government employees near the creek evacuated buildings, emergency responders moved rescue equipment into place, and the hospital emergency room prepared to treat injury trauma victims. At the library near the creek, employees told patrons to leave for high ground and gave them maps on the best routes to safety. A local high school, senior center, and hospital set up plans for people to move to the second floor. The drill helped leaders discover problems in their planning and participants to understand the seriousness of a disaster.

All that said, local governments, like families and businesses, have more immediate concerns that compete for time and money with disaster preparation. Before Katrina, the New Orleans mayor and city council worried about problems of high crime, violence and murder, poor schools, poverty, drug use, and attracting tourists and new business. They had a written response plan but paid little attention to it. Other cities face the same problem. A survey of disaster managers found that they prefer less time-consuming tasks such as working with the media and other government agencies to more time-consuming but crucially important tasks such as organizing volunteers and training residents.[75]

Even with a plan and plenty of practice, those preparing for a disaster must recognize another fact: No one can foresee all the problems and possibilities for action that will occur in the response. The complexity of mobilizing a response to a disaster requires leaders to be creative in adapting to circumstances. They should collaborate with partners to solve unexpected problems rather than give orders to follow predisaster plans rigidly.

State and National Government

State governments chiefly help local governments and communities prepare for disasters. In the decentralized approach to disaster response in the United States, preparation begins with those closest to where a disaster strikes. Towns, cities, and counties know best the special risks they face and actions needed for preparedness. Indeed, they have the most to lose from a disaster and the strongest motives to protect themselves. States have emergency or disaster management divisions in their governments that assist (rather than control) local governments in their preparations. States also serve as the go-between in getting federal help for communities.

The states vary in the quality of disaster services they provide. For example, critics blame Louisiana governor Kathleen Blanco for not preparing the state well for Katrina. Other states such as California and Florida, with long-standing worries about earthquakes and hurricanes, do a good job in emergency preparedness. In any case, governors and states should help communities get preparedness assistance from the federal government.

The national government works much the same way—it assists in preparation. FEMA has a number of programs to help local governments. Its

Capability Assessment for Readiness program evaluates the readiness of states to respond to a disaster. FEMA also manages the Comprehensive Exercise Program, which helps local, state, and federal officials set up exercises and evaluate the outcomes. More than money and grants, these programs share FEMA's technical knowledge and expertise with states and communities.

RESPONSE

Disaster response—actions taken just before, during, or just after a disaster to reduce casualties and damage—is the most dramatic and time-sensitive part of the disaster cycle. It sometimes involves search-and-rescue efforts and occasionally leads to special heroism and courage. Most important, disaster response involves individuals and families doing what they can to protect themselves and their property. Governments and disaster organizations will help with the most serious disasters, but victims need to rely first on their own resources to stay safe.

Disaster Behavior

Cities, towns, and counties have the first responsibility to alert residents of a likely disaster. A watch tells of a possible hazardous event, while a warning tells of a hazardous event that is imminent or has occurred. Alerts for watches or warnings include recommended or required actions such as leaving town, going to a shelter, taking cover, moving to high ground, or more generally getting to safety. Communicating clear recommendations requires cooperation with the media, which can best publicize watches and warnings. For terrorist alerts, however, DHS takes major responsibility by specifying threat levels ranging from low (green) to severe (red).

Public compliance with warnings is a crucial first step in response. However, even with a disaster approaching, people tend to discount or misunderstand warnings. Until they can see the danger themselves, they often carry on normal activities. People do the most to protect themselves when they receive a consistent message from all levels of government and reinforcement of the message by media, friends, and family. False alarms—warnings of a hazard that fails to occur—tend to weaken confidence in official sources. Because prediction of weather or terrorist events is uncertain, authorities must err on the side of caution. Explaining the reasons for a false alarm strengthens the credibility of future warnings.

During or immediately after an emergency, first responders—the police, firefighters, and emergency medical personnel—need to reach the trapped and injured quickly. Other disaster responders need to get water, food, and supplies to those who have lost their homes and belongings. Ideally, local governments will have emergency operations centers from which to manage an emergency response.

The media not only warns of an approaching disaster but also gives updates on the damage done. Indeed, large-scale disasters have become media events covered by national and local news shows. By one estimate, 25 percent of all news stories cover disasters.[76] The stories attract large audiences because they contain drama, action, bravery, failure, danger, and resolution. Local news can do more than report stories, however. The media passes on notices about where dangers remain, what areas to avoid, and how to get relief supplies.

Disaster experts recognize the critical role of the media in disaster response but also worry about the harm of bad reporting. On one hand, dramatic stories about the dangers and suffering caused by a disaster help encourage people to take disaster preparedness more seriously. On the other hand, reporters often overstate the damage of a disaster and perpetuate some myths of disaster behavior.[77] For example, stories about Katrina exaggerated the extent of looting and violence, which in turn slowed efforts to evacuate the stranded.[78]

Researchers have struggled to dispute a widely accepted myth that the media tend to encourage. Although many believe that the public responds to a disaster with mass panic, experts call this belief a myth. To the contrary, the public does surprisingly well during disasters. Panic flight is extremely rare and likely to occur in situations such as a building fire when all but one or two exits are blocked. After floods, hurricanes, earthquakes, tornadoes, and terrorist attacks, people typically behave in an orderly way and willingly help one another. Going into shock and acting disoriented are also rare. Grief from losing loved ones and valuables sets in eventually but typically does not hinder disaster response. Focus by the media on the rare instances of panic and shock gives a false impression of social behavior in crisis.

Researchers also dispute perceptions of widespread looting after a disaster. Although looting does occur, it is less common than reported, often involving the need for food and supplies rather than common theft. Perceptions that widespread looting follows a disaster have the unfortunate consequences of discouraging evacuation. People are less willing to leave if they worry about the safety of the property they leave behind.

Disaster Declaration Process

State governments help local governments and emergency responders with guidance and financial aid. Emergency management units in state governments are usually small and poorly funded. Although they cannot be generous with resources, these state units give two critical sources of aid. First, they can mobilize the National Guard to help in rescuing the stranded, delivering supplies, maintaining order, and protecting property. The National Guard receives little training in disaster response, and some believe its disaster duties should be minimal. However, the crucial help in response provided by the military after Hurricanes Andrew and Katrina have led to calls for better and more extensive use of this state resource.

Second, the state government takes responsibility for obtaining federal aid. In cooperation with local governments and state disaster agencies, the governor formally makes a request to the president for a major disaster declaration and release of federal disaster aid funds. A request from the state that clearly and completely lays out the needs of the disaster area will get funding more quickly. A request from the state that goes in quickly, sometimes even before an expected disaster occurs, will also lead to a faster response. More than local governments, state governments should understand the process of getting federal disaster aid.

The Stafford Act of 1988 and amendments since then list the steps for obtaining a presidential disaster declaration and receiving federal disaster aid. According to the law, all requests to the president come from the governor or chief executive of a state or territory. With the help of regional FEMA officials, the governor first prepares a preliminary damage assessment (PDA). This usually occurs after the disaster, but with a warning of a severe disaster, the request can come before the damage occurs. The PDA describes the extent of damage caused by the disaster and its impact on individuals and public facilities. It must further list what resources the state and local governments have committed to the response. The difference between needs and resources already committed determines the amount of funds requested from the federal government. However, the state must agree to pay 25 percent of the total costs.

The request from the governor goes to the regional director of FEMA, who reviews the on-scene damage and makes a recommendation to the FEMA director. The FEMA director then makes a recommendation to the president. Based on the extent of damage and losses, threats to life and safety, and the resources available from the state and local government, insurance, and voluntary agencies, the president then decides whether to declare a major disaster or a less serious emergency. Notice of a declaration goes to the governor, the media, members of Congress from the affected area, and federal departments that help in the response. Then FEMA prepares a document called the FEMA-State agreement that lays out the details of the assistance.

Unless FEMA has already put people in place before an expected disaster, federal action begins with the declaration and agreement. FEMA appoints a federal coordinating officer to direct and coordinate the federal response and a disaster field office and emergency response team to work at the site of the disaster. FEMA, its officers, and its team do not manage the response work themselves. Rather, they coordinate the actions of other federal departments that can deal with specific problems of transportation, communication, firefighting, health and medical services, energy, food, and other functions. All governmental agencies involved in a major disaster must work closely together, but as shown by the response to Hurricane Katrina, cooperation across agencies remains a problem.

The president commonly approves disaster declaration requests. From January 1 to August 15, 2006, there were 36 major disaster declarations and three emergency declarations.[79] In January, for example, counties in North Dakota, Minnesota, Kansas, and Nebraska were designated as major disaster areas for severe winter storms; counties in Texas and Oklahoma were designated for severe or extreme wildfire threat; and counties in South Carolina were designated for a severe ice storm. In June, counties in North Dakota, California, Minnesota, and Pennsylvania were designated for severe storms, flooding, mudslides, landslides, or ground saturation. Despite these declarations, states and communities handle most disasters without presidential declarations. According to a FEMA publication, "Although the exact number of disasters successfully handled without requests for Federal assistance is not known, it is estimated at 3,500 to 3,700 annually."[80]

One of the first things FEMA does after a major disaster declaration is to provide emergency information. A public affairs effort not only announces the declaration and the counties and states it includes but also tries to get information to victims of the disaster. Some say that getting information can be as important as getting food and water in times of a disaster. Toward that end, FEMA distributes a newsletter called the *Recovery Times* through its field offices and makes up-to-date information available to radio and television stations.

Also immediately after a major disaster declaration, FEMA may need to send search-and-rescue teams to the sites. The teams, recruited from police, fire, rescue, and emergency medical organizations, help find, remove, and treat disaster victims trapped in collapsed buildings, in flooded areas, and near hazardous materials. FEMA has dozens of such teams across the country that can be ready for transport to a site within four hours. The teams include engineers, physicians, dog trainers, and hazardous materials experts. Search-and-rescue teams gave critical help after the terrorist attacks in Oklahoma City, New York City, and Washington, D.C. They also help in earthquake and hurricane response.

Besides FEMA, other government agencies help with disaster response and recovery. For example, the Department of Health and Human Services assists with sanitation measures, and the Food and Drug Administration helps make sure food and drugs remain safe. The Department of Defense supplies equipment and military personnel to help clear debris and restore buildings to working order, and the U.S. Army Corps of Engineers helps repair damaged flood-control structures. The U.S. Forest Service helps with forest or grassland fires.

After helping to get food, water, clothing, and essentials to victims, the disaster response turns to helping those without housing to find shelter. Many will have already gone to emergency shelters located in sturdy buildings or safe zones. Those who cannot return to their homes after the disaster need temporary shelter. Staying in group shelters works only for a few days (hence the terrible conditions in the New Orleans Superdome and convention center after tens of thousands had to stay there for nearly a week). FEMA provides trailers for disaster victims who lost their homes and vouchers to pay for rent. Congress has set aside $400 million for a pilot program to replace trailers with small homes (called "Katrina cottages") for Katrina victims. These cottages are said to be more affordable and comfortable than trailers and may prove successful enough to use after future disasters.

Private and Volunteer Organizations

The most important private relief organization is the American Red Cross. Chartered by Congress in 1905 to carry on relief during great national calamities, the organization takes on a variety of duties in disaster response. To meet the needs of disaster victims, it operates shelters and provides meals and snacks to victims. Next, according to Red Cross materials,

Trained Red Cross interviewers meet one on one with families to determine their needs. The assistance may include providing the means for them to pay for groceries, new clothes, rent, emergency home repairs, transportation, medicines, and tools. The Red Cross also lets people know about other community or government resources available to them and helps those needing long-term recovery assistance when other resources are inadequate.[81]

To meet the needs of disaster workers, who can face stress as extreme as that of the victims, the Red Cross provides food and support. After the 9/11 attacks, it sent 57,000 workers, almost all volunteers, to help survivors and rescue workers. It also received and distributed nearly a billion dollars in outside donations to survivors, family members, and relief workers. These funds helped pay for medical needs such as prescriptions, supplies, and emergency treatment related to the disaster. The Red Cross collects blood and blood products for the physically injured, and it offers mental health counseling to the psychologically injured.

The Salvation Army likewise devotes considerable resources to disaster relief. The Stafford Act of 1988 affirmed the Salvation Army's long tradition of relief work by listing it as a disaster assistance organization. Using donations it receives, the Salvation Army gives material support in the form of food, drink, and shelter to first responders and survivors of disasters. Reflecting its Christian beliefs, it also gives emotional and spiritual support to those who want it. Later in the relief effort, it collects materials and funds to help repair and rebuild homes. The organization offers these services as an act of faith but helps those of all religious beliefs.

Many other faith-based organizations contribute to disaster response. The National Volunteer Organizations Against Disasters (NVOAD) has 34 national members, including Catholic Charities, United Jewish Communities, Christian Disaster Response, Friends (Quaker) Disaster Service, and disaster organizations representing Episcopal, Lutheran, Mennonite, Presbyterian, Southern Baptist, and United Methodist churches. The George W. Bush administration has advocated a greater role for faith-based organizations in dealing with social problems, and disaster relief represents an area of need for these organizations.

Spontaneous volunteer activity of community residents emerges after a disaster as well. According to a survey conducted after the Loma Prieta earthquake, 60 to 70 percent of the residents said they helped during the emergency.[82] Many chipped in by joining the search and rescue, providing food and water, assisting with cleanup, and sheltering those without homes. These activities arise spontaneously, as the tragedies heighten solidarity of community residents (and for extreme disasters, people across the country and around the world).

RECOVERY

It is difficult to define a clear point at which disaster response ends and recovery begins. Recovery involves actions taken after a disaster to repair, rebuild, and restore community life to normal, but such actions can begin immediately after a disaster and overlap with response efforts to reduce casualties and damage. Despite the overlap, recovery is a continuing process that contrasts with the response to immediate needs. It can take years to get back to normal, and even longer to improve the safety and security of the community. At least initially, however, victims most want financial assistance to help return to normalcy.

Assistance Programs for Individuals and Businesses

With a disaster declaration, numerous forms of assistance become available to communities and states. A 2005 publication from FEMA called *Disaster Assistance: A Guide to Recovery Programs* lists nearly 100 programs that cover work, housing, health, transportation, community development, and conservation.[83] The funds for the assistance programs come from dozens of agencies and relate to a variety of types of disasters. A brief summary of some of the largest and most important ones follows:

Food Assistance   The U.S. Department of Agriculture donates surplus food commodities to help feed disaster victims. Government or charitable agencies typically apply for food and then distribute it to individuals and families. In addition, assistance comes from the Disaster Food Stamp Program. State or local service agencies distribute food stamps to eligible households, whose members can use them at local stores.

Housing Assistance   The federal government makes funds available to homeowners and renters who can demonstrate that a disaster damaged their home or rental unit. The Disaster Housing Program pays for repairs to housing and for the cost of renting until repairs are made or other housing is found.

Disaster Loans   The federal government offers low-interest loans to individuals and businesses damaged by disasters. Although they charge low interest rates, these loans must be paid back and thereby differ from direct housing assistance. Renters and homeowners can get these loans to repair property, if they can prove that the damage to the property came from a disaster and they can repay the loan. Businesses likewise can get loans from the Small Business Administration to repair damaged property, restore inventories, and obtain needed supplies. They can sometimes get loans to keep the business going during the down times after a disaster.

Individuals and Households Program   This program offers assistance for housing (like the Disaster Housing Program) and other needs. It gives up to $5,000 for repair, $10,000 for replacement, $25,000 for permanent housing construction, and $25,000 for rental assistance. For those ineligible for other programs, this program also helps pay for household items, clothing, vehicles, storage, medical costs, and flood insurance.

Disaster Unemployment Assistance   This program provides unemployment benefits to those who lose their job because of a disaster or helps them find another job. To receive the benefits, victims must first register with the state employment office.

Legal Services   FEMA coordinates efforts to give legal aid to low-income victims of disasters. The aid services help in filing insurance claims, signing home repair contracts, and replacing lost documents.

Crisis Counseling   Loss of loved ones, property, and a way of life caused by a disaster obviously creates stress, grief, and depression. The federal government pays for counseling services such as mental health screening, symptom diagnosis, and short-term therapy for a period of 60 days following the disaster declaration. When needed, funds for regular counseling services can be extended for a period of nine months.

Cora Brown Fund   Cora Brown, a private citizen concerned about disasters, founded a private relief fund that assists victims otherwise ineligible for government assistance. The funds are used for disaster-related home repair, health and safety measures, and help to self-employed workers restarting their business.

Those eligible can apply to most of these programs with a simple phone call to FEMA service centers. The application must describe the location of the property, the nature of the damage, and the amount of insurance available to cover damage. FEMA inspectors then visit the property to verify the damage and eligibility for assistance. Applicants certify that the information they provided is correct and prove they own and previously occupied the property. Applicants also need to prove they are a citizen, a noncitizen national, or a qualified alien. Since others are not eligible for federal assistance, disasters can be especially costly for undocumented workers.

Along with directly funding individuals and businesses, FEMA and the federal government make grants after a disaster declaration. The grants go to state and local governments, Indian tribes, and some nonprofit organizations. Immediately after a disaster, the grants help communities pay for removal of debris, search and rescue, demolition of damaged buildings, and protection of lives and property. Later, the grants help communities pay for repair or rebuilding of roads, bridges, dams, levees, reservoirs, police stations, hospitals, libraries, water treatment plants, power generation, sewage treatment facilities, public parks, playgrounds, boat docks, and golf courses.

All these programs have eligibility requirements. Businesses, governments, and individuals must qualify for assistance rather than merely request it. Disaster relief laws aim to help victims while also preventing waste of resources. Government disaster assistance therefore covers only costs not otherwise paid by insurance, other government programs, or other sources of aid. Receiving duplicate funds is illegal. FEMA has programs to discover duplication and will require repayment of the extra funds or, in cases of fraud, prosecute offenders. However, as shown by the misuse of disaster funds after Katrina, preventing fraud is not an easy task. Along with being criticized for not helping enough, FEMA is criticized for helping unnecessarily.

Even legally given aid has limits. The amount of aid made available depends on the damage assessment and the resources of state and local governments. When state and local governments can deal with recovery, the federal government limits its assistance. For major disasters such as the 9/11 terrorist attacks and Hurricane Katrina, the federal government contributes generously to recovery. For most disasters, however, the federal government fills the gaps in aid left by state and local governments.

Disaster Response

Inequality in Recovery

FEMA and federal agencies responding to disasters often face high expectations. Victims of disasters naturally want as much help as they can get and want it as quickly as they can get it. By law, however, the role of the federal government is limited to certain tasks. FEMA is responsible for coordinating actions across levels of government and multiple agencies but cannot give orders to other government officials. Cooperation and strong partnerships work best. FEMA is quick to correct the misconceptions that arise about its responsibilities.

First, the federal government does not have total responsibility for disaster response and recovery. As noted, state and local governments have primary responsibility for dealing with disasters; the federal government helps only when resources of other governments are overwhelmed. Second, the federal government is not responsible for restoring all lost and damaged property. Disaster assistance can rarely restore homes, businesses, and property to their state before the disaster. Third, the federal government does not provide funds for everyone affected by the disaster. Applicants have to prove they meet the eligibility rules. Fourth, the federal government does not replace insurance. Federal assistance aims to supplement private insurance but only in certain situations. Individuals need to insure their property rather than count on the government to take care of everything after a disaster. Fifth, recipients must follow rules in using government assistance. They cannot spend the funds as they would prefer.

Given limits to disaster assistance, some groups recover more quickly and fully than other groups. Groups that are most vulnerable to the harm of disasters—the poor, minorities, immigrants, the less educated, and rural residents—are also those that have the most difficulty recovering. Inequality in social and economic life thus spills over to affect disaster recovery. Government assistance rarely can overcome these effects of inequality.

Consider some of the advantages in disaster recovery that come from higher education, more prestigious jobs, and greater income. Education gives persons the knowledge to understand and respond to disaster warnings. Skills developed in professional and executive jobs give people experience to work effectively with government agencies and bureaucracies to get help. And high income gives people the ability to buy insurance, get loans, and draw on savings to repair damage. The uneducated and poor have few such resources. Moreover, minority race and ethnic groups, often concentrated in lower social classes, sometimes face discrimination in obtaining relief. Immigrants have trouble communicating with the government, and other disadvantaged groups such as the disabled have special relief needs.

Social inequality may help explain the slow response and recovery in New Orleans. The affluent groups living in the Garden District and a few other neighborhoods fended for themselves. The city's large population of poor, minority, and infirm residents needed more help—and most did not get it. Sociologist Kathleen Tierney argues that assisting poor people of color during a disaster is sadly not regarded as a priority. She contrasts the situation in New Orleans with what would happen if, for example, an earthquake damaged homes in the richest neighborhoods in Los Angeles, such as in Beverly Hills, Santa Monica, and Bel Air. "It is inconceivable that the experiences of west Los Angeles residents would in any way resemble those of the poor African American residents of New Orleans."[84]

Sometimes social inequality creates political conflict between groups with different visions for future development. In New Orleans, disputes over the direction to take in rebuilding have made it difficult to settle on plans for redevelopment. These disputes pit lower-income African Americans who want to rebuild their homes against city leaders and planners who want to redevelop flood-prone areas with less housing. Although hard to reach, political consensus that overcomes these divisions speeds recovery. Strong leadership and political consensus can help avoid recovery battles.

MITIGATION

Mitigation involves sustained actions taken both after one disaster and before another to reduce the physical impacts of hazards on a community. One way to encourage mitigation efforts is to begin them after a disaster, when people are most motivated to protect themselves from another. Mitigation, like preparedness, requires investment for an uncertain benefit. Expensive and time-consuming mitigation tasks do not have the immediate payoff that response and recovery do. Fresh experience with a disaster encourages—but does not ensure—investment for future protection.

Basic Strategies

Mitigation measures begin with designing and constructing safe buildings and homes. State and local codes can do much to reach this goal. They can require use of fireproof materials, installation of sprinkler systems and fire alarms, and use of building materials that withstand winds from hurricanes, shaking from earthquakes, and damage from terrorist bombs. Building engineers have developed disaster-resistant materials and devised safer buildings, but they can do more. Further, governments need to tighten building codes to make sure the new materials and designs get used. However, these codes raise the cost of homes and buildings for families and businesses. Pressures to keep prices affordable can block mitigation.

The dilemma between price and safety appears clearly in debates over the safety of mobile homes. Disaster experts criticize the failure of manufacturers and governments to set more stringent safety guidelines for mobile homes. The main attraction to buyers—the inexpensive price—comes from the light materials and weak structure. These are precisely the features that make them and anyone inside vulnerable to disasters. Stronger safety rules would price out those who depend on the low cost of mobile homes.

The locations of buildings and housing help in mitigation but likewise raise financial issues. Careful land-use planning to identify and restrict building in floodplains limits flood damage. Preventing development in areas of high risk for hurricanes and earthquakes also limits damage. However, as shown by the growth of Miami, development of resorts and vacation homes along the Atlantic and Gulf coasts, and spread of cities in southern California and the San Francisco Bay area, these kinds of mitigation efforts seldom succeed. To the contrary, governments often encourage such development by building roads, bridges, and power stations for the new communities. Blocking developments in attractive areas would cost developers lost income and potential residents lost opportunities to live where they would like. Yet the short-term gain of new development sometimes conflicts with the long-term risk of disaster.

Recent terrorist events have called attention to a new form of disaster mitigation—intelligence and security. Activities of DHS to check airline passengers for weapons, people passing into the country across borders for terrorist ties, and financial transactions and chat rooms for hints of terrorist plans represent new forms of disaster prevention and mitigation. They differ from traditional mitigation in their attention to bombs, crime, and people rather than to natural hazards.

Some mitigation practices once thought effective have come under criticism. Efforts to protect cities from disasters by building levees, dams, and seawalls or by draining wetlands often worsen problems. These practices allow development of areas that otherwise would prove too dangerous for people to live. If the mitigation efforts then fail, it brings catastrophe. Residents of New Orleans and towns along the Mississippi now know all too well that levees break. Beach residents similarly know that seawalls can protect them from storm surges but also cause slow erosion of beaches. One other example illustrates the failure of technological solutions to disaster risks: Although cities once thought that draining wetlands would make areas safe from flooding, the practice in fact destroyed natural forms of water control and made some cities more vulnerable to flooding.

Concerns that large projects place too much confidence in technology have led experts to advocate a new approach to mitigation.[85] The approach focuses on sustainable local practices that preserve the environment while protecting people from disasters. It does so by protecting fragile coastal areas and wetlands from development and keeping people away from the natural flow of water during storms. The strategy limits urban growth and the freedom of property owners to build and landscape as they please. Reductions in poverty and inequality are needed as well. Then fewer persons will be forced by low income to live in unsafe housing and on cheap but disaster-prone land. The interests of environmentalists and disaster experts coincide in these recommendations, but the strategy demands new thinking about disaster policy by government leaders and developers.

FEMA Mitigation Programs

FEMA encourages mitigation in its response to disasters. It recommends that disaster victims rebuild stronger, safer homes and buildings as a way to reduce potential future losses. Those in earthquake-prone areas can anchor bookcases to walls, brace walls to foundations, and use flexible connections between gas and water pipes. Those in flood-prone areas can use water-resistant materials, raise wires for the electrical system, and install valves that prevent sewer water from backing up. Those in areas prone to high winds can reinforce walls and doors, secure roofs and shingles, and install window covers. These renovations are expensive but may save much more money in the future.

FEMA helps with mitigation costs but can do only a small part of what communities need. Its Hazard Mitigation Grant Program offers grants to states and communities (but not individuals) to implement mitigation measures after a disaster. Communities that are part of a declared disaster area may apply and use grant funds for a variety of purposes. They can retrofit buildings, pay for flood-control projects (not covered by other government programs), and buy houses and buildings in flood-prone areas to be replaced with open space, parks, and golf courses that can withstand flooding.

Funds available from the program are small compared to those for disaster response and recovery. The program makes up only 7.5 percent of the total disaster grants from FEMA. However, the Disaster Mitigation Act of 2000 amended the 1988 Stafford Act by requiring that funds for mitigation be part of disaster planning. Those states that commit to enhanced mitigation planning also become eligible for more funds. The goal of the act is to make mitigation part of a comprehensive disaster response effort.

FEMA points to some successes of its mitigation program. For example, after the 1993 Great Midwest Flood, the Hazard Mitigation Grant Program gave more than $100 million to the state of Missouri to buy property that had flooded. The state in turn contributed $2.3 million, all of which helped some 37,000 state residents displaced by the floods. Under the program, residents living on floodplains were paid for their property, which was then turned into open space and parks. One participant in the program, Joe Moore of Arnold, Missouri, received full preflood value for his house and used the funds to build a new house on the other side of town, outside the floodplain. The efforts worked, as only minimal damage occurred during a 2002 flood of areas participating in the program.

FEMA also has a Pre-Disaster Mitigation Competitive Grant Program. The program stemmed from efforts in the 1990s to do more than help communities with mitigation after a disaster. It also made sense to save money in the end by preparing communities before a disaster occurred. In the 2000s, the program asked states, territories, and tribal areas to submit applications for funding. Tulsa, Oklahoma, for example, applied for and received funds to include reinforced and anchored "safe rooms" in new housing that protect against tornadoes. Since the payoffs for such investments appear only when a disaster strikes, success is hard to evaluate right now. Yet projects done in the 1990s appear effective. Pre-disaster funds given to Seattle, Washington, as part of the program helped reduce the damage of a 2002 earthquake.[86]

Other mitigation programs focus on specific hazards. The National Earthquake Hazard Reduction Program, the National Hurricane Program, and the National Dam Safety Program help states protect themselves against these hazards. However, these programs provide more in the way of knowledge and guidance than dollars. The Assistance to Firefighters Grant Program provides funds to fire departments to deal with new terrorist threats, such as explosions, chemical contamination, and biological weapons, and with continuing threats from wildfires.

INTERNATIONAL DISASTER RESPONSE

The special risks from hurricanes, tornadoes, flooding, and earthquakes faced by the United States represent only a small part of global disasters. By far the worst disasters occur in developing countries. According to one estimate, "90 percent of disaster-related injuries and deaths occur in countries with per-capita income levels that are below $760 per year."[87] Consider a few examples of the world's worst recent disasters.

- A 1976 earthquake in Tangshan, China, perhaps the most severe in modern times, killed at least 255,000 (and up to 655,000 by some estimates).

Introduction to Disaster Response

- A 1985 volcanic eruption and resulting mudslide in Colombia killed 25,000.
- A series of 1991 floods in Bangladesh killed 139,000.
- A 2003 earthquake in Bam, Iran, killed 26,271.
- A 2004 tsunami killed about 230,000 in a dozen Southeast Asian nations.
- A 2005 earthquake centered in Pakistan killed more than 50,000.
- A May 2006 earthquake in Indonesia killed more than 5,000.

The huge number of deaths from these disasters defies comprehension, but such disasters occur regularly. If one adds the millions in Africa who have died from drought and disease epidemics, the problem becomes even worse.

Other forms of global disasters have worsened in recent decades. The 1984 release of poison from a Union Carbide pesticide plant in Bhopal, India, killed 15,000 and injured hundreds of thousands. A 1986 explosion that released radiation from the Chernobyl nuclear power plant in the Ukraine (then part of the Soviet Union) led to permanent evacuation of areas around the plant. Safety regulations for businesses working with dangerous materials may not be as strict in poor nations as in high-income nations. Terrorism also threatens nations outside North America and Europe: A 1998 terrorist bombing in Kenya and Tanzania and a 2002 terrorist bombing in Indonesia each killed about 200 people.

Low- and middle-income nations of the world are particularly vulnerable to disasters for several reasons. Perhaps most obvious, areas in central and Southeast Asia are prone to earthquakes. However, the problems go beyond the physical characteristics of the Earth—they are also social in nature. Poor residents in overpopulated, fast-growing nations are forced to locate on floodplains, riverbanks, steep hillsides, and areas already cleared once by disasters. With billions of people in China and India, and with hundreds of millions in Indonesia, Pakistan, Iran, and Bangladesh, it is hard to avoid locating communities in vulnerable spots. Contributing to the problem, governments of low-income nations often lack the authority or resources to control the settlements. Even when they are illegal, shantytowns develop quickly on hillsides, floodplains, near fault lines, and close to volcanoes. Residents may have little other choice on where to live; clearing the area would merely move the residents somewhere equally dangerous.

Low- and middle-income nations also face limitations in response. Since they must deal with immediate needs for food, roads, schools, and national defense, disaster response has a low budget priority. Nations suffering through famine, civil war, religious conflict, or disease epidemics can do even less for disaster response. Even when they have disaster supplies, governments often cannot deliver them to the places where they are needed—

the roads, bridges, and airports outside the major cities are not good enough. Great poverty likewise makes it difficult for victims of disasters to fend for themselves.

INTERNATIONAL RELIEF AGENCIES

Many nations, especially low- to middle-income ones, must rely on help from international organizations and richer countries for disaster relief. Leaders in disaster-prone nations sometimes worry that turning over relief to outsiders limits their autonomy and control. Despite such concerns, poorer nations depend on a variety of international organizations for help.

The United Nations (UN) takes the lead in international disaster response. The Undersecretary-General for Humanitarian Affairs and Emergency Relief Coordinator in the Office for the Coordination of Humanitarian Affairs oversee relief efforts for both human-caused and natural disasters. The latter office has a budget of more than $152 million and staff of more than 1,100. It maintains an emergency alert system and response unit that can travel quickly to the location of sudden disasters. It can also give technical assistance to nations experiencing a disaster. However, the office does not have the funds to pay for international relief. Rather, it coordinates the activities of other groups and agencies and helps raise charitable donations.

In March 2006, the UN announced a new effort to expand its role. It set up a $500 million fund called the Central Emergency Response Fund to improve its relief efforts. With funds in place, the UN hopes to make relief funds available in a few days rather than a few months. The first two allocations of the funds went to Kenya and other African nations suffering from drought and to Côte d'Ivoire, which was suffering from civil war. The new fund improves significantly on the $50 million previously available for relief but still depends fully on voluntary contributions from member states and private donors. Fund-raising remains a major task for UN disaster relief.

Along with providing relief after a disaster, the UN aims to prevent harm from natural and human-caused disasters. Toward that end, the UN General Assembly has set up the Inter-Agency Task Force on Disaster Reduction. The task force developed the International Strategy for Disaster Reduction, which has the goal of promoting awareness of disaster mitigation throughout the world. It does so by publishing research, articles, and guidelines on disaster mitigation and sponsoring the World Conference on Disaster Reduction.

Another UN initiative also focuses on disaster preparation. The UN Development Programme has goals of fostering national economic and social development and reducing inequality and poverty. To reach these goals, it advocates democratic rule, protection of the environment, public health efforts, and the empowerment of women. In addition, it has a Disaster Reduction Unit that helps developing nations protect themselves against the harm of disasters. Besides causing death, a natural disaster can create economic damage that sets back economic progress by decades. The Disaster Reduction Unit thus measures vulnerability to disasters, makes recommendations for mitigation, and provides information on the latest research and knowledge. It also encourages all new development projects to include risk-reduction components in their plans.

The International Federation of Red Crescent and Red Cross Societies has humanitarian goals similar to those of the 185 national organizations that make up the federation (the red crescent symbol is used in Islamic nations, the red cross symbol elsewhere). The Office of the Secretariat in Geneva, Switzerland, coordinates and mobilizes efforts of national societies to respond to disasters in any part of the world. It also leads international efforts to raise funds for disaster relief. According to its statements, the federation uses its funds to assist 30 million people each year. A sharp increase in worldwide natural disasters in recent years has led the organization to devote more attention to preparedness.

The federation does much the same in its international response as its members do in national response. It initially provides assistance for shelter, water, food, and basic health care, and it provides personal contact to show that someone cares. It later helps with reconstruction. Given the fragile nature of health care, water supply, and sanitation in many counties, repairing and rebuilding hospitals and utilities is particularly important. Other humanitarian assistance addresses problems that go beyond natural disasters. The federation handles problems of population movement, refugees, civil war, poor health care, and food insecurity. In 2006, the list of current relief efforts includes responding to the May 2006 Indonesian earthquake, the spread of cholera in several nations, floods in Tanzania, landslides in Serbia and Montenegro, a cyclone in Myanmar, drought in Ethiopia, an earthquake in Russia, and possible outbreaks of avian flu.

Other organizations help with international disaster relief. The World Health Organization monitors disease outbreaks after a disaster and offers technical assistance on how to control such outbreaks. The International Monetary Fund and the World Bank help financially. They provide emergency funds or loans to deal with short-term financial problems caused by a disaster and with long-term needs for rebuilding and mitigating. Private relief organizations representing the major religious denominations such as Catholic Charities and the Salvation Army and nonreligious charitable groups such as Rotary International and Oxfam contribute as well. These organizations, like the Red Cross, aim to stay independent and neutral in their dealings with national governments. This approach allows them to work with nations throughout the world.

The United States has special programs devoted to international disaster relief. The U.S. Agency for International Development (USAID) contains the Office of U.S. Foreign Disaster Assistance (OFDA), which coordinates overseas emergency assistance. When a disaster occurs in another country, the U.S. ambassador or Chief of Mission can declare a disaster. The OFDA will help when 1) the disaster exceeds the ability of the affected country to respond and 2) the country's government requests or is willing to receive the assistance. Then the office sends a response team to the nation to assess the damage and recommend the level of assistance. Besides USAID, the U.S. military sometimes assists in disaster response, although many countries hesitate to allow foreign troops on their soil. In addition to emergency assistance, the United States will give longer-term assistance. As USAID states, "OFDA funds mitigation activities to reduce the impact of recurrent natural disasters and also provides training to build a country's capacity for local disaster management and response."[88]

TSUNAMI DEATHS AND RELIEF

One of the most deadly disasters in the last century occurred only recently—on December 26, 2004. The event illustrates both the peril of developing nations to natural disasters and the willingness of nations, organizations, and individuals across the world to help. On that day, a strong earthquake (the fourth-strongest ever recorded) shifted the floor of the Indian Ocean near the Indonesian island of Sumatra. The earthquake created enormous and fast-moving sea waves called a tsunami that traveled in all directions. The Japanese term *tsunami* means "harbor wave" and refers to the damage that comes when the waves crash into land and overflow low-lying coastal cities. In this case, the tsunami hit thousands of miles of shoreline across more than a dozen countries.

Although some residents and tourists recognized the early signs of a tsunami—receding water at the shore—most did not. Walls of water washing over coastal towns left no time for escape. With 186,983 confirmed deaths and 42,883 missing, the death toll has reached 229,866. Children made up about one-third of the deaths, and about 9,000 were tourists vacationing on the sunny beaches during the winter season. Indonesia suffered the most deaths; more than 167,000 died there, largely in the territory of Aceh at the upper tip of the island of Sumatra, nearest to the earthquake. Deaths reached 35,000 in Sri Lanka, 18,000 in India, and 8,000 in Thailand. Well over 1 million survivors lost their homes. Death and devastation to this extent are almost unimaginable, but the world learned of the tragedy through stories of survivors and pictures of the devastation.

Introduction to Disaster Response

After the tsunami hit, the survivors most needed water and food. Saltwater from the tsunami contaminated many water sources, destroyed crops and food supplies, and killed food animals. Survivors who lost their homes and belongings also needed tents, beds, and clothes. Doctors and nurses worried about the spread of infectious diseases because of the poor sanitation, destruction of toilets, and dead bodies scattered about. The two nations most hurt, Indonesia and Sri Lanka, had the most trouble getting supplies to victims.

Nations throughout the world and international organizations stepped forward to help. The World Bank estimated that the relief effort would require $5 billion. A coalition of nations made up of Australia, India, Japan, and the United States began to organize the relief, and the UN soon took over leadership. Some controversy followed when one UN leader suggested that rich nations were stingy in their contributions. U.S. officials vigorously denied the accusation. In fact, nations across the world gave generously to the relief fund. According to recent figures, tsunami relief has received more than $12 billion. Combining both government and private donations, the United States gave the most, $2.63 billion, followed by Germany, Britain, Australia, and Japan.

The United States helped in ways other than donating funds. The USAID mobilized its Disaster Assistance Response Team to work with the military in delivering freshwater, building shelters, and repairing fishing boats. The Department of Defense also acted quickly. Commanders sent 15,000 military personnel, 26 ships, 58 helicopters, and 43 fixed-wing aircraft.

The supply of so much aid so quickly inevitably produced waste and corruption. In Sri Lanka, for example, hundreds of thousands in relief funds went to families unaffected by the tsunami; in India, officials appeared to have taken a cut of the relief funds; and in Indonesia, officials inflated the number of survivors needing compensation. Other problems came from civil conflict in Sri Lanka and Indonesia. The area worst hit by the tsunami, Aceh in Indonesia, had been battling a well-armed separatist movement. The conflict sometimes made it hard to get relief to those most in need.

Still, a special evaluation coalition made up of members from the United Nations, Red Cross, and nongovernmental organizations lauded the local response. A report from the coalition on the relief effort said that local communities and governments did better than many expected.[89] Rather than working closely with local leaders and agencies, international organizations sometimes went around them. The knowledge of locals about the areas damaged could have helped the relief effort. Relief workers from USAID agreed that they wanted to help the local people rather than impose on them. Others did not do as well.

That said, the coalition report evaluated the relief effort as largely effective. Donations from around the world broke records, and the public proved remarkably generous. Charity events put on by athletes, musicians, and performers helped raise funds. The huge private donations created a new form of globalized relief that no longer depended only on international organizations. Combined with generous funding, the quick action of relief workers led to some notable successes. Within just a few months, schools and health facilities reopened, and within six months, some 500,000 homeless had returned to new or repaired housing in Aceh. In Sri Lanka, 80 percent of damaged fish markets, boats, and equipment were restored.

The report did suggest some areas that needed improvement, however. For one, the international disaster relief efforts lacked the coordination needed to be most effective. Too many organizations, funds, and governments acted independently of others. As the report summarized, the generous funding "led to the proliferation of new actors with insufficient experience (and therefore competence), as well as established actors venturing into activities outside the normal areas of expertise."[90] In some cases, relief groups appeared more interested in the publicity of their efforts than in helping those in need. Funds went too often to places and people who managed to get the most attention from the media and exerted the most political pressure.

Designating leaders or coordinators could have avoided duplication and inefficiency. With the advice of independent experts, leaders could have guided spending to places and people most in need and regulated organizations that wanted to join the relief efforts. Such leadership could improve international efforts in another way. It could allocate funds to disasters that receive less publicity. The enormous attention given to the tsunami reduced donations to famine relief in Sudan, for example. The 2003 earthquake in Iran received only a small fraction of the funds it needed. International coordination of disasters could distribute funds more evenly.

While the relief effort did well, long-term issues of recovery present another challenge. Recovery requires economic development and less poverty, goals difficult to reach under the best of circumstances. Relief efforts from the outside did little to help with these goals. They may instead have made the situation worse by giving aid to local communities without focusing on long-term needs. Outside funds used for relief must now be replaced, but it is easier to raise emergency funds than recovery funds.

THE FUTURE OF FEMA

The United States has more than 100 years of experience with disaster response both here and in helping with international disasters. Despite that experience, the most recent major national disaster, Hurricane Katrina, revealed deep-set problems. The blame for the problems falls to FEMA, the federal government organization with the major responsibility for disaster preparation, response, recover, and mitigation. While it prepares for coming disasters, the agency's future remains in dispute.

At one extreme, some in Congress, such as Democratic senator Hillary Clinton and Republican senator Trent Lott, have called for restoring FEMA to its previous prominence. That change would include moving FEMA from DHS and making it a cabinet-level agency, much as it was in the 1990s. With more authority, clear lines of power, direct access to the president, and greater visibility, FEMA could improve its performance. It could avoid the divisional battles over funding that occur within DHS and ease the tension between terrorism and natural disaster preparation and response. It might even regain the respect it had under James Witt. Others oppose the move. They say that it will not address FEMA's problems of disorganization, weak management, and inadequate funding. Solutions must involve more than relocating the organization. The George W. Bush administration also opposes this proposal, arguing that the goals of terrorism and natural disaster response belong in the same organization.

Others in Congress suggest reorganizing FEMA within DHS. One proposal suggests abolishing FEMA and creating a new National Preparedness and Response Authority. The head of the new agency would have more power and greater opportunity to advise the president than the current FEMA director. Another proposal suggests overhauling the Army Corps of Engineers. Many blame the corps for the failure of the New Orleans levees. Again, however, DHS and the Bush administration oppose such changes.

Some critics call for giving more responsibility to private organizations in disaster response. They point to a few facts: Private hospitals performed better than public hospitals in getting sick patients out of town; corporations such as Wal-Mart, Home Depot, and Budweiser delivered supplies faster than FEMA; and (once let into the city) private charities such as the Salvation Army performed better than the government response agencies. The solution? According to one critic, "When massive and bloated governments at all levels disappoint, the solution is not to give them more money. Rather, the solution lies in a government limited in scope and ambition, and focused on its essential functions."[91] FEMA and other government agencies, some suggest, should receive fewer funds, while private sector and charitable organizations should be given more responsibility.

Most likely, FEMA will have its future role in disasters narrowed and its power curtailed but will remain the primary organization for disaster response. Power now resides in DHS under Secretary Michael Chertoff. The secretary proposed moving preparedness and mitigation activities out of FEMA into a new preparedness directorate. FEMA can then focus exclusively on response and recovery. Critics of DHS see this action as inadequate to solve disaster response problems.

Some places have a special concern with these changes. On the 100-year anniversary of the 1906 San Francisco earthquake, experts calculated that an earthquake today of the same size as in 1906 would kill 3,400, leave 225,000 homeless, and cost $150 billion. Experts rank California as one of the states best prepared for a disaster, and the state has done much to strengthen buildings, roads, and bridges since the 1989 earthquake in San Francisco. Even so, a major earthquake will cause chaos. San Franciscans will depend greatly on whatever federal agency takes charge of the disaster response.

Other major disasters are inevitable. Hurricanes that hit major cities on the Atlantic Coast are all but certain in decades to come. The location of large populations in dangerous areas puts increasing numbers of people at risk. The tendency to focus on short-term problems rather than prepare for rare but dangerous events increases the risks. Hurricanes, flooding, earthquakes, terrorist attacks, hazardous chemical accidents, and tornadoes will continue to cause harm in the United States and across the world. Events such as volcanic eruption, tsunamis, and severe drought will affect other parts of the world. All these types of disasters will continue to occur regularly. Other new forms of disaster involving loss of power, Internet sabotage, or release of biological weapons could threaten the country in the future. As the occurrence of disasters increases, the ability to respond will need to keep pace.

---

[1] E. L. Quarantelli, ed., *What Is a Disaster? Perspectives on the Question*. London: Routledge, 1998.

[2] Ronald W. Perry and E. L. Quarantelli, eds., *What Is a Disaster? New Answers to Old Questions*. Philadelphia: Xlibris, 2005.

[3] National Research Council, *Facing Hazards and Disasters: Understanding Human Dimensions*. Washington, D.C.: National Academies Press, 2006.

[4] Dennis S. Mileti, *Disasters by Design: A Reassessment of Natural Hazards in the United States*. Washington, D.C.: Joseph Henry Press, 1999, p. 96.

[5] "U.S. Annual Total Number of Weather Related Fatalities 1940–2003," University of Nebraska–Lincoln High Plains Regional Climate Center. Available online. URL: http://www.hprcc.unl.edu/nebraska/weather-related-fatalities1940-2003. html. Downloaded in May 2006; "Deaths from Earthquakes in the United States," USBS Earthquake Hazard Program. Available online. URL: http://earthquake. usgs.gov/regional/states/us_deaths.php. Updated on March 7, 2006.

[6] Ted Steinberg, *Acts of God: The Unnatural History of Natural Disaster in America*. Oxford: Oxford University Press, 2000, p. 72.

[7] Steinberg, *Acts of God*, p. 152.

8 Quoted in "Timeline: U.S. Storm Disasters," American Experience, PBS Online. Available online. URL: http://www.pbs.org/wgbh/amex/hurricane38/timeline/index.html. Downloaded in April 2006.

9 Quoted in Matthew Mulcahy, "A Tempestuous Spirit Called 'Hurri Cano': Hurricanes and Colonial Society in the British Greater Caribbean," in Steven Biel, ed., *American Disasters*. New York: New York University Press, 2001, p. 12.

10 Mulcahy, "A Tempestuous Spirit Called 'Hurri Cano,'" pp. 11–35.

11 Steinberg, *Acts of God*, p. 69.

12 "Rescue and Relief," The Great Chicago Fire and the Web of Memory, Chicago Historical Society. Available online. URL: http://www.chicagohs.org/fire/rescue/essay-6.html. Downloaded in June 2006.

13 Deana C. Hipke. "The Great Peshtigo Fire of 1871." Available online. URL: http://www.peshtigofire.info. Downloaded in May 2006.

14 Quoted in "The Marinette and Peshtigo Eagle," Wisconsin Electronic Reader. Available online. URL: http://www.library.wisc.edu/etext/wireader/WER2001-1.html. Downloaded in May 2006.

15 Quoted in Renée Montagne, "Remembering the 1906 San Francisco Earthquake," NPR. Available online. URL: http://www.npr.org/templates/story/story.php?storyId=5334411. Posted on April 11, 2006.

16 Peter S. Felknor, *The Tri-State Tornado: The Story of America's Greatest Tornado Disaster*. Ames: Iowa State University Press, 1992, p. 92.

17 John M. Barry, *Rising Tide: The Great Mississippi Flood of 1927 and How It Changed America*. New York: Touchstone, 1997.

18 Rick Shenkman, "Interview with Peter Daniel: The Great Flood of 1927," History News Network. Available online. URL: http://hnn.us/articles/15370.html. Posted on September 6, 2005.

19 Stephen Ambrose, "Great Flood: Expedition Journal," National Geographic News. Available online. URL: http://news.nationalgeographic.com/news/2001/05/0501_river4.html. Posted on May 1, 2001.

20 Kevin R. Kosar, "Disaster Response and Appointment of a Recovery Czar: The Executive Branches Response to the Flood of 1927," CRS Report to Congress. Available online. URL: http://fpc.state.gov/documents/organization/55826.pdf. Posted on October 25, 2005.

21 "As Drought, Fires, Floods, and Revolution Wreak Havoc around the Globe, the 'Red Cross Mothers the World,'" American Red Cross. Available online. URL: http://www.redcross.org/museum/history/20-39_c.asp. Downloaded in May 2006.

22 R. A. Scotti, *Sudden Sea: The Great Hurricane of 1938*. Boston: Little, Brown, 2003, p. 213.

23 Roger A. Pielke, Jr., Chantal Simonpietri, and Jennifer Oxelson, "Thirty Years after Hurricane Camille: Lessons Learned, Lessons Lost," Center for Science and Technology Policy Research. Available online. URL: http://sciencepolicy.colorado.edu/about_us/meet_us/roger_pielke/camille. Posted on July 12, 1999.

24 R. Steven Daniels and Carolyn L. Clark-Daniels, "Transforming Government: The Renewal and Revitalization of the Federal Emergency Management Agency," PricewaterhouseCoopers Endowment for the Business of Government. Available

online. URL: http://www.fema.gov/pdf/library/danielsreport.pdf. Posted in April 2000, p. 24.

[25] Martin Elliot Silverstein, *Disasters: Your Right to Survive*. Washington, D.C.: Brassey's, 1992. p. ix.

[26] George D. Haddow and Jane A. Bullock, *Introduction to Emergency Management*. Amsterdam: Butterworth Heinemann, 2003, p. 6.

[27] Steinberg, *Acts of God*, p. 186.

[28] Haddow and Bullock, *Introduction to Emergency Management*, p. 8.

[29] Daniels and Clark-Daniels, "Transforming Government," p. 10.

[30] Daniel Franklin, "The FEMA Phoenix," *Washington Monthly*, vol. 27, July/August 1995, pp. 38–43. Also available online. URL: http://www.washingtonmonthly.com/features/2005/0509.franklin.html. Posted in July/August 1995.

[31] Quoted in "Hurricane Hugo," Wikipedia: The Free Encyclopedia. Available online. URL: http://en.wikipedia.org/wiki/Hurricane_Hugo. Downloaded in June 2006.

[32] "Opening Statement of Senator Barbara Boxer," Barbara Boxer, United States senator from California. Available online. URL: http://boxer.senate.gov/students/resources/features/1906/committee.cfm. Posted on April 18, 2006.

[33] Quoted in Franklin, "The FEMA Phoenix."

[34] Erik Auf der Heide, *Disaster Response: Principles of Preparation and Coordination*. St. Louis: C. V. Mosby, 1989, p. 34.

[35] Franklin, "The FEMA Phoenix."

[36] United States General Accounting Office, *Disaster Management: Improving the Nation's Response to Catastrophic Disasters*. Washington, D.C.: United States General Accounting Office, 1993. Also available online. URL: http://archive.gao.gov/t2pbat5/149631.pdf. Posted in July 1993.

[37] Quoted in Franklin, "The FEMA Phoenix."

[38] Mileti, *Disasters by Design*, p. 93.

[39] "Effects of Catastrophic Events on Transportation System Management and Operations," U.S. Department of Transportation. Available online. URL: http://www.its.dot.gov/JPODOCS/REPTS_TE/13775.html. Posted on April 22, 2002.

[40] Haddow and Bullock, *Introduction to Emergency Management*, p. 92.

[41] "9/11 by the Numbers," *New York Magazine*, September 15, 2002. Also available online. URL: http://www.newyorkmetro.com/news/articles/wtc/1year/numbers.htm. Posted on September 15, 2002.

[42] "How Much Did the September 11 Terrorist Attack Cost America?" Institute for Analysis of Global Security. Available online. URL: http://www.iags.org/costof911.html. Downloaded in August 2006.

[43] Quoted in David Alexander, *Principles of Emergency Planning and Management*. Oxford: Oxford University Press, 2002, p. 236.

[44] U.S. General Accounting Office, *Combating Terrorism: FEMA Continues to Make Progress in Coordinating Preparedness and Response*. Washington, D.C.: U.S. Government Accounting Office, 2001. Also available online. URL: http://www.gao.gov/new.items/d0115.pdf. Posted in March 2001.

[45] "Federal Response: Examples of Government Action since September 11: Responding to the September 11 Terrorist Attacks," The White House, President

George W. Bush. Available online. URL: http://www.whitehouse.gov/news/releases/2001/10/20011003.html. Posted in October 2001.

46 "FEMA Assistance Available for Victims of WTC," FEMA. Available online. URL: http://www.fema.gov/news/newsrelease.fema?id=5663. Posted on September 23, 2001.

47 "Executive Order Establishing Office of Homeland Security," The White House, President George W. Bush. Available online. URL: http://www.whitehouse.gov/news/releases/2001/10/20011008-2.html. Posted on October 8, 2001.

48 "The Storm: A Short History of FEMA," Frontline, PBS Online. Available online. URL: http://www.pbs.org/wgbh/pages/frontline/storm/etc/femahist.html. Posted on November 22, 2005.

49 U.S. General Accounting Office, *Major Management Challenges and Program Risks: Federal Emergency Management Agency*. Washington, D.C.: U.S. Government Accounting Office, 2003. Available online. URL: http://www.gao.gov/pas/2003/d03102.pdf. Posted in January 2003.

50 Department of Homeland Security, *National Response Plan*. Washington, D.C.: U.S. Department of Homeland Security, 2004.

51 "Fact Sheet: National Response Plan," Department of Homeland Security. Available online. URL: http://www.dhs.gov/dhspublic/interapp/press_release/press_release_0581.xml. Downloaded in August 2006.

52 "National Response Plan Brochure," Department of Homeland Security. Available online. URL: http://www.dhs.gov/interweb/assetlibrary/NRP_Brochure.pdf. Downloaded in August 2006.

53 "The Storm: Interview Leo Bosner," Frontline, PBS Online. Available online. URL: http://www.pbs.org/wgbh/pages/frontline/storm/interviews/bosner.html. Downloaded in August 2006.

54 Douglas Brinkley, *The Great Deluge: Hurricane Katrina, New Orleans, and the Mississippi Gulf Coast*. New York: William Morrow, 2006, p. 399.

55 Quoted in "The Storm: 14 Days: A Timeline," Frontline, PBS Online. Available online. URL: http://www.pbs.org/wgbh/pages/frontline/storm/etc/cron.html. Downloaded in August 2006.

56 "President Addresses Nation, Discusses Hurricane Katrina Relief Efforts," The White House, President George W. Bush. Available online. URL: http://www.whitehouse.gov/news/releases/2005/09/20050903.html. Posted on September 3, 2005.

57 "DHS Inspector's Report: FEMA Deserved Criticism after Katrina," FoxNews.com. Available online. URL: http://www.foxnews.com/story/0,2933,191702,00.html. Posted on April 14, 2006.

58 Lisa de Moraes, "Kanye West's Torrent of Criticism, Live on NBC," *Washington Post*, September 3, 2005, p. C1. Also available online. URL: http://www.washingtonpost.com/wpdyn/content/article/2005/09/03/AR2005090300165.html. Posted on September 3, 2005.

59 "Florida State Emergency Response Team and FEMA Continue Joint Response to Hurricane Wilma," FEMA Disaster Information. Available online. URL: http://www.fema.gov/news/newsrelease.fema?id=20060. Posted on October 25, 2005.

[60] Quoted in "Florida State Emergency Response Team and FEMA Continue Joint Response to Hurricane Wilma," FEMA Disaster Information.

[61] The White House. *The Federal Response to Hurricane Katrina.* Washington, D.C.: White House, 2006. Also available online. URL: http://purl.access.gpo.gov/ GPO/LPS67263. Posted in February 2006; U.S. Government Accountability Office, *Statement by Comptroller David M. Walker on GAO's Preliminary Observations Regarding Preparedness and Response to Hurricane Katrina.* Washington, D.C.: U.S. Government Accountability Office, 2006; Select Bipartisan Committee to Investigate the Preparation for and Response to Hurricane Katrina, *A Failure of Initiative: The Final Report of the Select Bipartisan Committee to Investigate the Preparation for and Response to Hurricane Katrina.* Washington, D.C.: U.S. House of Representatives, 2006. Also available online. URL: http://katrina.house.gov/ full_katrina_report.htm. Posted on February 15, 2006.

[62] Select Bipartisan Committee, p. 2.

[63] Quoted in "FEMA Chief Touts High-Tech Hurricane Response," CNN.com. Available online. URL: http://www.cnn.com/2006/WEATHER/06/01/hurricane.forecast/index.html. Posted on June 1, 2006.

[64] U.S. Government Accountability Office, "Expedited Assistance for Victims of Hurricane Katrina and Rita: FEMA's Control Weaknesses Exposed the Government to Significant Fraud and Abuse," Washington, D.C.: U.S. Government Accountability Office, 2006. Also available online. URL: http://www.gao.gov/new. items/d06403t.pdf. Posted on February 13, 2006.

[65] Quoted in Joby Warrick, "Multiple Layers of Contractors Drive up Cost of Katrina Cleanup," *Washington Post*, March 20, 2006, p. A1. Also available online. URL: http://www.washingtonpost.com/wp-dyn/content/article/2006/03/19/ AR2006031901078.html. Posted on March 20, 2006

[66] Quoted in Martin Wolk, "Katrina: Contractors Rake It in as They Clean It Up," CorpWatch. http://www.corpwatch.org/article.php?id=13629. Posted on May 31, 2006.

[67] Gary Rivlin, "Some People Return, but Only One in 10 Businesses Has Reopened," *New York Times*, April 5, 2006, p. 1.

[68] Quoted in Michael Kunzelman, "Betting on Recovery," Courier-Journal. com. Available online. URL: http://www.courier-journal.com/apps/pbcs.dll/ article?AID=/20060807/BUSINESS/608070346/1003. Posted on August 7, 2006.

[69] Eric Klinenberg, *Heat Wave: A Social Autopsy of Disaster in Chicago.* Chicago: University of Chicago Press, 2002.

[70] Amanda Ripley, "Floods, Tornadoes, Hurricanes, Wildfires, Earthquakes ... Why We Don't Prepare," *Time Magazine*, August 28, 2006, p. 54.

[71] Cited in Kathleen J. Tierney, Michael K. Lindell, and Ronald W. Perry, *Facing the Unexpected: Disaster Preparedness and Response in the United States.* Washington, D.C.: Joseph Henry Press, 2001, p. 55.

[72] Greg Bluestein, "Helping Firms Survive Disaster," MercuryNews.com. Available online. URL: http://www.mercurynews.com/mld/mercurynews/business/14963863. htm?source=rss&channel= mercurynews_business. Posted on July 4, 2006.

[73] Mileti, *Disasters by Design*, p. 218.

[74] Haddow and Bullock, *Introduction to Emergency Management*, p. 138.

[75] Cited in Tierney, Lindell, and Perry, *Facing the Unexpected*, p. 50.

[76] Auf der Heide, *Disaster Response*, p. 216.

[77] Mileti, *Disasters by Design*, p. 225.

[78] Kathleen Tierney, Kristine Bevc, and Erika Kuligowski, "Metaphors Matter: Myths, Media Frames, and Their Consequences in Hurricane Katrina," *Annals of the American Academy of Political and Social Science*, vol. 604, March 2006, pp. 57–81.

[79] "2006 Federal Disaster Declarations," FEMA. Available online. URL: http://www.fema.gov/news/disasters.fema?year=2006. Downloaded in August 2006.

[80] FEMA Emergency Management Institute, *A Citizen's Guide to Disaster Assistance*. Washington, D.C.: FEMA, 2003, p. 3–4.

[81] "Our Services," American Red Cross. Available online. URL: http://www.redcross.org/services/disaster/0,1082,0_561_,00.html. Downloaded in August 2006.

[82] Cited in Tierney, Lindell, and Perry. *Facing the Unexpected*, p. 112.

[83] *Disaster Assistance: A Guide to Recovery Programs*. Washington, D.C.: FEMA, 2005.

[84] Kathleen Tierney, "Social Inequality, Hazards, and Disasters," in Ronald J. Daniels, Donald F. Kettl, and Howard Kunreuther, eds., *On Risk and Disaster: Lessons from Hurricane Katrina*. Philadelphia: University of Pennsylvania, 2006, p. 123.

[85] Mileti, *Disasters by Design*, pp. 17–41.

[86] Haddow and Bullock, *Introduction to Emergency Management*, p. 45.

[87] Haddow and Bullock, *Introduction to Emergency Management*, p. 165.

[88] "Disaster Assistance," USAID from the American People. Available online. URL: http://www.usaid.gov/our_work/humanitarian_assistance/disaster_assistance. Downloaded in August 2006.

[89] "Introduction to the Synthesis Report," Tsunami Evaluation Coalition. Available online. URL: http://www.tsunami-evaluation.org/The+TEC+Synthesis+Report. Downloaded in August 2006.

[90] "Executive Summary. Joint Evaluation of the International Response to the Indian Ocean Tsunami: Synthesis Report," Tsunami Evaluation Coalition. Available online. URL: http://www.tsunami-evaluation.org/The+TEC+Synthesis+Report/Executive+Summary.htm. Posted in July 2006.

[91] David Boaz, "Catastrophe in Big Easy Demonstrates Big Government's Failure," Cato Institute. Available online. URL: http://www.cato.org/pub_display.php?pub_id=4819. Posted September 19, 2005.

CHAPTER 2

THE LAW AND
DISASTER RESPONSE

Disaster response in the United States is now guided by local, state, and federal laws, but for most of its history, the nation relied on spur-of-the-moment decisions and last-minute legislation. Both existing laws and past practices come from the federalist system of government in the United States. Federalism places primary responsibility for emergency management on localities and states. Some experts suggest that ceding authority to states and localities makes for weak leadership and fragmented disaster response. They favor the adoption of a comprehensive set of laws that apply to all states and localities. Most European nations have a centralized system of disaster response, but there has been little movement in the United States toward this model.

If not comprehensive, federal laws still set rules and regulations for how the federal government can aid states and communities. These laws accumulated slowly and have undergone revisions on a regular basis. Today they specify conditions that states and communities must meet to qualify for federal assistance and set up a process to follow in providing this assistance. Otherwise, guidance for disaster response relies on rules, directives, and advice rather than on legal mandates. As a result, few legal disputes have arisen over the laws and regulations. Only recently have court decisions help set policy and guide disaster response.

LAWS AND REGULATIONS

Federal Law

The first piece of federal disaster legislation came in 1803. After a fire burned much of a New Hampshire town, Congress passed a bill that provided economic relief in the form of lower tariffs. This legislation set a pattern for the next 150 years. Congress would respond more than 100 times with makeshift bills to help communities and states damaged by hurricanes, floods, earthquakes, and other natural disasters. Politics as well as need guided this legislation. Representatives and senators fought over which states and communities deserved the relief and which did not.

Perhaps the most enduring legislation for disaster response came in 1905. Congress chartered the American Red Cross that year. The charter established the Red Cross as a nonprofit, tax-exempt charitable organization and gave it responsibilities for, among other things, disaster relief. The legislation did not set aside funding for the Red Cross, which remains an independent agency. It did treat the organization as a partner to support relief efforts of the armed forces and federal government. For many decades to follow, this legislation came as close as anything else to a federal disaster policy.

One small step toward new kinds of government involvement in disaster relief came in the mid-20th century. The Federal Disaster Relief Act of 1950 created the first formal role for federal agencies. It authorized the federal government to grant relief funds to states harmed by a disaster without Congress having to first pass a relief bill. Instead, when the president declared that a disaster had occurred, funds could go directly to the affected areas. The law intended that the funds would supplement rather than replace state and local spending, however. The president was to declare a disaster only when major damage had occurred and state and local governments had committed funds to response and recovery. At least initially, the law had only a small financial impact. It restricted federal contributions to restoring public buildings and facilities and did not give direct help to individuals. Its importance came instead from shifting decision-making authority from Congress to the president.

The legislation reaffirmed the federalist approach that guided most disaster response in the past. Under federalism in the United States, federal and state governments share power. The federal government in principle defers to states and localities in many activities, as states and localities defer to the federal government in others. For disasters, federalism meant that the federal government would help only when demands outstripped the resources of other levels of government. In case of any confusion, President Harry Truman made this philosophy clear in 1952. He signed an executive order stating that federal assistance did not replace state and local assistance. This principle continues to guide disaster policy today.

Congress took some more formal but still tentative steps toward a federal disaster policy with legislation in the 1960s and 1970s. It passed the National Flood Insurance Act of 1968, the Disaster Relief Act of 1970, and the Disaster Relief Act of 1974. Each gave the federal government a larger role in disaster assistance. These actions still left states dissatisfied, however. Although they appreciated help, the various laws made for confusion in dealing with the federal government. After a call for a more comprehensive policy in the 1970s, the White House and Congress took steps to create such a policy.

PRESIDENTIAL DIRECTIVE 12148: CREATION OF FEMA

On July 20, 1979, President Jimmy Carter ordered that federal government emergency functions be transferred to the newly established Federal Emergency Management Agency (FEMA).[1] These functions had resided in the Defense Civil Preparedness Agency in the Department of Defense, the Federal Disaster Assistance Administration in the Department of Housing and Urban Development, the Federal Preparedness Agency in the General Services Administration, the Office of Science and Technology, and numerous other parts of the government. The directive consolidated all these into a single government organization. Given the dispersion of disaster responsibilities, consolidation made good sense.

The directive also laid out duties for FEMA. The new agency would establish federal policies for disaster response and coordinate all civil defense and emergency planning, management, mitigation, and assistance. These tasks were broad. FEMA would lead efforts to improve dam safety, natural and nuclear disaster warning systems, and preparation and planning for major terrorist incidents. In so doing, it needed to work with state and local governments and charities spread across the country. Disaster policies at all levels of government would need to be reviewed, evaluated, and changed. The FEMA director, who represented the president in dealings on disaster policy, had to report back on the state of disaster programs and make recommendations for change.

The directive defined civil emergency widely to include accidents, natural events, human-caused events, and wartime events that caused substantial injury to the population or substantial damage to property. Giving FEMA a role in civil defense and wartime emergencies meant it had to work with the Department of Defense, which had its own policies in this area. However, the natural hazards and civil defense units of FEMA never worked well together, and eventually, civil defense responsibilities were moved out of FEMA.

Along with creating FEMA, the directive established a new Federal Emergency Management Council to advise the president. The director of FEMA chaired the council, while the director of the Office of Management and Budget and others appointed by the president served as members. The council would give advice to both the president and to the FEMA director. Ideally, a council would involve the president in disaster activities and give FEMA more support from the White House.

Strong in its goals but short in its details, the directive left many questions about the new agency unanswered. The new director faced the challenge of dealing with rivalries and trying to get all of its new parts to work smoothly. It would in fact take more than a decade for FEMA to become a highly effective organization.

THE ROBERT T. STAFFORD DISASTER RELIEF AND EMERGENCY ACT OF 1988

Robert T. Stafford, a Republican from Vermont, served in the Senate from 1971 to 1989. His work on disaster relief led Congress to name this bill after him. The bill amended the Disaster Relief Act of 1974. After being amended several times since then, the 1988 law guides government relief and assistance today. It intends "to provide an orderly and continuing means of assistance by the Federal Government to State and local governments in carrying out their responsibilities to alleviate the suffering and damage which result from such disasters."[2] Toward that end, it broadens the scope of previous disaster legislation by providing more assistance and by encouraging states, communities, and individuals to do more to prepare for disasters.

The Stafford Act makes a distinction between an emergency and a major disaster. An *emergency* refers to circumstances in which federal assistance is needed to supplement state and local efforts to save lives, protect the safety of the public, and limit damage. A major disaster is more serious. It occurs when, in the view of the president, a catastrophe is serious enough to require major disaster assistance to alleviate damage, loss, hardship, and suffering. Most major disasters are caused by natural events, but they can also come from fires, explosions, and other human-caused events. The cause is less important than the severity of death and damage for declaring a major disaster. The legislation does not define severity but gives authority to the president, who relies on advice from experts to determine whether an emergency is serious enough to become a major disaster.

The law has several subchapters that deal with the core elements of disaster response:

Preparedness and Mitigation   State and local communities (defined widely to include territories, American Indian tribal areas, and unincorporated areas) have primary responsibility to prepare for and mitigate disasters. The law recognizes, however, that states and localities need incentives to devote time and money to preparedness and mitigation. Otherwise, they will use scarce tax dollars to deal with immediate problems rather than invest for a less certain gain in disaster protection. To help encourage long-term investment, the federal government offers financial assistance for preparedness and mitigation. It also calls on FEMA to give states and localities technical assistance in identifying unmet needs and following guidelines.

The Law and Disaster Response

All communities should begin disaster preparation by installing warning systems. The Stafford Act allows the federal government to enter into agreements with private or commercial companies that own communication systems and can provide warnings. The emergency warnings announced by television and radio stations illustrate this kind of cooperation between the public and private sector. In dealing with state and local governments, the president and the federal government are authorized to help create a civil-defense communication system that can warn those endangered by disasters. The federal government can give technical assistance to communities setting up local warning systems such as sirens placed around cities and towns.

Other forms of preparedness involve emergency planning and practice. City governments need a comprehensive disaster plan that involves city residents and includes regularly scheduled drills. The Stafford Act authorizes grants up to $250,000 for states to develop such disaster plans. To receive a grant, states must submit an application that lays out how they will use the funds to prepare residents for a disaster and how the state government agencies will train staff, formulate regulations, and set up exercises in disaster preparation. Those already with plans can request an additional $50,000 to maintain and update them. The federal grant pays 75 percent of the total costs, requiring a contribution of 25 percent from the state and community.

Pre-disaster mitigation to minimize the threat of disasters involves more extensive and expensive action than preparedness. The Stafford Act accordingly offers larger grants for this purpose. The federal government awards up to $500,000 for pre-disaster mitigation but, as in other programs, requires states to contribute 25 percent of the total. The awards are selected from five local projects recommended by the governor of each state. The criteria for the awards include the ability of the mitigation project to reduce the vulnerability of the population to a serious disaster, the strength of commitment and funding from the state, and the involvement of impoverished communities that can afford to do little on their own. Successful projects must also have private businesses and organizations to partner with local governments.

To help identify locations of greatest need for mitigation, the law authorizes the federal government to develop multi-hazard advisory maps. These maps show the areas within each state that face the greatest risks from hazards and those that face multiple, overlapping hazards. When shared with state governments, the maps can help in designing mitigation projects and guiding applications for pre-disaster mitigation grants. The maps may also inform the public of the risks of natural disasters they face.

An interagency task force coordinates the implementation of pre-disaster mitigation projects. The director of FEMA chairs the task force, while members come from federal agencies involved in disaster mitigation, state and local governments (including Indian tribes), and the American Red Cross. A 2005 report from FEMA lists expenditures of about $290 million. California, Florida, Iowa, and Missouri received the largest number of grants, but nearly all other states in the country received awards. Examples of awards include preparing water districts in California for seismic events, adding building reinforcement to health centers and public buildings in Florida, and developing multi-hazard mitigation plans in Iowa. The largest awards of $3 million went to Washington State to retrofit schools for an earthquake, to San Diego to retrofit water pipelines for an earthquake, and to Maine to acquire and demolish property on a floodplain.

Administration Under the Stafford Act, most administrative duties for a major disaster go to a federal coordinating officer appointed by the president. The officer first assesses the most urgent needs for relief. Based on the assessment, the officer sets up field offices near the disaster and coordinates the activities of private relief groups such as the Red Cross, the Salvation Army, and Mennonite Disaster Service. Most important, the officer works to get prompt assistance to victims. The president may also request that the state governor appoint a state coordinating officer to work closely with the federal coordinating officer.

The federal coordinating officer supervises federal emergency-support teams. These teams go to the damaged areas, where they work directly with responders and victims. However, they organize others rather than do the work themselves. The law says that federal funds to clear debris, distribute supplies, repair buildings, and give other emergency assistance should go to individuals and firms that normally conduct business in the area. The law also says that selection of private individuals and firms for paid disaster work should be done equitably and without discrimination.

In helping local communities, the government can cover only those costs for privately owned buildings and housing that are not paid by private insurance or other federal programs. The law prohibits victims from getting duplicate benefits and requires that federal agencies take steps to prevent such duplication. Anyone receiving undeserved benefits must return them and is liable for fines and criminal prosecution. However, disaster assistance does not count as income used in determining eligibility for other federal assistance programs (such as food stamps, welfare, and Medicaid).

State, local, and tribal governments also have administrative duties. To obtain assistance funds, local governments must submit a mitigation plan. The plan should lay out the actions the government will take to reduce risks and vulnerabilities of its citizens from the natural hazard and present a strategy to implement the actions. State governments must also explain how they will support local mitigation efforts, provide technical assistance to local communities, and take mitigation actions on its own. Recipients of disaster assistance must further demonstrate that they comply with safe land use and construction practices.

Major Disaster Assistance　Major disaster assistance comes only after the president has declared a major disaster. All requests for a major disaster declaration must come from the governor of the state in which the disaster occurred. The governor should have already executed the state emergency plan but found that the response needs exceed the capabilities of the state. The application furnishes information on state and local resources already committed to alleviating the effects of the disaster and on the additional resources needed from the federal government. Based on the request, the president may conclude that a major disaster exists.

With the declaration of a major disaster, the resources of the federal government become available, as needed, to support state and local assistance efforts. These resources include federal equipment, supplies, facilities, and personnel. Although it leaves most work to local agencies and companies, the federal government assists with removing debris, leading search-and-rescue teams, repairing roads and bridges, demolishing unsafe structures, warning of further risks, and finding technical information. The federal government also coordinates the distribution of medicine, food, and other consumable supplies by charitable organizations such as the American Red Cross, the Salvation Army, and Mennonite Disaster Services. Under special circumstances, the state government may request assistance from the military and resources from the Department of Defense.

The assistance from the federal government gives priority to repairing federal facilities damaged by the disaster (unless the repair can be deferred until Congress appropriates special funds). Under certain conditions, however, the federal government can contribute to the repair of state and local public facilities. The facility must provide critical services such as power, water, sewage disposal, wastewater treatment, communication, and emergency medical care. Any contribution of more than $20 million made to repair these facilities requires notification of Congress and the appropriate committees. If state or local governments decide that restoring a public building would not be wise, they can request 75 to 90 percent of the estimated repair funds in cash to use for other disaster recovery costs. For example, a public building likely to be harmed again by a flood or earthquake can be demolished and the funds used for a new building elsewhere. In fact, the law prohibits the repair of buildings that lie in special flood-zone areas designated by FEMA.

Under a major disaster declaration, the president can assign federal departments and agencies to assist in removal of debris. Funds can also go directly to state and local governments or to private companies that help remove wreckage from public and private property. The state or local government must agree to protect the federal government from any claims for damages caused by the removal.

Sometimes local governments suffer loss of tax and other revenues because of a disaster. The federal government under the Stafford Act can make loans to cover these shortfalls. The local government must show that it cannot perform crucial functions because of disaster-related income losses. The amount shall not exceed $5 million or 25 percent of the yearly operating budget of the local government. Repayment may be canceled if, during the next three years, local government income does not rise to meet its operating budget. To also help communities, the federal government can furnish emergency public transportation. This transportation helps workers get to jobs, students to attend school, and government staff to help those in need— all steps needed for the community to resume its normal pattern of life.

In addition to repair of public buildings, removal of debris, and loans to local governments, major disaster assistance includes federal programs for individuals and households. Those forced out of their homes by damage from the disaster may need housing assistance. They can apply for temporary assistance in the form of funds for fair-market rent and the cost of utility hookups. Sometimes FEMA supplies housing units that victims can live in for up to 18 months. If they desire, occupants can purchase the units at the end of the temporary use period. Victims can also apply for grants of up to $5,000 for repairs to make their housing livable. Alternatively, they can apply for grants of up to $10,000 to replace housing damaged by the disaster. Besides housing, assistance for individuals and families includes funds for medical and dental services, funeral costs, and important transportation needs. However, the Stafford Act limits assistance to those individuals and households that lack the money to meet the disaster-related expenses on their own.

The law also provides for unemployment assistance. Those workers who lost their jobs because of the disaster can get unemployment benefits for up to 26 weeks or until they find another job. The amount of assistance depends on the unemployment compensation law of the state. The federal government can also help pay for crisis counseling to victims of major disasters and to private mental health organizations that serve disaster workers.

For most forms of assistance offered under major disaster declarations, the federal government contributes 75 percent of the total, and state and local governments contribute 25 percent. However, if the extraordinary nature of a disaster or a series of disasters leaves the state unable to pay its 25 percent portion, the federal government can lend or advance the funds. In exceptional circumstances, the president can agree to cover all the costs. The formula differs for programs to assist families and individuals. The federal government fully covers these costs.

The Law and Disaster Response

Emergency Assistance Programs An emergency occurs when federal assistance can help state and local governments to lessen or avert the threat of a catastrophe, but the threat does not involve the severe damage of a major disaster. Although the assistance available to state and local governments under emergency declarations is smaller than for major disaster declarations, the application procedures are much the same. The state governor requests emergency assistance by describing the extent of the damage, resources already committed by the state and local government, and unmet needs.

The federal government contributes much the same kind of support for emergencies as for disasters (though not the same amount). It puts agencies of the federal government on notice to help support state and local efforts, and it coordinates cross-government and private organization relief efforts. It also gives technical advice and helps distribute medicine, food, and other emergency supplies. A limit of $5 million is placed on federal assistance for a single emergency. This amount can make up 75 percent of the total, with state and local governments contributing the other 25 percent. Under exceptional circumstances, the president can exceed the $5 million limit but must report the extra spending to Congress and possibly propose legislation to cover additional costs.

Emergency Preparedness The Stafford Act includes provisions for preparing for emergencies. These provisions differ from others in the law by giving primary attention to terrorist events. Emergency preparedness falls jointly to the federal government, the states, and the political subdivisions of the states. The federal government coordinates and guides preparedness so that a comprehensive emergency system exists for all hazards—including both natural and human-caused events. The director of FEMA takes major responsibility for emergency preparedness under the Stafford Act (although the Department of Homeland Security has recently shifted most such responsibilities to another unit within the department).

The law describes activities and measures the FEMA director should take to minimize the effects of hazards on the population. The director collaborates with state agencies to plan and delegate preparedness responsibilities. Research may be needed to determine the best methods for limiting the effects of hazards, developing shelter designs and materials to withstand hazards, and setting standards for equipment and facilities used in emergency response. The director coordinates this research. Further, the director sets up training programs for emergency personnel and disseminates disaster information.

This subchapter gives attention to security considerations that are not addressed elsewhere in the law. It states that the director shall establish security requirements for access to information. Persons filling certain positions designated of critical importance for national security must undergo an investigation.

By law, all employees of FEMA must take a loyalty oath in which they affirm to support and defend the Constitution and that they are not a member of an organization that advocates overthrow of the U.S. government.

THE HOMELAND SECURITY ACT OF 2002

This legislation established the Department of Homeland Security (DHS), its mission, and its main offices, effective January 2003.[3] The primary mission of the new department is to prevent terrorist attacks in the United States and to minimize the damage and assist in the recovery of any attacks that may occur. This law has four subsections on 1) information analysis and infrastructure protection; 2) chemical, biological, radiological, and nuclear countermeasures; 3) border and transportation security and weapons; and 4) emergency preparedness and response. However, the legislation lays out only the broadest guidelines for integrating agencies involved with each subsection into a single department.

The undersecretary for emergency preparedness and response ensures that the country is prepared for terrorist attacks and major disasters and coordinates the federal response to such events. Toward these ends, the law transfers the following agencies and functions into DHS: FEMA, the Office for Domestic Preparedness, and Public Health Emergency Preparedness. In connection with an actual or expected nuclear attack, certain parts of the Department of Energy and Environmental Protection Agency would serve as part of DHS. DHS would also work closely with the Department of Health and Human Services in responding to biological, chemical, or radiological attack.

State Laws

State and local governments handle most emergencies, seeking assistance from the federal government only when a disaster overwhelms their resources. State and local laws generally follow the lead of federal laws in creating emergency management agencies and assisting victims. However, state laws vary in how they organize and fund emergency response agencies. Without trying to summarize the statutes of all 50 states, the District of Columbia, and other territories, a few examples from three states—California, Florida, and Louisiana—illustrate similarities and differences in state disaster laws.

Chapter 7 of the California Government Code, the California Emergency Services Act, established the Office of Emergency Services (OES) under authority of the governor. The act requires the office and the governor to put procedures in place for preparedness and response to events such as war, oil spills, natural disasters, and release of toxic substances or hazardous materials. When local authorities cannot cope with an emergency, the governor can declare a state emergency and use funds legally available to the government to aid in the response.

The OES takes the lead in coordinating the state response to a disaster. Before a disaster, the office maintains a state emergency plan to organize the response to fires, floods, earthquakes, dam breaks, hazardous material incidents, and nuclear power plant emergencies. The OES Earthquake Program gets special emphasis. It provides earthquake preparedness planning and technical assistance to local governments, businesses, schools, hospitals, and the public. During a disaster, the OES activates state response centers, takes requests from local governments for funds, and distributes funds from the federal government to local governments. For help in the response, it can call on other state agencies such as the National Guard, the Department of Health Services, and the Department of Transportation.

Chapter 252 of the Florida Statutes outlines emergency management. The law recognizes the special circumstances of the state. It says that the state's vulnerability to natural and technological disasters is increased by "the tremendous growth in the state's population, especially the growth in the number of persons residing in coastal areas, in the elderly population, in the number of seasonal vacationers, and in the number of persons with special needs. This growth has greatly complicated the state's ability to coordinate its emergency management resources and activities."[4] Given this challenge, the law intends to promote preparedness, response, recovery, and mitigation and to give resources to local governments in the case of a major or catastrophic disaster.

The law creates the state-level Division of Emergency Management and authorizes the creation of local emergency agencies. The Division of Emergency Management works with federal and local governments to coordinate preparation for and response to a disaster. It further must prepare a comprehensive state emergency plan that includes components for evacuation, sheltering, post-disaster response and recovery, use of state resources such as the National Guard, a warning system, and training and exercise programs. The governor has responsibility for declaring a state of emergency when a disaster has occurred or is imminent. During a state of emergency, the governor can issue rules and directives that have the force of law, including issuing mandatory evacuations and mobilizing the National Guard.

The law gives attention to persons with special needs. It says that local agencies must keep records of citizens with special needs for assistance and have plans to help these persons. Government agencies should also contact care providers of people with disabilities to ensure that plans and provisions are in place for an emergency or disaster.

Disaster Response

The Louisiana Homeland Security and Emergency Assistance and Disaster Act, Chapter 6, aims to protect people and property of the state "from emergencies and disasters of unprecedented size and destructiveness resulting from terrorist events, enemy attack, sabotage, or other hostile action, or from fire, flood, earthquake, or other natural or man-made causes."[5] To do so, the law designates the Military Department of the state of Louisiana as the homeland security and disaster preparedness agency and authorizes the creation of local emergency preparedness agencies. These agencies should prepare, approve, and maintain state and local disaster plans. The plans should include actions for evacuation, rescue, care, and treatment of persons victimized or threatened by a disaster.

The Louisiana governor has responsibility for addressing the dangers presented by emergencies and disasters. This responsibility includes making emergency declarations and giving parish (the Louisiana equivalent of a county) presidents special emergency powers. During an emergency, the governor may suspend certain state regulations, transfer resources and personnel from state offices to help in the disaster response, and direct or compel evacuations of all or parts of areas threatened by a disaster. Under the governor, the adjutant general of the Military Department serves as the director of the Office of Homeland Security and Emergency Preparedness and leads emergency preparedness and response programs. The adjutant general works with the federal government and local governments during a disaster.

The law gives special responsibilities to parish presidents. Along with establishing a local office of homeland security and emergency preparedness, a parish president may declare a local state of emergency. When the emergency extends beyond the resources of the parish, aid from the state government may be requested. Like the governor, a parish president can during an emergency suspend regulations, direct local resources to emergency assistance, and force evacuation.

Laws in all three states authorize or require the creation of emergency agencies at the local level to work with state agencies. For example, San Francisco, California, has an Office of Emergency Services and Homeland Security that develops emergency plans and, in the case of a disaster, manages emergency operations. It receives $80 million in grant funds from the federal and state government for equipment, planning, training, and exercise needs. In Miami, Florida, the Office of Emergency Management coordinates the multiagency response to a disaster affecting the 2.4 million residents of Miami-Dade county. In New Orleans, Louisiana, the Office of Emergency Preparedness advises the mayor, works with city departments and the state government in responding to a disaster, and makes requests for additional federal disaster assistance.

Multiplying the state laws and agencies by more than 50 and the local regulations and agencies by thousands gives a sense of the network of government disaster preparedness and response organizations. The laws for states and communities follow the pattern of the federal laws but differ in details and implementation. This approach reflects the federalist policy of governing that guides the United States. To encourage cross-government consistency and cooperation, FEMA has over the last decade tried to standardize agency procedures and knowledge with its training programs and guidelines. Yet the U.S. system of law continues to allow for state and local autonomy.

COURT CASES

Disaster response laws and policies have not come under much scrutiny by the courts. Although courts occasionally have to resolve disputes over the eligibility of individuals for disaster assistance, they rarely have considered disaster-related cases that involve constitutional issues of civil rights, personal freedoms, and misuse of government powers. In one exception involving disaster mitigation (*United States v. Sponenbarger*), the Supreme Court ruled in 1939 that diverting riverwater to private land as part of comprehensive flood control did not constitute a "taking" of the land or require payment to the owner of the land. With this case and others, the authority of the government to take special action during a threatened or actual disaster has seldom been challenged.

In the few cases FEMA or other disaster response agencies have been sued for wrongdoing, they have successfully defended themselves. Two cases, one involving a 1986 Supreme Court decision and the other a 2003 federal district court opinion, illustrate the successful defense of the federal government from suits involving disaster response and relief. However, in a 2006 case involving Hurricane Katrina, the federal district court forced FEMA to change its response policies.

Supreme Court Decisions

LYNG, SECRETARY OF AGRICULTURE, ET AL. V. PAYNE, ET AL. 84-1948 (1986)

Background

On May 26, 1973, President Richard Nixon declared 13 counties in northern Florida a major disaster area after torrential rains badly damaged farm crops and property. Disaster relief at this time, before the creation of FEMA, came through several agencies. For farm damage, the Department of Agriculture and the Farmers Home Administration (FmHA) took responsibility. Following its rules, FmHA announced the availability of emergency loans for victims of the disaster, but none of the eligible farmers filed an application in the months after the damage occurred. On January 2, 1974, however, Congress passed a new law that provided loans under more generous conditions and created a 90-day application period. FmHA sent out press releases about the new law and benefits, and at least two newspapers published a story on the availability of the loans. This time, four applications were submitted by the end of the 90-day application period.

In 1976, 2,500 northern Florida farmers filed a class-action suit against the Department of Agriculture. They claimed they had been eligible for disaster relief loans but did not know of the program. According to the suit, the press release in 1974 did not explain the availability of more generous benefits. The loans had only a 1 percent interest rate, could be combined with other sources of credit, and forgave payment of up to $5,000. The farmers complained that the failure of FmHA to publicize the program more fully violated the agency's own regulations and deprived them of property without due process of law. The respondents asked the courts to direct the FmHA to reopen the loan program under the terms prevailing during the period "up to and including April 2, 1974."

The Florida district court granted the request for an injunction to have the Department of Agriculture reopen the program. It ruled that FmHA had failed to give adequate notice. For example, the ruling noted that many farmers had left a 1973 meeting with the wrong impression that they did not qualify for the loans, and FmHA did nothing to correct the misimpression. The district court also found that the details in the press release were incomplete and FmHA had failed to notify various state and country officials about the loans. It ordered the agency to reopen the program for 60 days.

The appeals court next affirmed the lower-court decision. It agreed that FmHA had not followed its own procedures and promises to notify the public of the new loan program. The information sent out in the press release did not, according to the appeals court decision, adequately explain the generous terms. After a review, however, the Supreme Court voided the decision, sending it back to the appeals court to reconsider its decision. The reconsideration should take into account a 1984 Supreme Court ruling on the need for those dealing with the government to know the law. Even after the review, the appeals court reinstated its earlier decision. The Supreme Court then agreed to hear the case.

Legal Issues

Several aspects of the district court's decision to reopen the application period raised legal issues. First, was it proper to respond to violations of administrative procedures by reopening the application period? The farmers claimed that the meager publicity about the program deprived them of government relief. The only way to rectify this problem was to allow farmers to reapply now that others had made the information available to them. The Department of Agriculture responded that, even if inadequate notice had been given, reopening the application period was inappropriate. Only when the agency misstated the policy or deceived those eligible would it be proper to reopen the application period. Since the agency never misrepresented the policies or eligibility rules, it should not have to revive the program.

Second, was the notice of the program so inadequate as to deprive the farmers of property without due process of law? The farmers argued that the failure of FmHA to publicize the program more fully in essence deprived them of property to which they were entitled. Since this loss of property occurred without due process of law, it violated the Fifth Amendment. This amendment states that no person shall "be deprived of life, liberty, or property, without due process of law; nor shall private property be taken for public use, without just compensation." Not receiving the benefits they were due was thus unconstitutional. The Department of Agriculture responded that not widely publicizing opportunities for benefits differed significantly from taking property that people already owned. The Fifth Amendment might apply if the government took possession of the farmers' land but not when the government failed to fully notify the farmers about a program.

Third, did the FmHA fail to make appropriate public announcements? The farmers argued that the announcements of the disaster benefits did not meet the agency's own standards and legal requirements. FmHA rules required the agency to notify potential borrowers of the availability of disaster relief by making public announcements and informing various public officials and agricultural leaders. The failure of the farmers to learn of the program and its generous terms proved that the agency did not meet this requirement. The Agriculture Department responded that the press release and notice of the program in the *Federal Register* met its requirements.

Decision

The decision authored by Justice Sandra Day O'Connor reversed the district and appeals courts by ruling in favor of the government. The ruling concluded that FmHA did not violate its procedures but gave adequate notice—even if not ideal in its clarity—of the program. The agency therefore could not be held responsible for the lack of applications (nor be expected to reopen the application period). Referring to the statutes governing publication of program notices, the Court found no requirements beyond those followed by the agency. The ruling also rejected the claim that eligible nonapplicants were deprived of property without due process of law.

Applicants for benefits cannot rightly claim they have a constitutional entitlement to those benefits. Even if they did have such an entitlement, the notice given by the agency satisfied due process concerns. A dissent by Justice John Stevens held that the ruling gave too much discretion to government agencies in meeting the intent of congressional legislation, but his counterarguments failed to sway the other justices.

Impact

As one of the few recent Supreme Court cases involving disaster relief, the decision absolved the government agency from responsibility for the failure of victims to take advantage of relief programs. In a sense, those who need disaster benefits from the government are expected to learn about the programs. This reduces the responsibility of government agencies (and in years to come, FEMA) to ensure that those eligible actually apply for benefits. Good agencies will do all they can to widen the pool of applications, but they are not legally liable for meeting the highest standards of publicity. Meeting a minimum standard is sufficient. This case helped remove the threat of suits based on the performance of disaster response agencies.

Federal Appeals Court Decisions

HOWARD G. DAWKINS, JR., AND ANNETTE DAWKINS V. JAMES LEE WITT, DIRECTOR OF THE FEDERAL EMERGENCY MANAGEMENT AGENCY 318 F.3D 606 (2003)

Background

The Dawkins owned a two-story home on an island near Wilmington, North Carolina, that was elevated aboveground by posts. Hurricane Fran damaged their house on September 5, 1996, but the Dawkins had purchased a government-sponsored insurance policy against flood damage through the National Flood Insurance Program. They expected this policy to cover the damage. The policy required that proof of damage and claims for losses be submitted within 60 days of the damage. The Dawkins had also purchased an insurance policy against wind damage from a private insurance company.

After a visit by the FEMA adjuster, the Dawkins sent in the required documents to FEMA, which paid the claim for flood damage. A private insurance adjuster also examined the property for wind damage but refused to pay the claim. The adjuster said that damage to the top story came not from wind but from floodwater twisting the foundation of the house. The Dawkins then requested that FEMA reopen their case to pay for the newly discovered flood damage to the top story. FEMA refused, claiming that the request could not be evaluated. Other completed repairs of the house made it impossible to identify any other flood damage.

The Dawkins filed a complaint against FEMA in the Eastern District of North Carolina. They claimed that FEMA breached their insurance contract, leaving them with costs of more than $10,000. FEMA moved to dismiss the case because the request came after the 60-day deadline (although FEMA had said nothing earlier about sticking to the 60-day limit). The district court agreed with FEMA and dismissed the case, at which time the Dawkins appealed.

Legal Issues

The main legal issue concerns whether FEMA could use its 60-day limit to reject the second request of the Dawkins for more funds. As plaintiffs, the Dawkins asked the appeals court to reject the district court dismissal and allow the case to go forward. They claimed that it was impossible for them to meet the deadline for the second set of repairs and that FEMA could not use the deadline now after they had ignored it earlier. FEMA had accepted the first claim, although it was submitted after the 60-day deadline. Several people involved in the first request had in fact stated that the 60-day requirement was not enforced. The Dawkins argued that ignoring the deadline in their first request for damage represented a waiver from future enforcement of the deadline. FEMA therefore should not have imposed the deadline for the second request for damage.

The Dawkins also claimed that FEMA could not use the 60-day deadline to reject the claim under the doctrine of equitable *estoppel.* This legal term refers to barring someone from making a claim or taking a position that contradicts a previous claim or position. In this case, the misleading information received earlier—that the 60-day limit would not be enforced—should prevent the government from enforcing the rule later. According to the plaintiffs, the conditions of the case met those traditionally required for estoppel: FEMA knew the facts about enforcing the 60-day limit, the plaintiffs had good reason to believe FEMA did not intend to enforce the 60-day limit, and the plaintiffs relied on the misinformation in their actions.

As the defendant, FEMA made a straightforward response. By FEMA rules, those wanting damages after the 60-day deadline must request and receive a written waiver. The Dawkins neither requested nor received the waiver. The insurance policy they signed stated in Article 9, Paragraph D that "no action we [FEMA] take under the terms of this policy can constitute a waiver of any of our rights." This implies that accepting a late request in one instance does constitute a waiver from the deadline in another instance. The defendant also claimed that no misconduct occurred on its part to justify equitable estoppel. FEMA representatives may have not followed rules strictly, but they did not intentionally mislead or lie to the plaintiffs.

Decision

The appeals court sided with the defendant by affirming the district court decision and ordering dismissal of the suit against FEMA. The court agreed that, according to the policy contract, the plaintiffs needed a written waiver from the 60-day limit, which they never received. The ruling further justified the decision by referring to Supreme Court precedent. Earlier decisions concluded that misinformation alone did not justify equitable estoppel— there had to be evidence of affirmative misconduct, a higher standard than existed in this case. Even if the Dawkins found it difficult to get the claim and proof of the damage into FEMA by the 60-day deadline, it was not impossible. Absent the waiver, the policy required such a deadline regardless of the difficult circumstances. The Dawkins therefore had not made a sufficient case to justify a full trial.

Impact

Like *Lyng v. Payne*, this decision placed primary responsibility on applicants for disaster relief to follow the standards of the government funding agencies. Even if FEMA does not always enforce its policies, applicants must follow them in applying for aid. The decision thus gives government disaster organizations considerable discretion in their actions but gives applicants less choice in following the rules.

Federal District Court Decisions

BEATRICE B. MCWATERS, ET AL. V. FEDERAL EMERGENCY MANAGEMENT AGENCY, ET AL. 408 F. SUPP. 2D 221 (2006)

Background

This class-action suit was submitted on behalf of residents of Louisiana, Mississippi, and Alabama who live in declared major disaster areas, lost their homes from Hurricane Katrina, and have failed to receive assistance for temporary housing. The suit, first submitted on November 10, 2005, about two months after the hurricane, demanded that FEMA provide temporary housing assistance that it had earlier denied. The plaintiffs claimed that they were displaced from their primary place of residence before the hurricane and therefore deserve housing assistance. FEMA's denial of these benefits violated the Stafford Act and federal law. They sued FEMA to receive the assistance they believed was due to them.

Legal Issues

As plaintiffs, McWaters and other victims of Katrina made several legal claims based on the FEMA response or lack of response to the hurricane. First, they argued that FEMA's shared household rule, which gave assistance to only one of the persons living in the same household before a disaster, violated the legal right of displaced persons for assistance. Many persons who had shared the same housing ended up in different locations across the country after the hurricane. They could not share housing but also could not get their own assistance.

Second, many persons received initial rental assistance without notice that the funds could be used only for rent. Some spent the $2,358 on food and clothing, which then disqualified them from more rental assistance. Because FEMA representatives did not fully explain the limits on the funds, the victims believed they should not have been penalized.

Third, some victims were told, in violation of the Stafford Act, that they had to apply for a small-business loan before becoming eligible for housing assistance. Applying for the loan slowed their applications for housing benefits.

Fourth, the law states that FEMA must provide assistance equal to fair market rental value, but FEMA chose rates for its rental assistance that were inadequate. The $2,358 meant for three months' rent of a two-bedroom apartment fell well below rents in many cities to which the victims moved. According to the plaintiffs, all these actions, including both delays in providing assistance and denials of assistance, violated federal laws and regulations that FEMA must follow. The suit claimed that decisions made by FEMA were arbitrary, capricious, and inconsistent with standards and requested the court to order changes.

As the defendant, FEMA moved to dismiss the case on several grounds. First, it argued that the district court does not have jurisdiction over FEMA actions. The Stafford Act states that the government shall not be liable for any claim based on a federal agency's performance or failure to perform a duty. The decisions FEMA made about eligibility for assistance are part of the agency's duty and involve policy judgments rather than violation of procedure and law. This makes FEMA immune from a suit such as this one. To make their case, the plaintiffs would need to cite a law holding that a presidential disaster declaration eliminates FEMA's discretion in applying policy. Without such a law, the court has no jurisdiction, and the suit should be dismissed.

Second, FEMA argued that it had already responded to most of the concerns of the plaintiffs. It had waived the shared-household rule, allowed use of the first housing assistance payment for other purposes, and speeded up processing of applications for assistance. Even if the right existed to sue FEMA, most of the concerns had become irrelevant.

Third, FEMA argued that no laws, regulations, or constitutional rights required the agency to act on applications by a certain deadline or set benefits at certain levels. The actions of FEMA fall within its legal limits.

Decision

In support of the plaintiffs, the district court ruling held that FEMA is not immune from a suit and judicial review. The Stafford Act, the ruling said, does not prohibit judicial review of agency actions. If it did, it might create the unconstitutional state of affairs in which Congress could pass laws that are shielded from review by the judicial branch. Such laws would violate the Constitution's provision of checks and balances. The court thus has authority to review FEMA actions. The ruling further agreed with the plaintiffs that, at least in some cases, actions of FEMA harmed the property interest of Katrina victims.

To correct inappropriate actions, FEMA had to make several changes. The court restrained FEMA from making false claims that those wanting assistance needed first to apply for a small-business loan and from misstating the eligibility requirements for temporary housing assistance. FEMA must notify those who, as a result of miscommunication, unnecessarily filled out small-business loan applications of the error. The correct policy requires that only those asking for special assistance (not temporary housing assistance) must apply for the loan. In addition, the ruling required FEMA to give those participating in the short-term lodging programs two weeks' notice before ending their participation. Such notice gives victims time to apply for temporary housing assistance before their short-term housing assistance ends.

In support of FEMA, the ruling dismissed other claims of the plaintiffs. In the case of providing temporary housing, the ruling concluded that delays were inevitable and that FEMA showed no economic discrimination in its slow processing of claims. The ruling also concluded that FEMA did not violate constitutional rights in failing to notify recipients about the assistance it provides. The judge criticized FEMA for not doing so but could not say it violated the law or constitutional rights. The ruling also did not overturn FEMA's decisions about shared housing eligibility and rental assistance levels.

The Law and Disaster Response

Impact

The ruling favored the Katrina victims in some of their claims and favored FEMA in others. However, allowing victims of disasters to sue FEMA for improper action represented a change. In the past, FEMA had rarely come under judicial review and evaluation. In this case, the ruling made FEMA liable for certain actions. In addition, the ruling harshly criticized FEMA, even when it ruled in FEMA's favor. The court said that it hesitated to "reward" FEMA for its indecision and bureaucratic bumbling by ruling in the agency's favor. The judge said that it "defies reason that such an agency would be seemingly more concerned with fraud on the individual level than with actually helping those persons whose lives have been literally turned upside down through no fault of their own." The court saw little evidence of FEMA's desire for openness and clarity in its communications. Although not legally required to take certain actions, FEMA failed in its mission by not doing so.

Besides presenting its own decision, the ruling made recommendations for others. For FEMA, it said,

> *Rather than hiding behind bureaucratic double-talk, obscure regulations, outdated computer programs, and politically loaded platitudes such as "people need to take care of themselves," as the face of the federal government in the aftermath of Katrina, FEMA's goal should have been to foster an environment of openness and honesty with all Americans affected by the disaster. Sharing information in simple, clear, and precise terms and delineating the terms and conditions of available assistance in an up-front and forthright manner, does just that.*

For Congress, it said,

> *The Court finds that FEMA is not legally required to notify applicants or recipients of assistance about what FEMA provides or how to obtain such assistance. Regrettably this Court must leave any dissatisfaction with the law in this regard for those in the legislative branch to remedy.*

Even partial victory by FEMA in this case did little to enhance its reputation.

---

[1] "Executive Order 12148—Federal Emergency Management," The American Presidency Project. Available online. URL:http://www.presidency.ucsb.edu/ws/index.php?pid=32625. Downloaded in August 2006.

[2] "Robert T. Stafford Disaster Relief and Emergency Assistance Act, as Amended by Public Law 93-288, June, 2006," FEMA. Available online: URL:http://www.fema.gov/about/stafact.shtm. Downloaded in August 2006.

[3] "Analysis for the Homeland Security Act of 2002," The White House. Available online. URL: http://www.whitehouse.gov/deptofhomeland/analysis. Downloaded in August 2006.

[4] "The 2006 Florida Statutes," The Florida Senate. Available online. URL: http://www.flsenate.gov/Statutes/index.cfm?App_mode=Display_Statute&URL=Ch0252/titl0252.htm&StatuteYear=2006&Title=%2D%3E2006%2D%3EChapter%20252. Downloaded in August 2006.

[5] "The Louisiana Homeland Security and Emergency Assistance and Disaster Act," Free Republic. Available online. URL: http://www.freerepublic.com/focus/f-news/1483555/posts. Posted on September 13, 2005.

CHAPTER 3

CHRONOLOGY

This chapter presents a timeline of significant events related to disaster response. It lists major disasters; the creation of laws, policies, and programs for helping disaster victims; and the successes and failures of disaster response. The historical events in this chronology shaped today's strategies of disaster response in the United States.

1495

- Christopher Columbus writes of the terrible storms he experienced during his trips to the new continent. He says that these storms, much more severe that those in Europe, had winds powerful enough to pull up trees by their roots.

1635

- Only 15 years after the Pilgrims sailing on the *Mayflower* landed at Plymouth Rock, the Great Colonial Hurricane sweeps through southern New England. Massachusetts governor William Bradford says, "Such a mighty storm of wind and rain as none living in these parts, either English or Indian ever saw."

1686

- A hurricane strikes Charles Town (later Charleston), South Carolina, driving ships ashore, blowing houses down, and ruining settlements. Witnesses describe the area as a map of devastation, with heaps of trees, fences, and the remains of houses scattered about.

1803

- After a fire burns much of a New Hampshire town, Congress passes its first piece of disaster legislation. The bill provides economic relief for the town in the form of lower tariffs.

Disaster Response

1878

- *October 8:* The Great Chicago Fire spreads from one closely built wooden structure to another and burns throughout the night. It razes most of the downtown, kills 200 to 300, causes $222 million in damage (worth $3.8 billion today), and leaves 100,000 of the 300,000 population homeless. The Chicago mayor appoints Civil War hero Lieutenant General Philip Sheridan to preserve order, and the city goes under a form of martial law. The Chicago Relief and Aid Society organizes relief efforts, using contributions that come in from around the country. Rebuilding moves forward quickly, but this time new fire codes protect the city from another such disaster.
- *October 8:* A strong forest fire near the logging town of Peshtigo, Wisconsin, starts the same day as the Chicago fire. With discarded piles of brush near railroads serving as tinder and strong winds fanning the flames, the fire moves through woods and towns at 80 miles per hour. The destruction of 11 towns and deaths of up to 2,500 lead to new practices in forest fire safety.

1889

- *May 31:* During heavy rains, a dam located in the hills above Johnstown, Pennsylvania, breaks and releases 20 million tons of water toward the town. A massive wall of water reaches Johnstown in 10 minutes, killing 2,209 people and destroying a four-mile section of downtown.
- Five days after the Johnstown flood, Clara Barton, founder of the American Red Cross and 67 years old, comes to Johnstown with five Red Cross workers. Established initially to aid those wounded in war, the American Red Cross takes a new step with this peacetime relief effort.
- Relief after the Johnstown flood relies on the charitable donations from across the country. Pennsylvania governor James A. Beaver appoints the Pennsylvania Relief Committee to help and calls out the state militia. President Benjamin Harrison orders army engineers to help with the cleanup. Within six weeks, cleanup efforts have removed debris and rebuilding begins.

1900

- *September 8:* The deadliest natural disaster in U.S. history occurs when a hurricane with winds of 130 miles per hour and a storm surge of 15 feet moves through Galveston, Texas. More than 6,000 Galveston residents die, most drowned or crushed by debris. Three-quarters of the city and 3,600 homes are destroyed.

- Relief comes slowly to Galveston after the hurricane. Houston sends water and supplies, Texas sends militia, and the Red Cross sends Clara Barton and volunteers. Locals bury the dead, remove the wreckage, and restore facilities. Leaders decide to raise up the town and build a seawall to protect it from future hurricanes.

1906

- *April 18:* One of the strongest earthquakes ever recorded in the United States shakes San Francisco. Along with toppling buildings and splitting roads, the earthquake triggers fires that destroy a good part of the city. In the end, 3,000 to 6,000 die, 300,000 lose their homes, and 500 city blocks burn.
- Armed forces located in San Francisco lead the relief effort after the earthquake. Along with setting up tent cities for survivors and distributing supplies, the army troops follow shoot-to-kill orders from the mayor as a way to keep order. Soldiers also force able-bodied males to help clear the wreckage and begin rebuilding.
- Responding to the San Francisco earthquake, Congress passes a $500,000 appropriation and gives responsibility to Secretary of War (and future president) William Howard Taft to deliver supplies from army bases across the country. Congress and President Theodore Roosevelt provide $2.5 million for emergency relief (the equivalent today of $56.9 million).

1925

- *March 18:* A tornado arising in Missouri moves 219 miles through Illinois and Indiana during the next three-and-a-half hours. The deadliest and longest tornado in U.S. history, it kills 695 people (more than twice as many as the next deadliest), injures 2,027 people, destroys 15,000 homes, and causes $16.5 million in damage ($193.3 million in today's dollars).
- After the tornado, the response to the death and destruction in the rural areas of the Midwest moves slowly. Most help comes several days or weeks later from the Red Cross, Salvation Army, and donations from the nearby cities of St. Louis and Chicago. The state sends militia, but the federal government contributes little.

1927

- *April 15:* Rising water in the Mississippi River causes levees to break in 145 places, doing the most damage to the Mississippi Delta, an area of low-lying ground east of the river in the state of Mississippi used for cotton growing. Overall, the flood covers 16.5 million acres in seven states, kills 250 to 500 people, dislocates 637,000 people, causes $102 million in crop losses, floods 162,000 homes, and destroys 41,000 buildings.

- Reflecting racism and discrimination in the South, the flood-rescue efforts ignore stranded African Americans, giving priority to white victims. African Americans are later forced, sometimes at gunpoint, to stay in the refugee camps and do relief work.
- Breaking with tradition, the federal government leads the flood relief effort. Secretary of Commerce (and future president) Herbert Hoover takes charge of coordinating the response of eight federal agencies, the Red Cross, and other private agencies. Congress passes several relief bills to help, and President Calvin Coolidge asks the public to contribute to the Red Cross.

1928

- *September 26:* One of the nation's deadliest hurricanes, the Great Okeechobee Hurricane, moves through south Florida, where it kills about 2,500. When the storm surge from hurricane winds causes Lake Okeechobee to overflow the dike that surrounds one part of the lake, flooding kills thousands of black migrant laborers living in nearby small towns. Palm Beach suffers extensive damage as well.

1931

- Responding to a series of droughts in the southern prairie states of Kansas, Oklahoma, Texas, New Mexico, and Colorado, the Red Cross distributes hot lunches to 3,600 rural schools. The Red Cross also gives out millions worth of food, clothing, medical aid, shelter, crop seeds, and other assistance to 2.7 million people.

1932

- Responding to the economic damage caused by the Great Depression, President Herbert Hoover establishes the Reconstruction Finance Corporation (RFC). Although primarily aimed at helping banks, the RFC receives authority to make loans for the repair and reconstruction of facilities harmed by earthquakes and, later, other disasters.

1934

- During the administration of President Franklin Delano Roosevelt, the Bureau of Public Roads receives funding to repair roads and bridges damaged by disasters. Although the funds going to disasters remain modest, they reflect a change in the federal government's philosophy about leaving disaster recovery to states and localities.

Chronology

1938

- *September 21:* The Great New England Hurricane of 1938 destroys much of the shore along Long Island and Rhode Island. It kills 682, fells 275 million trees, and causes $600 million in damage ($8.7 billion today). President Franklin Roosevelt sends in 100,000 relief workers from the Works Progress Administration, the Civilian Conservation Corps, the U.S. Army, and the U.S. Coast Guard.

1949

- After the Soviet Union tests its first nuclear bomb, the federal government shifts attention to preparing for a nuclear attack and urges communities to appoint civil-defense directors to manage emergency response. In years to come, the attention to civil defense creates warning plans that natural disaster response programs can adopt but also directs government funds away from natural disasters.

1950

- Congress passes the Federal Disaster Relief Act, which creates the first formal role for federal agencies in disaster response. It authorizes the federal government to grant relief funds to states harmed by a disaster without Congress having first to pass a relief bill. However, Congress will continue to respond to disasters with specially legislated disaster assistance.

1964

- Congress passes the National Plan for Emergency Preparedness. By focusing on preparation for disasters from both nuclear war and natural hazards, this legislation gives new federal attention to natural disasters.

1968

- Congress passes the National Flood Insurance Act, which creates the National Flood Insurance Program (NFIP). For communities that join the NFIP, residents can obtain low-cost government flood insurance. However, the communities must restrict future development on floodplains.

1969

- *August 17:* Hurricane Camille, one of the strongest hurricanes to strike the United States, kills 256 people and causes $1.4 billion in property damage (the equivalent of $7.8 billion today). About 200,000 residents evacuate and 50 civil-defense shelters open just before Camille reaches the Mississippi coast, but a tidal surge 22.6 feet high washes away much coastal property.

- *August–September:* Marking the start of a new period of disaster response, the federal government takes the lead in providing shelter, water, and food for the 15,000 left homeless by Hurricane Camille. The Department of Housing and Urban Development brings in 5,000 mobile homes for victims, and the Department of the Treasury sponsors loans of $25 million (the equivalent of $140 million today).
- *October 1:* President Richard Nixon signs the Disaster Relief Act of 1969. The legislation creates a new position called the federal coordinating officer, who, under the authority of the president, has responsibility for coordinating and managing disasters. The act also allows the federal government to grant modest disaster benefits for housing, education, unemployment, and small businesses.

1970

- Congress passes the Disaster Relief Act of 1970, which incorporates many of the provisions in previous legislation but also adds more assistance for temporary housing, legal services, unemployment insurance, and individual needs.

1972

- *June:* Hurricane Agnes makes landfall in Florida and eventually moves through the mid-Atlantic states of Pennsylvania and New York State, where drenching rains cause severe flooding. Agnes ends up killing 129 and causing $3.1 billion in damage ($15.2 billion in current dollars), becoming the costliest disaster to hit the United States.

1974

- Congress passes the Disaster Relief Act of 1974, making a crucial change in federal policy. Assistance from the federal government now becomes available after a major disaster declaration to individuals and families as part of the Individual and Family Grant Program. The Federal Disaster Assistance Administration, established in the 1960s as part of the Department of Housing and Urban Development, will lead relief efforts.
- *April 3–4:* A huge storm moves through 13 states and spawns 148 separate tornadoes. Six of the tornadoes have winds of 261 to 318 miles per hour and reach the maximum of F5 on the Fujita-Pearson tornado intensity scale. The tornadoes cover 2,500 miles, kill 330, and injure 5,484, justifying the name of the super (or jumbo) outbreak of 1974.

Chronology

1976

- *July 28:* An earthquake in Tangshan, China, perhaps the most severe in modern times, kills at least 255,000 (and up to 655,000 by some estimates).

1979

- *March 28:* Problems with the nuclear reactor at the Three Mile Island Nuclear Generating System near Harrisburg, Pennsylvania, lead to the release of deadly radiation into the atmosphere. Despite fear of the danger among nearby residents, no clear evacuation plans existed. FEMA works to make sure in the future that areas surrounding nuclear power plants have such plans in place.
- *May 21:* President Carter declares a state of emergency at Love Canal, a neighborhood in Niagara Falls, New York, used decades earlier as a dump for toxic chemical waste. With growing evidence that the buried chemicals had increased the risk of cancer and genetic damage among the residents, FEMA helps evacuate families.
- *July 20:* To consolidate the disaster activities of some 100 separate agencies, President Jimmy Carter submits an executive order to create the Federal Emergency Management Agency (FEMA). FEMA will also deal with civil-defense tasks, which are transferred to the agency from the Defense Civil Preparedness Agency in the Department of Defense.

1980

- *May 18:* The most deadly and damaging volcanic eruption in U.S. history occurs at Mount St. Helens, Washington. The eruption kills 57 and destroys 250 homes, 47 bridges, 15 miles of railway, and 185 miles of highway.

1984

- *December 3:* The release of poison from a Union Carbide pesticide plant in Bhopal, India, kills 15,000 and injures hundreds of thousands.

1985

- A volcanic eruption and resulting mudslide in Colombia kills 25,000.

1986

- *April 26:* An explosion that releases radiation from the Chernobyl nuclear power plant in the Ukraine (then part of the Soviet Union) leads to permanent evacuation of areas around the plant.

Disaster Response

1989

- *September 21:* Hurricane Hugo strikes the South Carolina coast near Charleston and moves through the state to North Carolina. Although evacuation before the storm creates a good deal of confusion and gridlock, it saves lives. Hugo causes $7 billion in damage on the U.S. mainland but kills relatively few—estimates range from 32 to 56.
- *September 21–27:* FEMA is harshly criticized for responding slowly to Hurricane Hugo. It takes six days for sufficient quantities of food and clothing to reach Charleston and 10 days for FEMA to set up a disaster center in heavily damaged rural areas. Some 1,200 families do not receive help after nine months.
- *October 17:* The Loma Prieta earthquake damages San Francisco, Oakland, Santa Cruz, and other cities around the San Francisco Bay. At least 63 die (most when a double-decked highway collapses), 3,757 are injured, and 12,000 are left homeless. President George H. W. Bush declares seven counties as major disaster areas.
- *October–November:* Six weeks after the Lome Prieta earthquake, some 50,000 people, many homeless, still have not received assistance. California senator Barbara Boxer calls FEMA's response chaotic, overly bureaucratic, and even arrogant. California congressman Norman Mineta says FEMA "could screw up a two-car parade."

1991

- A series of floods in Bangladesh kills 139,000.

1992

- *August 24:* Hurricane Andrew moves through a 50-mile swath of south Florida. Having just missed heavily populated Miami, Andrew severely damages the town of Homestead and surrounding areas. Its high winds and storm surge leave nearly 200,000 residents homeless and 1.3 million without electricity. Although only 25 die, the damage reaches $30 billion.
- *August 25–31:* FEMA does not appear in Homestead for three days after the hurricane. Once there, the agency acts so slowly in bringing water, food, and medical supplies that most federal aid does not reach victims until six days after the storm. Those in need instead rely on army troops and private organizations for relief.

1993

- Congress debates eliminating FEMA because of its poor performance after Hurricane Andrew. It instead amends the Stafford Act to increase federal relief.

- President Bill Clinton appoints James Witt, the former director of the Arkansas Office of Emergency Services, as FEMA director. With the support of the president, Witt will succeed in improving the performance and reputation of the agency.
- *July:* A report from the General Accounting Office (GAO) suggests some solutions to the problems revealed by Hurricane Andrew. The GAO report urges FEMA to act before state and local authorities make a formal request and the president declares a major disaster. FEMA needs to do more planning so that it can respond within hours of a disaster.
- *July 11–29:* Extensive summer rains raise the Raccoon River in Iowa. In Des Moines, the river overflows the city's water treatment plant. As a result, the city has no running water for 19 days.
- *April–September:* The nation's worst flood since 1927 occurs along the Mississippi and Missouri Rivers. The Missouri overflows hundreds of levees, while the Mississippi crests at 49.6 feet above sea level at St. Louis. President Clinton declares all of Iowa and parts of eight other states as disaster areas. The flooding kills 50, causes $15 billion in damage, and destroys 10,000 homes. By moving quickly to help and maintaining close ties to state and local emergency offices during the disaster, FEMA earns unfamiliar praise for its response to the flooding.

1994

- *January 17:* An earthquake centered in the community of Northridge in the San Fernando Valley of Los Angeles causes numerous fires, the collapse of some apartment buildings, and breaks in busy highways. It kills 51 people and seriously injures 9,000. The damage of $25 billion makes it the most expensive earthquake since 1906. Working closely with Los Angeles officials, FEMA quickly organizes search-and-rescue operations and solicits help from other federal government agencies. In the afternoon, President Clinton declares a national disaster for Los Angeles Country. FEMA again earns praise for its response.

1995

- *April 19:* A bomb contained in a rented truck explodes in front of the nine-story Alfred P. Murrah Federal Building in Oklahoma City. The partial collapse of the building kills 168 people, including 19 children. The bomb injures 800 others, damages 300 nearby buildings, and shuts down offices in downtown Oklahoma City. FEMA responds quickly to the disaster by providing search-and-rescue teams and coordinating the delivery of relief supplies. Cooperation among federal authorities, state and local governments, and charitable organizations goes so smoothly that the "Oklahoma standard" becomes a goal for future disaster response efforts.

- *July:* During an eight-day heat wave, more than 700 people die in Chicago. Those who die—largely elderly persons—live in neighborhoods with high poverty and crime where they are afraid to go out or even open their windows.

1996

- President Clinton elevates FEMA to cabinet status in 1996. The elevation raises the profile and authority of the agency, allowing FEMA to work as an equal with other federal departments.

1997

- FEMA establishes a new mitigation program called Project Impact. The project funds community mitigation activities such as adding reinforced safe rooms to homes damaged by tornadoes in Ohio and installing hurricane shutters on homes in Key West, Florida. FEMA expects that spending money before a disaster will save money afterward.

1999

- *September 15:* Hurricane Floyd, one of the largest Atlantic hurricanes on record makes landfall in North Carolina and moves up through Virginia to the mid-Atlantic. Largely from flooding caused by hurricane rains, Floyd kills 57 people and causes $4.5 billion in damage. Activating emergency response teams even before landfall, FEMA delivers water, food, and medical care almost immediately to many areas affected by Hurricane Floyd. Some heavily flooded rural areas with primarily African-American residents prove difficult to reach, however.

2000

- The Disaster Mitigation Act of 2000 amends the 1988 Stafford Act by requiring that funds for mitigation be part of disaster planning. Those states that commit to enhanced mitigation planning also become eligible for more funds. The goal of the act is to make mitigation part of a comprehensive disaster response effort.

2001

- *February:* President George W. Bush appoints Joe Allbaugh as the new director of FEMA. The former national campaign manager for the Bush 2000 Election Campaign plans to trim the agency and concentrate more on its primary goals. He expresses concern that FEMA has become bloated and wants to reorganize and streamline the agency.

- *September 11:* Nineteen men affiliated with an alliance of militant and radical Islamic groups called al-Qaeda hijack four commercial passenger jets. The hijackers crash two jets into the Twin Towers of the World Trade Center, one into the Pentagon, and a fourth into a field in Pennsylvania (after passengers tried to retake control). With the collapse of the two towers, nearly 3,000 people die.
- *September 11:* Local responders race to the World Trade Center, where thousands evacuate before the towers collapse. The heroic actions of city police, city firefighters, and Port Authority police are hampered by problems of radio communication and lack of coordination.
- *September 11:* All but essential federal workers are ordered to leave Washington, D.C., at 10:45 A.M. Washington, D.C., mayor Anthony Williams declares a state of emergency in the city at 1:27 P.M.
- *September 11:* President Bush orders the release of federal disaster resources and funds to New York City. A major disaster declaration for the five New York counties most affected by the attacks provides federal funds to be used to purchase and deliver food, water, heavy machines, medical supplies, and lifesaving equipment.
- *September 18:* President Bush agrees to cover 100 percent of the costs for the New York counties most affected by the recent terrorist attack. Typically, federal funds pay 75 percent of the cost for emergency services, debris removal, and building repair, while the state pays the other 25 percent.
- *October:* A White House memo states that 3,571 federal personnel, including 1,596 from FEMA, worked directly on the response to the terrorist attacks. Congress and the president also approve a $40 billion emergency response package. About $2 billion goes to FEMA for rescue and clearing operations and for individual and family assistance.
- *October 8:* An executive order from the president establishes the Office of Homeland Security (OHS), a precursor to the Department of Homeland Security (DHS). The office will lead efforts to secure the United States from terrorist threats or attacks. Former Pennsylvania governor Tom Ridge will lead the office.

2002

- *November 22:* Congress passes the Homeland Security Act, which authorizes the creation of the new Department of Homeland Security.

2003

- *January 24:* The Department of Homeland Security officially begins operation.

- *March 1:* FEMA is transferred into the Department of Homeland Security.
- *December 26:* An earthquake in Bam, Iran, kills 26,271.

2004

- *July 23:* A FEMA-sponsored exercise called Hurricane Pam concludes. The exercise aims to predict the damage and to plan required action if a severe hurricane were to hit New Orleans and southeast Louisiana. FEMA expects that the exercise will help the agency should the real thing occur.
- *November:* DHS announces a new framework for disaster response. Called the National Response Plan (NRP), it presents an all-hazards approach for responding to both natural and terrorist disasters. Critics call the plan complex and difficult to understand.
- *December 26:* A strong earthquake (the fourth-strongest ever recorded) shifts the floor of the Indian Ocean near the Indonesian island of Sumatra, creating an enormous and fast-moving tsunami that moves in all directions. The tsunami hits thousands of miles of shoreline, killing about 230,000. Indonesia suffers the most deaths, followed by Sri Lanka, India, and Thailand. A coalition of nations made up of Australia, India, Japan, and the United States organizes the relief, and the United Nations soon takes over leadership. Nations across the world will give generously—more than $12 billion—to the relief fund.

2005

- *June:* A formal proposal circulates to move emergency preparedness from FEMA to another part of DHS. FEMA director Michael Brown objects, arguing that separating preparedness activities from response activities will harm the performance of his agency.
- *August 28:* With Hurricane Katrina looming, New Orleans mayor Ray Nagin orders mandatory evacuation. However, with the late warning, those without transportation are unable to leave and no arrangements have been made to bus them out. Tens of thousands left in the city move to the New Orleans Superdome and Ernest Morial Convention Center.
- *August 29:* Hurricane Katrina makes landfall on the Gulf Coast of Louisiana, Mississippi, and Alabama, where it will cause at least 1,863 confirmed deaths and leave 1,840 persons missing and presumed dead. With winds reaching 130 miles per hour, covering 93,000 square miles, and causing a storm surge to reach 27 feet, the hurricane displaces 770,000 people, destroys the homes of tens of thousands of residents, and causes $96 billion in damage.

Chronology

- *August 30–September 1:* Due to breaks in the levees protecting the city, New Orleans continues to flood after Katrina passes through. Looting breaks out in parts of the city; people stranded run out of food, water, and medical supplies; and reporters call the situation desperate. Yet federal help in rescuing the stranded and delivering supplies comes slowly.
- *September 2:* President Bush flies into the New Orleans airport, where he admits to the failed relief effort and promises to correct the problem. Those stranded in the city become increasingly angry and unruly about the lack of help.
- *September 5:* New Orleans workers close a major gap in the levees, while evacuation of the city speeds up.
- *September 7–8:* With the worst of the Hurricane Katrina crisis over, President Bush calls for $52 billion in aid to supplement the $10.5 billion already provided by Congress. Congress passes the supplement the next day.
- *September 9:* FEMA director Michael Brown, accused of bungling the Katrina response operation, is removed from control and sent back to Washington.
- *September 12:* Michael Brown resigns as FEMA director. David Paulison, a career firefighter with experience in emergency preparedness, later takes his place as acting director.
- *September 24:* Less than a month after Katrina, Hurricane Rita makes landfall near the Louisiana-Texas border, killing 120 and causing $10 billion in damage. Rita forces evacuation of New Orleans, several Louisiana parishes, and coastal areas of Texas.
- *October 8:* An earthquake centered in Pakistan kills more than 50,000.
- *October 24:* After passing through parts of Mexico and Cuba, Hurricane Wilma, one of the strongest Atlantic hurricanes ever recorded, makes landfall in Florida. Officials earlier ordered mandatory evacuation of areas in the Florida Keys, and FEMA promises to have supplies in place to deliver immediately. At least 35 residents of south Florida die directly from the storm.
- *November 30:* By the conclusion of the hurricane season, Katrina, Rita, Wilma, and other hurricanes make the 2005 season the most active in recorded Atlantic history. During the period, a record 28 tropical and subtropical storms formed, and 15 became hurricanes. Florida suffered through eight hurricanes over a period of 14 months.
- *December:* In a repeat of the confusion between federal and local authorities, FEMA says that it has 125,000 trailers ready but cannot deliver them until parish officials say where the trailers should go. Locals complain about the continued slow action of FEMA.

Disaster Response

2006

- **February:** Three government reports are released that investigate the response problems after Katrina and recommend improvements. Reports from the General Accounting Office, the House Select Committee, and the White House agree that Katrina brought catastrophic problems that would challenge even the best response system but strongly criticize all levels of government for their inaction.

- **March 13:** The United Nations announces a new $500 million fund called the Central Emergency Response Fund to improve its relief efforts. The new fund adds significantly to the previous fund of $50 million but still depends fully on voluntary contributions from member states and private donors.

- **April 7:** President Bush nominates David Paulison as the permanent undersecretary for FEMA in the DHS. Paulison, who served as acting undersecretary after Michael Brown resigned, was selected after several others declined the position.

- **April 18:** On the 100-year anniversary of the San Francisco earthquake, experts calculate that an earthquake today of the same size as in 1906 would kill 3,400, leave 225,000 homeless, and cost $150 billion.

- **July:** More than 120 people die from the heat in California—more than in the most recent California earthquake. Government officials have difficulty helping the victims, often poor, elderly, and isolated from family and community.

- **July 28:** The UN Human Rights Committee weighs in on the Katrina disaster response, criticizing the U.S. government for not protecting the rights of the poor and disadvantaged during the disaster.

- **August 23:** As the nation approaches the one-year anniversary of Hurricane Katrina, President Bush reassures the victims that the government has not forgotten them but admits it will take a long time to rebuild.

- **October 31:** Responding to complaints about how it handles disasters, the Red Cross announces that it will change its leadership structure. It plans to reduce the size of the Board of Governors and give more responsibility to its professional managers.

- **December 26:** A story from the Associated Press two years after the Indian Ocean Tsunami reports scientific predictions that another earthquake occurring along the same fault will likely occur within the next few decades and cause a tsunami as severe as the last one. Towns along the coast of Indonesia report on efforts to create warning systems to protect the dense population.

Chronology

2007

- *January 19:* A Senate hearing held in the French Quarter of New Orleans includes complaints from senators and citizens about the slow pace of recovery. Many blame federal rules that limit government assistance for the problem.

- *May 4:* A tornado destroys 90 percent of the 1,400-person town of Greensburg, Kansas. While many begin to relocate nearby, residents debate whether to rebuild the town. The strong attachment of many residents to the town is balanced by a decline of agricultural jobs in the area.

- *May 11:* Several governors say that the deployment of National Guard troops to Iraq has left their states poorly prepared to respond to disasters.

- *May 15:* FEMA chief R. David Paulison tells lawmakers at a House Homeland Security hearing that most of the problems exposed in the response to Hurricane Katrina have been fixed. Lawmakers express concern that FEMA will not be fully prepared when the hurricane season begins on June 1, but Paulison promises an active response.

- *June 25:* A report from the Center for Philanthropy at Indiana University reports only a slight increase in charitable giving in 2006. The report says that the absence of a major or highly publicized disaster that year led to a drop in disaster giving and slow growth of overall giving.

- *July 24:* A report from the agency's inspector general says that the Small Business Administration improperly cancelled loans to victims of the 2005 Gulf Coast hurricanes. Many have criticized the agency for its slow response to the needs of those whose properties were damaged by Hurricanes Katrina, Rita, or Wilma.

- *August 1:* The Interstate 35W Bridge connecting Minneapolis and St. Paul, Minnesota, collapses during the evening rush hour, sending cars on the bridge into the Mississippi River below. The collapse of the bridge, which inspectors had said as early as 1990 needed major repair or replacement, kills 13 and injures more than 100. Some predict that the poor state of many bridges across the country will result in other disasters involving the failure of technology.

- *August 7:* A report on the population of New Orleans, Louisiana, says that the number of residents has risen to 273,000. Although only about 60 percent of the pre-Katrina level, the number reflects steady growth over the last year and leads to hopes of continued growth in years to come.

CHAPTER 4

BIOGRAPHICAL LISTING

This chapter contains brief biographical sketches of leaders, experts, and politicians who have been involved in major disasters, policymaking, and disaster response.

Joe Allbaugh, director of FEMA from 2001 to 2002. The former national campaign manager for the George W. Bush 2000 Election Campaign planned to trim FEMA and concentrate more on its primary goals. As the new director, Allbaugh wanted to reorganize and streamline the agency. During his term, FEMA dealt with the 9/11 terrorist attacks and prepared the agency for a move to the newly established Department of Homeland Security.

Haley Barbour, Republican governor of Mississippi since 2003. Before Katrina made landfall, he declared a state of emergency for Mississippi and ordered evacuation of areas along the Gulf Coast. In contrast to other state governors, he received praise for his leadership during the response to Katrina.

Clara Barton, founder of the American Red Cross and leader of the organization's early disaster relief mission. In 1889, at the age of 67, she traveled to Johnstown, Pennsylvania, to help victims of the recent flood. With this effort, the Red Cross took a first step toward becoming the primary private disaster relief organization in the country. She later traveled to Galveston, Texas, to help with relief efforts after the 1900 hurricane.

James A. Beaver, governor of Pennsylvania at the time of the 1889 Johnstown flood. He appointed the Pennsylvania Relief Committee to take over leadership from local residents and called out the militia to assist the recovery. He further persuaded President Benjamin Harrison to order army engineers to help with the cleanup. With this aid, the town recovered and rebuilt quickly after the flood.

Kathleen Blanco, Democratic governor of Louisiana since 2004. She was faulted for not taking more aggressive action to prepare her state for

Hurricane Katrina and for not doing more to help the hurricane survivors who remained stranded in New Orleans. She defends her actions, blaming the federal government for not responding to her pleas for help.

Leo Bosner, a long-term FEMA employee who criticized the move of the agency to the Department of Homeland Security (DHS). He stated that the National Response Plan, the formal guide for response to an Incident of National Significance, was difficult to understand and faulted FEMA and the DHS for failed leadership in response to Hurricane Katrina.

Barbara Boxer, California Democratic representative from 1983 to 1993 and senator since 1993. She criticized FEMA for its poor 1989 response to the Loma Prieta earthquake and the Department of Homeland Security and the George W. Bush administration in 2006 for not doing enough to prepare for another possible earthquake in the San Francisco Bay area.

Aaron Broussard, president of Jefferson Parish, south of New Orleans, since 2003. He gained national attention for his appearance after Hurricane Katrina on *Meet the Press,* when he complained about the lack of federal help. He also criticized the federal government for turning back trucks with water sent by Wal-Mart.

Cora Brown, a resident of Kansas City, Missouri. On her death, she left a portion of her estate to the United States for the purpose of helping victims of natural disasters.

Michael Brown, FEMA counsel from 2001 to 2003 and FEMA director from 2003 to 2005. While leading FEMA after its move to the Department of Homeland Security, he expressed concern that lack of funding would prevent the agency from responding as it should in the next major disaster. When FEMA performed so poorly after Hurricane Katrina, he took the blame and resigned. Many claimed that he lacked the qualifications to lead FEMA.

George H. W. Bush, president of the United States from 1989 to 1993. At the time he became president, FEMA suffered from problems of disorganization and poor morale. The problems showed in the slow responses to Hurricane Hugo in 1989, the Loma Prieta earthquake in 1989, and Hurricane Andrew in 1992. In 2005–06, he co-led with former president Bill Clinton a fund-raising effort for victims of Katrina.

George W. Bush, president of the United States since 2001. In response to the September 11 terrorist attacks, he established the Department of Homeland Security and made FEMA part of the new department. Critics claimed too much attention went to national security and too little to natural disaster response. The events after Hurricane Katrina largely validated the claims.

Biographical Listing

Andrew Card, the secretary of transportation from 1992 to 1993. Responding to criticism over the slow response to Hurricane Andrew in 1992, President George H. W. Bush appointed Card to head a special task force to handle the disaster. Card then met with the Florida governor, offering aid and insisting that the state could not handle the relief. He ended up taking a leadership role that normally belonged to FEMA.

Jimmy Carter, president of the United States from 1977 to 1981. Responding to calls for a single federal agency to coordinate federal disaster response, he issued a presidential directive in 1979 that established the Federal Emergency Management Agency (FEMA). During his administration, FEMA responded to two new kinds of disasters—the release of radiation from the Three Mile Island Nuclear Generating System near Harrisburg, Pennsylvania, and the threat to the health of residents of Love Canal in Niagara Falls, New York, from the leakage of toxic chemicals buried underground.

Michael Chertoff, secretary of the Department of Homeland Security (DHS) since 2005. As secretary, he had authority over FEMA and some responsibility for the poor performance of the agency after Hurricane Katrina. While most blame fell on Michael Brown for the failed response, Chertoff and the DHS also came under criticism. He promises that the DHS and FEMA are prepared for the next major hurricane.

Isaac Cline, Galveston Weather Bureau section director in 1900, when the city was hit by a powerful hurricane. About nine years earlier, he dismissed the worry that a hurricane could devastate Galveston as an absurd delusion. The hurricane in fact remains the nation's most deadly natural disaster, having killed 6,000 in Galveston and nearly as many along other parts of the Texas coast.

William Jefferson Clinton (Bill Clinton), president of the United States from 1993 to 2001. He invigorated FEMA in 1993 by appointing James Witt as director and filling key positions with professionals who had emergency experience. He further raised the profile of the agency by elevating it to cabinet status in 1996. FEMA received unfamiliar but well-earned praise during the Clinton administration.

Calvin Coolidge, president at the time of the 1927 Great Mississippi Flood. He believed that only the federal government had the resources to handle the disaster and appointed Herbert Hoover, then the secretary of Commerce, to lead the response effort. He also asked the public to contribute $10 million to the Red Cross for the relief effort.

Frederick Funston, brigadier-general and commander of army troops located in the Presidio base at the time of the 1906 San Francisco earthquake. He led about 2,000 troops in the disaster response. Vigorous efforts by the military to keep order led some to claim that San Francisco had become a military dictatorship after the earthquake, but Funston and the army did much to get housing, food, and supplies to the victims.

Rudolph Giuliani, Republican mayor of New York City from 1994 to 2001. He led the disaster response to the September 11 terrorist attacks on the World Trade Center. Under his authority, the response avoided many of the conflicts between federal, state, and local governments that have impaired the response to other disasters. *Time* magazine named him Person of the Year in 2001 for his leadership in a time of crisis.

James Gooden, an African-American resident of Greenville, Mississippi. Gooden was shot in the back after refusing to work a second cleanup shift after the 1927 Great Mississippi Flood. Blacks complained that planters and the National Guard forced them at gunpoint to stay in the relief camps and do repair work.

Ernest Frederick Hollings (Fritz Hollings), Democratic senator from South Carolina from 1966 to 2005. Critical of FEMA for its slow response to Hurricane Hugo in 1989, he called the agency a "bunch of bureaucratic jackasses." Like many others in Congress at the time, he believed FEMA's poor performance required reforms to overhaul the agency.

Herbert Hoover, secretary of Commerce at the time of the 1927 Great Mississippi Flood and president from 1929 to 1933. An engineer by training, he took charge of coordinating the response of eight federal agencies, the Red Cross, and other private agencies. With full leadership authority, he avoided a struggle between federal, state, local, and private agencies in setting policy. As president, in 1932 he established the Reconstruction Finance Corporation (RFC), which gave loans to repair public facilities damaged by earthquakes and, later, other disasters.

Jesse Jackson, African-American civil rights leader; former candidate for the Democratic presidential nomination; and president, founder, and chief executive officer of the Rainbow/PUSH Coalition. He criticized FEMA in 1999 for not doing enough to help African Americans in rural parts of North Carolina and South Carolina recover from Hurricane Floyd. He later criticized FEMA for not helping the largely African-American population of New Orleans after Hurricane Katrina.

John Macy, the first permanent director of FEMA from 1979 to 1981. While director, he set up the Integrated Emergency Management System, a set of procedures to deal with all kinds of disasters, including weather-related events, technological breakdowns, and nuclear war. However, he was unable during his term to fully integrate the separate units of the agency.

Norman Mineta, Democratic representative from California from 1975 to 1995. He served as the chairman of the House Public Works and Transportation Committee, which oversaw FEMA. Highly critical of FEMA in the 1980s, he came to praise the agency in the 1990s for its improved performance.

Ray Nagin, Democratic mayor of New Orleans since 2002. As leader of the city during the preparations for and response to Katrina, he faced near insurmountable problems, some of his own making. He was criticized for failing to order mandatory evacuation earlier, properly prepare shelters for the tens of thousands of people that needed them, and ensure buses could be used to take people out of the city. He in turn blamed the federal government and FEMA for not responding to his requests for help. He won reelection as mayor in 2006.

Richard M. Nixon, president of the United States from 1969 to 1974. During his presidency, he sent federal troops to help in the response to Hurricane Camille and signed disaster legislation in 1969 and 1970 to create a comprehensive federal policy for disaster response.

David Paulison, a career firefighter who became acting director of FEMA in 2005 and was nominated by President George W. Bush in 2006 to become the director. He began as FEMA acting directorship at a difficult time—after the failed response to Katrina and the resignation of Michael Brown as director. While acting director, he has moved to correct the flaws in FEMA revealed by the Katrina response and promised that the agency would be well prepared for the next major disaster.

Rick Perry, Republican governor of Texas from 2000 to the present. Having seen the damage to Louisiana and Mississippi from Hurricane Katrina in early September 2005, he ordered mandatory evacuations of coastal areas in his state and mobilized the National Guard as Hurricane Rita approached. Rita did not cause major destruction in Texas but closed many refineries and led to a nationwide rise in gas prices.

Ronald Reagan, president of the United States from 1981 to 1989. During his term, he shifted the focus of disaster response from natural disasters to nuclear war. Critics accused the administration of staffing FEMA with political appointees and failing to support the agency's goal of effective disaster response.

Tom Ridge, special assistant to the president for homeland security from 2001 to 2003 and secretary of the Department of Homeland Security (DHS) from 2003 to 2005. The former congressional representative and governor of Pennsylvania led efforts to integrate FEMA and disaster response into the new DHS. He argued that the move benefited FEMA by making it part of an organization devoted to preparedness and security.

Geraldo Rivera, a high-profile television reporter for Fox News. Stranded in New Orleans while reporting on Hurricane Katrina, he expressed the dismay and anger he and others felt over not getting rescued or even getting word out on when the rescue would come. Rivera called it "hell on earth."

Franklin Delano Roosevelt, president of the United States from 1933 to 1945. While president, he developed several programs that took initial steps to involve the federal government in disaster assistance. For example, the Bureau of Public Roads received funding to repair roads and bridges damaged by disasters. He also sent federal relief workers to the New England coast after the 1938 hurricane.

Theodore Roosevelt, president of the United States at the time of the 1906 San Francisco earthquake. He signed legislation that provided $2.5 million for emergency relief to the city (the equivalent today of $56.9 million).

Philip Sheridan, Civil War hero and lieutenant general who lived in Chicago at the time of the 1871 fire. Appointed by the mayor to preserve order in the city, he put together a mix of militia, police, and volunteers to patrol the city. For two weeks after the fire, the city stayed under a form of martial law.

Robert T. Stafford, Republican senator from Vermont from 1971 to 1989. His work on disaster relief led Congress to name the Disaster Relief and Emergency Act of 1988 after him. The bill and amendments since 1988 guide disaster policy today.

William Howard Taft, secretary of war at the time of the 1906 San Francisco earthquake and future president. After the earthquake, he took responsibility for having supplies delivered from army bases across the country and overseeing the assistance provided by the army (as best he could when located thousands of miles away in Washington, D.C.).

Kathleen Tierney, sociologist and director of the Natural Hazards Center at the University of Colorado, Boulder. She has studied inequality in disaster response and argued that the poor and people of color get little attention and support during and after a disaster.

Harry S Truman, president of the United States from 1945 to 1953. He signed the Federal Disaster Relief Act of 1950, which created a formal role for federal agencies without Congress having first to pass a relief bill. He signed an executive order in 1952 affirming that federal assistance did not replace state and local assistance.

Henry Waxman, Democratic representative from California since 1974. He investigated problems in contracting for the Hurricane Katrina cleanup, claiming that the FEMA-led effort showed "widespread mismanagement, waste and fraud."

Kanye West, music producer and rap recording artist. He created controversy on an NBC relief telethon for the victims of Hurricane Katrina by saying that "George Bush doesn't care about black people."

Biographical Listing

Anthony Williams, mayor of Washington, D.C., from 1999 to 2007. After the terrorist attack on the Pentagon, the mayor's office issued conflicting orders to city workers, and the mayor did not declare a city emergency until 1:27 P.M. Although no damage occurred in Washington, D.C., many criticized the mayor and city for the poorly organized response.

James Witt, director of FEMA from 1993 to 2001. Having previously served as the state director of the Arkansas Office of Emergency Services under then-governor Bill Clinton, he brought emergency management experience to FEMA. As director, he overhauled the agency to make it more professional, built close ties to state and local disaster officials, and improved the speed of response to disasters. The agency received near unanimous praise during the years of his leadership.

CHAPTER 5

GLOSSARY

This chapter defines terms and phrases and titles of major legislation that those conducting research on disaster response will likely encounter.

avalanche The sudden movement of snow and ice down a steep slope or hillside.

blizzard A severe winter storm that lasts for several hours and is characterized by heavy snow, winds in excess of 35 miles per hour, and low visibility.

disaster An unusual and dramatic event that, in a relatively short time span, causes enough death and destruction as to disrupt normal patterns of living.

disaster cycle A four-step process of preparedness, response, recovery, and mitigation needed to limit the death and destruction of a disaster.

Disaster Mitigation Act of 2000 Legislation amending the 1988 Stafford Act to require that mitigation efforts be included in federally funded disaster planning.

Disaster Relief Act of 1974 Legislation that made assistance from the federal government available to individuals and families as part of the Individual and Family Grant Program. Before, all disaster relief funds went to states and communities to distribute.

drought A shortage of rainfall that causes water availability to fall below that needed by plants and humans.

earthquake Trembling or shaking of the Earth's surface due to the movement of fractures or faults below the surface. By damaging buildings, homes, and roads, it causes injuries and deaths.

emergency A situation that poses a threat to human life or serious damage to property and requires immediate action.

emergency declaration A decision that federal assistance is needed to supplement state and local efforts to save lives, protect the safety of the public, and limit damage from an emergency. An emergency declaration indicates a less serious problem than a major disaster declaration.

fault A fracture in the underlying rock formation that is caused by shifting of the Earth's crust and tends to produce earthquakes.

Federal Disaster Relief Act of 1950 Legislation that authorized the federal government to grant relief funds to states harmed by a disaster without Congress having first to pass a relief bill.

FEMA-State Agreement A document that lays out the details of federal assistance to a state after the president makes a major disaster or emergency declaration.

flood A rising body of water that overflows into normally dry land.

floodwall A concrete wall built on a levee to protect low-lying land from being flooded by nearby water sources.

Fujita-Pearson Scale A measure of the force or intensity of a tornado that varies between F0 (winds from 42 to 72 miles per hour) to F6 (winds greater than 319 miles per hour).

hazard A potential event that stems from nature, technology, or terrorist action and may lead to a disaster.

heat wave A period of unusually hot weather, sometimes measured as temperatures at least 90 degrees Fahrenheit and five degrees over normal and lasting for two or more days.

Homeland Security Act of 2002 Legislation to establish the Department of Homeland Security (DHS) and define its mission to prevent terrorist attacks in the United States, minimize their damage, and assist in the recovery from any attacks that may occur.

human-caused disaster A disaster relating directly to human action or error such as the release of radiation from a nuclear power plant or destruction of cities and buildings by terrorist bombs. Its technological or willful source contrasts with a natural disaster.

hurricane A violent tropical storm of large size that has wind speeds of more than 73 miles per hour and heavy rains (also known as a typhoon).

Incident of National Significance An event that threatens such extraordinary casualties, damage, and disruption as to require a coordinated response from all levels of government, the private sector, and nongovernmental organizations. A declaration of an Incident of National Significance gives the secretary of the Department of Homeland Security authority to manage a multiagency response.

index of hazardousness A ranking given to each state in the United States on the risk it faces from natural hazards and disasters. California, Texas, and Florida rank as most hazardous on the index.

Integrated Emergency Management System A system that defines procedures and roles for organizations to deal with all types of disasters, including weather-related events, technological breakdowns, and nuclear war.

Glossary

levee A high embankment or reinforced earthen wall that protects low-lying land from being flooded by nearby water sources.

major disaster declaration A catastrophe that, as determined by the president, is serious enough to require major disaster assistance to alleviate damage, loss, hardship, and suffering.

mitigation The actions taken both after one disaster and before another to reduce the physical impacts of hazards on a community.

multi-hazard advisory maps Maps showing the areas within each state that face the greatest risks from multiple, overlapping hazards.

National Flood Insurance Act Legislation in 1968 that created the National Flood Insurance Program and provided public flood insurance for homeowners who could not get private insurance.

National Incident Management System (NIMS) A set of procedures that lays out duties, actions, and guidelines for each partner in the response to an Incident of National Significance. It sets up a unified command to minimize confusion across towns, counties, states, and levels of government.

National Plan for Emergency Preparedness A creation of Congress in 1964 to prepare for disasters from both nuclear war and natural hazards.

National Response Plan (NRP) A plan developed to replace the Federal Response Plan by taking an all-hazards approach for responding to both natural and terrorist disasters. It goes into effect when an Incident of National Significance is declared.

natural disaster A disaster relating to weather—hurricanes, tornadoes, heat waves, droughts, winter storms, and floods—or to geological changes—earthquakes, volcanic eruptions, landslides, and avalanches.

one-hundred-year flood A flood with a 1 percent chance of being equaled or exceeded in any given year.

preparedness The state of being prepared for a disaster or actions taken before the disaster to allow effective response.

Presidential Directive 12148 A 1979 order by President Jimmy Carter that created the Federal Emergency Management Agency (FEMA) and authorized it to mobilize, coordinate, and manage federal disaster response.

al-Qaeda An alliance of militant and radical Islamic groups responsible for the hijacking of four commercial jets and the disasters that followed when two jets crashed into the Twin Towers of the World Trade Center, one into the Pentagon, and a fourth into a field in Pennsylvania (after passengers tried to retake control of the plane).

recovery The actions taken after a disaster to repair, rebuild, and restore community life to normal.

response The emergency actions taken just before, during, and just after a disaster to reduce casualties, damage, and disruption.

Richter scale A scale used to measure the severity of earthquakes that is based on the logarithm of the released energy. A Richter 3 earthquake causes slight damage, while a Richter 6 earthquake causes severe damage.

risk The susceptibility of death, damage, destruction, and disruption from a natural or human-caused hazard. Social factors such as the location of communities and requirements for buildings influence risk.

Saffir-Simpson scale A scale used by the National Weather Service to rate the severity of a hurricane. It ranges from Category 1 (a weak hurricane with winds from 74 to 95 miles per hour) to Category 5 (an extremely strong hurricane with winds in excess of 155 miles per hour).

Stafford Act of 1988 Legislation that created a more orderly system for requesting and giving federal assistance to state and local governments after a disaster. Amended several times since 1988, the Stafford Act is the main legal guide for disaster response.

storm surge An abnormal rise in the sea along a shore due primarily to high winds from a storm.

technological disaster A disaster relating to technology and human action such as the release of radiation from a nuclear power plant or a spill from a train car containing toxic chemicals.

tornado A violent, destructive windstorm that moves over ground in the shape of a funnel.

tropical storm A storm with rotating winds of less than hurricane force (ranging from 30 to 73 miles per hour) that sometimes turns into a hurricane.

tsunami A Japanese term meaning "harbor wave" that refers to enormous and fast-moving waves created by an undersea earthquake. The waves cause much damage when they crash into land and overflow low-lying coastal cities.

volcanic eruption The explosive release of liquid rock from the Earth's interior through an opening in the Earth's surface called a volcano.

vulnerability The lack of resources of a community to prevent, respond to, and recover from a disaster.

warning An alert that a hazardous event such as a tornado, hurricane, or flash flood is imminent or has occurred.

watch A forecast to alert the public of a possible hazardous event such as a tornado, hurricane, or flash flood.

willful disaster A disaster relating to intentional human action such as the destruction of cities and buildings and the killing of people by terrorist bombs.

PART II

GUIDE TO FURTHER RESEARCH

CHAPTER 6

HOW TO RESEARCH
DISASTER RESPONSE

In one sense, information on disasters is easy to find. Media reports regularly cover the warnings for and consequences of disasters, and viewers seem fascinated by potential or actual death and destruction. The interest in media reports spills over to interest in books, articles, and web documents on disasters and the response to them. The remarkable force of natural hazards, the evil behind terrorist attacks, and the mistakes causing technological emergencies deserve the attention they get. Nearly everyone faces threats from one or more of the major kinds of disasters: chemical, dam failure, earthquake, fire, wildfire, flood, hazardous materials, heat, hurricane, landslide, nuclear plant emergency, terrorism, thunderstorm, tornado, tsunami, volcano, and winter storm.

At the same time, however, all the information available can overwhelm those doing research on disaster response. As an aid to researching this topic, this chapter offers some general suggestions on using bibliographic resources as well as more specific suggestions on consulting key sources. Even with these suggestions, however, those researching disaster response will face several challenges.

First, writings on the topic span a variety of fields of study. Disaster response may relate to meteorology and geological science, the actions of terrorists, failures of technology, behavior under extreme conditions, the psychology of preparation, federal law and policy, programs for assistance and recovery, trauma experienced by survivors, charitable organizations, cross-government relations, or international humanitarian efforts. It may further relate to more specific knowledge about the Department of Homeland Security (DHS), the Federal Emergency Management Agency (FEMA), the 9/11 terrorist attacks, Hurricane Katrina, or the threat of disasters to come. Few can master all these specialized areas of study.

Second, the literature on the topic sometimes reflects strong political and moral views that make it hard to separate facts from opinions. These views come into play, for example, in debates over the proper role of the government in paying for disaster recovery and the competence of government agencies in aiding those in need. On one side, critics view disaster policies that pay for repair of housing and replacement of property of those who live in disaster-prone areas as encouraging people to take greater risk. They also suggest that large government bureaucracies move slowly and respond ineffectively, while private charitable organizations are much more effective. These critics favor more reliance on the private sector in disaster response. On the other side, many see disaster response as an essential duty of the government and problems as a result of too little rather than too many resources. With proper leadership, government organizations perform effectively, even heroically, in the face of disaster. These differences in viewpoints can lead to widely varying interpretations of the facts and issues.

Third, disaster response relies on complex legal and policy guidelines. Disaster response plans are often filled with names and acronyms of departments, committees, groups, centers, response teams, and actions. These names and acronyms are then linked by detailed and intricate flowcharts. So many agencies and departments at all levels of government get involved in major disasters that their roles and responsibilities get blurred. The same complexity occurs in relief and assistance programs. FEMA and other agencies strive to make eligibility rules and application procedures clear to victims of disasters. Yet the laws that guide assistance have many details, limits, qualifications, and exceptions that prevent simple summary. Researchers can benefit from some guidance on how to master such material.

TIPS FOR RESEARCHING DISASTER RESPONSE

How can researchers overcome these challenges? Here are some tips.

- **Define the topic and questions carefully.** Rather than researching disasters, the following topics would allow for more focused and in-depth research: the evolution of federal disaster policy, changes in FEMA since being moved to the Department of Homeland Security, the successes and failures of the response to the 9/11 terrorist attacks, the causes of the mishandled response to Hurricane Katrina, the importance of disaster mitigation, social behavior during disasters, special problems of international disaster response, and human settlement in disaster-prone areas. With so many choices available, making research manageable requires care and precision in selecting topics. A narrowly defined topic can prevent feeling overwhelmed by the material and allow for in-depth treatment.

- **Consider the underlying perspectives.** Relying on a variety of sources will help make sense of the differing values and belief that shape views on disaster response. Toward that end, the annotated bibliography in the next chapter includes a wide selection of readings that represent diverse perspectives. In addition, however, it helps to consider the background and potential biases of authors. Such information can help separate opinions and emotion from facts and reason.

- **Evaluate your sources.** In reviewing books and articles, check the date of publication to make sure the information is recent, confirm the qualifications of the author and the citation of sources to make sure the information is reliable, and look for the presentation of alternative views to make sure the information is presented fairly. Books and articles often differ in their audience, with some prepared for popular audiences and some written for scholarly audiences. Both popular and scholarly information is useful, but it helps to recognize how sources differ in the depth of information, citation of sources, and year of publication. In reviewing Internet sources, use even more care. Nearly anyone can post documents, and many documents lack checks on the reliability of their information. Evaluate the qualifications of the author, the legitimacy of the sponsoring organization, and the potential for bias.

- **Master the basic facts and terms.** Few can make sense of the material on disaster response without having some familiarity with common names, organizations, and acronyms in the area. Try to learn the basic terminology; careful and precise usage lends authority to research.

- **Search for balance.** Since complex questions about disaster response seldom have simple answers, do not accept claims at face value. It is easy to assign blame for failures in disaster response and to advocate simple solutions. To avoid this tendency, search for balanced presentations based on evidence—even if highly technical—and careful weighing of the alternatives. Researchers should seek to understand the complexity that underlies the topic and treat all sides of the debate fairly.

ONLINE RESOURCES

Given its ease in providing information, the Internet offers a good place to begin research on disaster response. The Web contains a wide variety of research, reference, and opinion pieces on the topic that can be easily accessed with an Internet connection. One can find useful facts and perspectives on nearly any aspect of disaster response by patiently working through even a small portion of available web pages. Finding one suitable site suggests links to others, which may in turn lead in new directions. Innovative ideas and fresh information emerge in this process. Indeed, many web documents are updated or created anew to keep up with recent events and the latest information.

However, the extraordinary wealth of information that the Internet makes available to researchers can be overwhelming. For instance, a Google search for "disaster response" results in nearly 38 million hits—an impressive but daunting number. The advice to define narrow research topics applies particularly to using the Internet. Otherwise, combing through all the web sites listed by searches can result in wasted effort. In addition, the information obtained does not always meet high standards of reliability and balance. Unlike books and articles, web documents generally do not go through a process of review and editing before publication. In some cases, they offer little more than the opinions of strangers.

Users must take care in relying on materials obtained from web sites and inquire into the background of the site sponsors. Is the organization reputable, or does the author have expertise? Does the web page aim for objectivity? Is it written well and based on careful thinking? Those web pages where one can answer these questions affirmatively will be the ones to rely on the most. With these qualifications in mind, Internet research can proceed in several ways.

GENERAL SITES

Popular and general search engines such as Google (http://www.google.com), Yahoo! (http://www.yahoo.com), AltaVista (http://www.altavista.com), Excite (http://www.excite.com), Lycos (http://www.lycos.com), Ask (http://www.ask.com), MSN (http://www.msn.com), and many others can direct you to web sites with information on disaster response. Using these search engines effectively requires thoughtful selection of search terms and patient effort but can lead to unexpected and intriguing discoveries. Broad searches might focus on disaster recovery, disaster plans, disaster relief, disaster preparedness, and disaster mitigation. Narrower searches might focus on types of disasters (hurricanes, earthquakes, technological hazards), organizations and programs (FEMA, National Response Plan, Individual and Family Program), and events (9/11, Hurricane Katrina, Indian Ocean tsunami).

The Web also includes directories with listings on disaster response. In Yahoo!, a helpful directory of web sites and organizations can be found by going to the Yahoo! home page and doing a directory search for "disasters." Under the categories for natural and human-made disasters, Yahoo! lists links to a variety of sites and has additional categories of sites based on types of disasters. Google likewise has a directory with a broad list of topics. On the Google home page, click "More" and then "Directory." Under "Science, Earth Science, and Natural Disasters and Hazards," Google lists links to numerous web pages. Other web pages collate links to disaster sites. CBS News Disaster Links (http://www.cbsnews.com/digitaldan/disaster/disasters.shtml) lists hundreds of web pages.

Wikipedia, a free, Web-based encyclopedia (http://en.wikipedia.org/wiki/Main_Page), has entries for most major disasters. Created in 2001, Wikipedia allows readers to collaboratively make and revise entries, which is particularly helpful in keeping up-to-date with current events and with fact checking. On the topic of disasters, the coverage is extensive, and the entries are generally, though not always, thorough and authoritative. Critics point out that the entries lack an authority or known author to ensure reliability, and many schools prohibit use of Wikipedia as a source for student papers. Sometimes the objectivity of writers and editors is disputed (this occurs for the entry on Hurricane Katrina). While recognizing these limitations, the entries for some disasters can, in combination with other sources, be useful to researchers.

ORGANIZATION SITES

Knowledge of key organizations—government, charitable, professional, and research—is crucial for researching disaster response. Chapter 8 lists a variety of such organizations, but consulting the home pages of a few of them can help in getting started with research.

Two federal government agencies deal most directly with disasters: the Federal Emergency Management Agency (FEMA) and the Department of Homeland Security (DHS). Nearly all links on the FEMA home page (http://www.fema.gov) contain information helpful to the public and researchers. The DHS web page (http://www.dhs.gov) under the preparedness and response menu option likewise contains much useful information. In addition to the federal government, each state government will have an office or department on disaster or emergency response. Finding the office or department requires a search within a state government web site. Among private organizations, the American Red Cross web page (http://www.redcross.org) has a section on disaster services that offers information on disaster safety, preparedness, post-disaster action, and organization resources. For more academic information, consult the web pages of the Natural Hazards Center at the University of Colorado (http://www.colorado.edu/hazards) and the Disaster Research Center at the University of Delaware (http://www.udel.edu/DRC). Both pages offer materials on disasters and disaster response.

Disaster Response

SITES ON SPECIFIC DISASTER RESPONSE TOPICS

Along with getting resources from broad—and perhaps overwhelming—general searches and from organizations with wide-ranging goals, it helps to begin a search with particular sites. Here are some recommendations organized by the major topics on disaster response.

History

Web pages on major disasters in U.S. history offer details of specific events, and Wikipedia has entries on nearly all of them. One general web document from the Congressional Research Service focuses more on policy history. "Federal Emergency Management and Homeland Security Organization: Historical Developments and Legislative Options" (http://www. mipt.org/GetDoc.asp?id=3052&type=d) describes the current organization of FEMA and historical developments that led to the current arrangements. It also relates past developments to post-Katrina deliberations over federal disaster policy.

September 11, 2001, Terrorist Attacks

The Wikipedia entry (http://en.wikipedia.org/wiki/September_11,_2001_attacks) is thorough and contains links to primary sources. It offers a good starting point for researching the response to this disaster. The most thorough discussion of the response to the attacks comes from the *9/11 Commission Report*. Chapter 9, "Heroism and Horror" (http://www.9-11commission. gov/report/911Report_Ch9.htm), discusses preparedness, the response of police and fire officials at the sites, and the problems encountered in evacuating those in the buildings.

Hurricane Katrina

To understand the failure of response in New Orleans, it helps to have a timeline of the events leading up to and following the hurricane. The Brookings Institution offers one (http://www.brookings.edu/fp/projects/homeland/katrinatimeline.pdf) that is detailed and precise. Another web site contains a timeline, a history of FEMA, interviews with nearly all the major participants, and information on the breakdown in communication. Based on an episode from the PBS television show *Frontline* called "The Storm," this web page (http://www.pbs.org/wgbh/pages/frontline/storm) is an excellent source on the causes of the failed response.

FEMA and Federal Disaster Policy

Two government web pages contain information on the response to and recovery from disasters. The description from FEMA of the National Incident

Management System (http://www.fema.gov/emergency/nims/index.shtm) summarizes how the response to a major incident should proceed (but often does not). Of the topics covered on the web page, those on basic principles and frequently asked questions (FAQs) will most aid readers unfamiliar with the system. The description from FEMA of the assistance programs for individuals and households harmed by a disaster ("Individuals and Households Fact Sheet," http://www.fema.gov/news/newsrelease.fema?id=5404) helps make sense of the ways that the government gets funds to disaster victims. The information on these two web pages can be overwhelming but gives the details needed to understand disaster response and recovery in the United States.

Personal and Social Aspects

Disaster response involves more in the way of social and policy science than natural science. For a summary of the contribution the social sciences make to disaster response, see the testimony of four social scientists brought before Congress to discuss the contributions of their disciplines (http://commdocshouse.gov/committees/science/hsy24463.000/hsy24463_0.htm).

International Response

For information on how the United States aids in international disasters, start with "Disaster Assistance," (http://www.usaid.gov/our_work/humanitarian_assistance/disaster_assistance), a web document from the U.S. Agency for International Development and its Office of Foreign Disaster Assistance. This agency is responsible for facilitating and coordinating U.S. government emergency assistance overseas.

PRINT SOURCES

Despite the ease of obtaining sources from the Internet, books and articles available from libraries and bookstores remain essential sources of information. Good books integrate material that is otherwise scattered, present information in a logical and understandable format, and allow for a comprehensive approach to the issues. Edited volumes provide multiple perspectives on a topic but usually with a meaningful framework, while other books present a single but in-depth viewpoint—both of which have advantages. Exploiting these advantages requires use of catalogues, indexes, bibliographies, and other guides.

BIBLIOGRAPHIC RESOURCES

Besides using catalogs at a city or university library, researchers can consult the comprehensive bibliographic resource of the Library of Congress catalog (http://catalog.loc.gov). To browse holdings by subject, click "basic search," then type in "disaster planning," "disaster preparedness," "disaster relief," or other specific terms and highlight "subject browse." A variety of subject headings will be listed, some deserving further investigation. Alternatively, a keyword search of "disasters" returns a list of 4,676 references. The list can be narrowed by adding limits to search results.

A listing of catalogs for specific libraries can be found through Yahoo! (http://dir.Yahoo.com/Reference/Libraries). A large list of libraries allows users to browse catalogs outside their local library and discover new references. Each library will have its own search procedures, but the general rule of searching for more specific keywords will work best in finding relevant materials.

Bookstore catalogs not only allow for searches of books currently in print on any variety of disaster topics but also have another advantage: They often include summaries and reader reviews of books that can help determine their relevance and value. In some cases, one can browse through an electronic version of parts of a book. At the same time, bookstore catalogs will not have as many books that are out-of-print, but still valuable, as libraries. Overall, electronic bookstores such as Amazon.com (http://www.amazon.com) and Barnes and Noble (http://www.barnesandnoble.com) are good bibliographic resources.

Periodical indexes used to search for print articles are available at most libraries. *OCLC First Search* contains an electronic version of *Reader's Guide Abstracts* that will list articles from a large number of magazines. However, users generally need access to a subscribing library for this database. *InfoTrac* also compiles articles for general-interest audiences and sometimes includes an abstract with the citation, or an abstract and a full text article. It again requires library privileges. *Ingenta Library Gateway* (http://www.ingenta.com) includes more than 19 million citations from nearly 20,000 journals and allows searches for scholarly articles in the areas of medicine, science, and social science. Searching *Ingenta* is free but delivery of an article requires a fee. Magazines such as *Time* (http://www.time.com/time) sometimes have a web site that allows users to search for articles, though many require fees to read the articles.

Libraries usually subscribe to catalogs of newspaper articles. In addition, many newspapers maintain a web page with an archive of past articles. The *New York Times*, for examples, allows searches of its stories (and presents the day's major news) at its web page (http://www.nytimes.com). Articles from the last seven days are free, but accessing earlier articles requires a fee. The *Washington Post* also provides a web page with a search option (http://www.washingtonpost.com) but also requires purchase of older articles. Otherwise, Yahoo! (http://dir.yahoo.com/News_and_

Media/Newspapers) lists links to many newspapers that can be accessed via the Web. Local libraries offer a better source for finding past articles without a fee. For all these sources, a search on disasters will typically return too many stories to sort through; narrower searches will provide more useful information.

SPECIFIC BOOKS AND ARTICLES ON DISASTER RESPONSE

Along with the above-mentioned general bibliographic resources for print materials and the full annotated bibliography in chapter 7, it helps to have a few books and print articles to get started. Here are some recommended books and articles organized by the major topics of disaster response.

History

One history of a major disaster brings together themes common to most other disasters: failed technology, inequality in damage and recovery, and efforts of the government and charitable organizations to help. *Rising Tide*, by Roger Barry (New York: Simon and Schuster, 1997), covers these themes in recounting the 1927 Great Mississippi Flood. The book makes for fascinating reading and offers a good starting place on the history of disaster response in the United States. For a book that focuses less on a specific disaster and more on the general failure of leaders and the public to limit the damage from natural disasters, see *Acts of God*, by historian Ted Steinberg (New York: Oxford University Press, 2000). Two very good articles contrast a failed and successful disaster response: The failed response to Hurricane Andrew in 1992 is described in "Catastrophe 101: Hurricane Andrew," by Cathy Booth (*Time*, vol. 140, September 14, 1992, pp. 42–43). On the other hand, the successful response to the Great Midwest Flood in 1993 is described in "Flood, Sweat and Tears" (*Time*, vol. 142, July 26, 1993, pp. 22–33).

September 11, 2001, Terrorist Attacks

As a supplement to the description of the response to the terrorist attacks on New York City and the Pentagon contained in the *9/11 Commission Report*, see *The 9/11 Report: A Graphic Adaptation*, by Sid Jacobson and Ernie Colon (New York: Hill and Wang, 2006). Another description of the response comes from the *New York Times* in "Ground Zero Diary: 12 Days of Fire and Grit" by C. J. Chivers (September 30, 2001, pp. A1, B9).

Disaster Response

Hurricane Katrina

Several fine books on Katrina came out soon after the disaster. Perhaps the most comprehensive and readable account of the events of the storm and its aftermath is *The Great Deluge*, by Tulane history professor Douglas Brinkley (New York: William Morrow, 2006). Others by the metro editor of the *New Orleans Times-Picayune*, Jed Horne (*Breach of Faith*, New York: Random House, 2006), and by *Wall Street Journal* reporters Christopher Cooper and Robert Block (*Disaster: Hurricane Katrina and the Failure of Homeland Security*, New York: Times Books, 2006) are also excellent. No article can cover all that happened with Katrina, but one clearly explains the problems behind the failed response: "Four Places Where the System Broke Down," by Amanda Ripley, Karen Tumulty, and Mark Thompson (*Time*, vol. 166, no. 12, September 19, 2005, pp. 34–41).

FEMA and Federal Disaster Policy

The best treatment of disaster policy comes from a textbook by two former high-level FEMA officials. Written for those interested in careers in emergency management, *Introduction to Emergency Management*, by George D. Haddow and Jane A. Bullock (Boston: Butterworth-Heinemann, 2003), covers the four components of the disaster cycle—mitigation, response, recovery, and preparedness—and includes other chapters on communication, terrorism, and international response. For a shorter treatment that focuses more specifically on disaster assistance programs for individuals and families; small businesses; and state, local, and tribal governments, see "Federal Disaster Programs" by the Congressional Research Service (*Congressional Digest*, vol. 84, no. 9, November 2005, pp. 260–262). The article presents the outlines of disaster assistance without excessive detail.

Personal and Social Aspects

Under the auspices of the National Research Council, a distinguished committee of experts summarizes social science research on coping with disasters and effectively reducing risk in *Facing Hazards and Disasters: Understanding Human Dimensions* (Washington, D.C.: National Academies Press, 2006). It gives special attention to how social changes in the population and economy have increased the risks of disasters and how disseminating knowledge about disasters can benefit society. While this volume is academic and careful in its language, a more popular article discusses social aspects of disasters in more personal terms. Rebecca Solnit in "The Uses of Disaster" (*Harper's*, vol. 311, October 2005, pp. 31–37) cites several examples of how the suffering and tragedy of a disaster brought people closer and led to surprising acts of kindness.

International Response

In *Large Scale Disasters: Lessons Learned* (Geneva: OECD, 2004), the Organization for Economic Cooperation and Development reviews the response to and recovery from famous disasters such as the September 11 attacks, Hurricane Andrew, the Kobe, Japan, earthquake, and the Chernobyl nuclear accident. For more on the largest recent international disaster, the Indian Ocean tsunami, see "The Borders of Healing" by Marianne Szegedy-Maszak (*U.S. News & World Report*, vol. 138, no. 2, January 17, 2005, pp. 36–37).

LEGAL RESEARCH

The search for federal laws on disaster response is relatively straightforward because the basic law and the amendments—the Stafford Act—is available on the Web (http://www.disastersrus.org/FEMA/Stafact.htm) and parts are reproduced here in Appendix C. For more detail—and more complexity—a search of the U.S. Code will locate a variety of more specific laws. Go to the Cornell Law School search web page (http://www4.law.cornell.edu/uscode/search/index.html) and type in "disaster." Then scroll through the 66 separate listings of the code to find those of most interest. However, finding the laws for individual states or cities requires separate searches.

Only a few court decisions directly address the issue of disaster response (see chapter 2). The suits usually involve victims protesting denial of assistance or slow action of the government. Information on the suits, jury decisions, awards, appeals, and final judgments can be found through searches of newspapers such as the *New York Times* (http://www.nytimes.com) and general search engines such as Google, Yahoo! and Ask. To obtain the written decisions in cases involving disaster response, electronic law libraries such as Westlaw (http://www.westlaw.com) and LexisNexis (http://www.lexisnexis.com) include court opinions but require a subscription. Opinions of the Supreme Court can be obtained from the Legal Information Institute (http://www.law.cornell.edu).

CHAPTER 7

ANNOTATED BIBLIOGRAPHY

The following annotated bibliography on disaster response contains six sections:

- disaster response history;
- response to the 9/11 terrorist attacks;
- Hurricane Katrina response;
- FEMA and federal disaster policy;
- personal and social aspects of disaster response; and
- international disaster response.

Within each of these sections, the citations are divided into subsections on books, articles, and Web documents. The topics and citations include technical and nontechnical works, in-depth and short treatments, and research and opinion pieces (see chapter 6 for an overview on how to use these materials most effectively).

DISASTER RESPONSE HISTORY

BOOKS

Barry, John M. *Rising Tide: The Great Mississippi Flood of 1927 and How It Changed America.* New York: Simon and Schuster, 1997. This detailed and fascinating book describes the nature of race relations in the South at the time and the efforts of engineers to control the Mississippi River. It then chronicles the flooding and the response that occurred in 1927, giving particular attention to events in Greenville, Mississippi. The flood did indeed have historic consequences: It led to the migration of hundreds of thousands of blacks from the South to the North, the shift of political allegiance of blacks from the Republican to the Democratic

Party, and the increased involvement of the federal government in disaster relief.

de Boer, Jelle Zeilinga, and Donald Theodore Sanders. *Earthquakes in Human History: The Far-Reaching Effects of Seismic Disruptions.* Princeton, N.J.: Princeton University Press, 2004. While discussing issues beyond disaster response in the United States, this book includes fascinating information on how earthquakes have changed history from the fall of Jericho to the 1906 San Francisco earthquake. It well supports its major theme, that geological events have important social and economic impacts.

Bolin, Robert, and Lois Stanford. *The Northridge Earthquake: Vulnerability and Disaster.* London: Routledge, 1998. This study of the 1994 earthquake in Los Angeles emphasizes the vulnerability of the city to a disaster. To examine how social relations affect this vulnerability, the authors compare two rural towns populated largely by Latino agricultural workers with two suburban towns populated largely by middle-class whites who commute into the city for work. The poor rural towns suffered more damage from the earthquake because of substandard housing, and they received less rapid attention from responders because of their low visibility. Since the well-off towns recovered more fully than the poor towns, the earthquake worsened inequality in the area.

Davis, Mike. *Ecology of Fear: Los Angeles and the Imagination of Disaster.* New York: Henry Holt, 1998. According to this study of Los Angeles, residents remain concerned, even paranoid, about the threat of wildfires, earthquakes, and other natural hazards. Davis argues that the concern is misplaced. The hazards faced by the city come less from nature than the tendency of leaders, developers, and residents to ignore common sense in dealing with the environment. Parts of the book describe the major disasters and responses that have occurred in southern California.

Felkner, Peter S. *The Tri-State Tornado: The Story of America's Greatest Tornado Disaster.* Ames: Iowa State University Press, 1992. The 1925 tornado that moved through Missouri, Illinois, and Indiana was indeed rare and amazing in how long it lasted and how far it traveled. With few historical documents available on the disaster, the author traveled along the route of the tornado to interview survivors, check old newspaper accounts, and find pictures. The book presents many personal and newspaper stories verbatim.

Fradkin, Philip. *The Great Earthquake and Firestorms of 1906: How San Francisco Nearly Destroyed Itself.* Berkeley: University of California Press, 2005. While several books describe the San Francisco earthquake and its aftermath, this book uses new sources to contend that the response worsened the damage of the earthquake. It describes efforts to stop the fire by dynamiting buildings, to deny the damage to avoid negative publicity about the earthquake, and to reconstruct buildings quickly with shoddy materials and design. Fradkin applies the lessons of 1906 to the present by arguing that San Francisco remains in as much danger as a century ago.

Klinenberg, Eric. *Heat Wave: A Social Autopsy of Disaster in Chicago.* Chicago: University of Chicago Press, 2002. This case study of the July 1995 Chicago heat wave that killed more than 700 focuses on the social aspects of the disaster. Those who died—primarily elderly persons—lived in neighborhoods with high poverty and crime where many were afraid to go outside or even open their windows. City leaders did little to recognize or respond to the risks of the heat wave for isolated elderly persons, but some neighborhoods with closer social ties between the elderly and neighbors had fewer deaths.

Lapierre, Dominique, and Javier Moro. *Five Past Midnight in Bhopal: The Epic Story of the World's Deadliest Industrial Disaster.* New York: Warner Books, 2002. This story of the disaster that occurred in an Indian city when an U.S.-owned chemical plant accidentally released poisonous gas illustrates the risks to modern society of technology and industry. Natural disasters generally cause more death and damage than technological disasters, but this one example—16,000 to 30,000 dead and 500,000 permanently injured—warns of the risks of technology.

Larson, Erik. *Isaac's Storm: A Man, a Time, and the Deadliest Hurricane in History.* New York: Crown, 1999. Along with describing the Galveston hurricane and its aftermath, this book traces the background and views of Isaac Cline, the Galveston scientist working for the U.S. Weather Service. Despite Cline's confidence in weather science, he failed to predict the strength of the hurricane and the vulnerability of Galveston Island to a major storm. The book clearly explains complex ideas about weather and fully describes what remains the nation's most deadly natural disaster.

McCullough, David. *The Johnstown Flood.* New York: Simon and Schuster, 1987. Famed historian David McCullough tells the story of the dam failure that flooded Johnstown. He treats the disaster as a technological failure caused by human mistakes rather than a natural disaster caused by the weather. The description of the flood includes heroic stories of response and survival to balance the foolishness that led to the flood.

Parchman, Frank. *Echoes of Fury: The 1980 Eruption of Mount St. Helens and the Lives It Changed Forever.* Kenmore, Wash.: Epicenter Press, 2005. The 1980 eruption of Mount St. Helens did not cause as many deaths as the worst hurricanes, but it did affect the lives of those living nearby. This book describes the eruption, the people whose lives were changed by the disaster, and the regeneration of areas around the volcano.

Peacock, Walter Gillis, Betty Hearn Morrow, and Hugh Gladwin. *Hurricane Andrew: Ethnicity, Gender, and the Sociology of Disasters.* New York:

Routledge, 1997. Less concerned with the specifics of the damage and response to Hurricane Andrew, this book examines how the hurricane affected different social groups in south Florida. The authors, based at Florida International University, suffered through the hurricane but go beyond their own experiences to study those of minorities and the very poor. They describe how these groups ended up in tent cities set up by the military, received less aid than better-off groups, and had more trouble finding permanent housing.

Reilly, Benjamin. *Tropical Surge: A History of Ambition and Disaster on the Florida Shore.* Sarasota, Fla.: Pineapple Press, 2005. This history of southern Florida highlights the battle between nature and developers. It describes the damage brought by hurricanes in 1919, 1926, and 1935 that slowed but did not end the growth of the population in this ecologically vulnerable area.

Scotti, R. A. *Sudden Sea: The Great Hurricane of 1938.* Boston: Little, Brown, 2003. This story about the hurricane that devastated Long Island and the coast of Rhode Island clearly describes the storm and the people affected by it. The final chapters also discuss the response, which involved the federal government more than previous disasters. New England has not faced another such severe hurricane since then but can expect one sometime in the future. This book gives a sense of the destruction that likely will occur.

Steinberg, Ted. *Acts of God: The Unnatural History of Disasters in America.* New York: Oxford University Press, 2000. A professional historian, Steinberg emphasizes the social and political nature of disasters by showing how decisions of leaders worsened the physical impact of earthquakes, floods, and other natural hazards (hence the use of the term *unnatural* rather than *natural* in the title). Leaders throughout history have blamed God and nature for disasters when the harm is under greater human control than people recognize. Steinberg calls for more action to protect the population—particularly the poor, elderly, and minorities—from harm and calls for stronger leadership from business and the government.

Zebrowski, Ernest, and Judith A. Howard. *Category 5: The Story of Camille, Lessons Unlearned from America's Most Violent Hurricane.* Ann Arbor: University of Michigan Press, 2005. The strongest-recorded hurricane to reach land in the United States, Camille not only demolished much of the Mississippi coast in 1969, but it also led to federal government efforts to improve its disaster response and eventually establish the Federal Emergency Management Agency (FEMA). The authors discuss how issues of politics and race in the South affected the response and recovery. Having reviewed the devastation brought by the hurricane, the authors remain pessimistic about the ability of the nation to learn from disasters like Camille.

Annotated Bibliography

ARTICLES

Akin, Wallace. "The Great Tri-State Tornado." *American Heritage*, vol. 51, no. 3, May/June 2000, pp. 32–36. This article highlights the humanitarian response to the nation's deadliest and longest-lasting tornado. News of the disaster was carried from the rural towns damaged by the tornado along railroad and telegraph lines to larger cities. On hearing of the news, medical teams and firefighters came from St. Louis and Chicago, as did trainloads of coffins. The author includes eyewitness accounts published at the time.

"Andrew's Wrath." *Newsweek*, vol. 120, September 7, 1992, pp. 16–24. A cover story in this news magazine describes the storm and the damage it brought to south Florida. It also discusses the criticism that followed the hurricane over FEMA's slow and ineffective response. Providing more than statistics on wind speeds, death, and building damage, the photographs included convey the damage of the storm.

Baker, Kevin. "The Future of New Orleans: Lessons from Past Cases of Disaster-Stricken Cities." *American Heritage*, vol. 57, no. 2, April/May 2006, pp. 23–25. This article describes how cities responded to destruction wrought by the 1871 Chicago fire, the 1900 Galveston hurricane, and the 1906 San Francisco earthquake. Some lessons for New Orleans after Katrina follow from the response of these cities to equally catastrophic events.

Barry, John M. "After the Deluge: Great Flood of 1927." *Smithsonian*, vol. 36, no. 8, November 2005, pp. 114–116, 118–121. John Barry, whose book *Rising Tide* describes the Great Mississippi Flood of 1927 in some detail, shows in this article that the same mistakes made in 1927 were made again with Hurricane Katrina. In 1927, efforts of the Army corps of Engineers to protect cities from flooding of the Mississippi actually made things worse. When the levees constructed by the corps broke, the damage was worse than it would have been had the levees never been built.

Boggs, Johnny D. "'Darkness Is Overwhelming Us': The 1900 Galveston Hurricane." *Weatherwise*, vol. 53, no. 5, September/October 2000, pp. 12–19. This article describes the events that took place when a Category 4 hurricane hit Galveston in 1900 and the death toll reached 10,000 to 12,000—still the deadliest natural disaster in U.S. history. It also describes the surprisingly quick recovery and rebuilding of Galveston.

Bolt, Bruce A. "Balance of Risks and Benefits in Preparation for Earthquakes." *Science*, vol. 251, January 11, 1991, pp. 169–174. The 1989 Loma Prieta earthquake in the San Francisco Bay area led policymakers and scientists to prepare for future risks. As described in this article, the preparation has been difficult. Scientists cannot yet predict where another earthquake will most likely occur, and legislation to require earthquake protection practices has not passed.

Booth, Cathy. "Catastrophe 101: Hurricane Andrew." *Time*, vol. 140, September 14, 1992, pp. 42–43. This article compares the quick and effective response of the army to Hurricane Andrew with the slow and ineffective response of FEMA. The complaints about FEMA led to debates about the role of soldiers versus bureaucrats in disaster response. Despite recommendations for a larger role of the armed forces in disaster response after Andrew, concerns about military intervention in domestic affairs, as described in this article, have limited the military to a role of last resort.

Bovard, James. "FEMA Money! Come and Get It!: Clinton Administration." *The American Spectator*, vol. 29, September 1996, pp. 24–26. An alternative and minority view of the claims that President Bill Clinton and Director James Witt successfully reformed FEMA in the 1990s makes the point that any success came from the excessive spending of the agency. The author criticizes the use of FEMA funds for what he views as political purposes and the unwillingness of the government to stop subsidizing buildings in dangerous areas.

Bower, Bruce. "Emotional Scars near Mount St. Helens: Study by James H. Shore and Others." *Science News*, vol. 127, June 1, 1985, p. 344. Although the eruption of this volcano in Washington State did not kill many people compared to other disasters in the last several decades, it traumatized those living in the nearby logging communities. Psychiatrist James H. Shore has documented this trauma, and the article describes his research. The findings can help understand how other major disasters affect the psychological well-being of those who survive.

Boyer, Peter J. "Gone with the Surge: Mississippi Coast after Hurricanes Camille and Katrina." *New Yorker*, vol. 81, no. 29, September 26, 2005, pp. 76, 78, 80–84, 86. The damage to the Mississippi coast from Katrina has similarities to damage done earlier. Hurricane Camille in 1969 devastated the coast even more than Katrina (Camille was one of the few Category 5 hurricanes to make landfall in the United States). This article describes the effects of Camille on the coastal areas and, in light of the potential for future damage, questions the continued construction of casinos in the area.

Brown, Jeremy K. "Witt, James Lee." *Current Biography*, vol. 61, no. 3, March 2000, pp. 88–92. This brief biography highlights Witt's success at FEMA and in responding to major disasters during his tenure as FEMA director from 1993 to 2000. It also describes some of the disasters during those years and how FEMA handled them. Witt's key innovation was trying to anticipate rather than just respond to disasters.

Annotated Bibliography

Burgan, Michael. "The Great Chicago Fire: Survivor C. Innes." *National Geographic World*, no. 277, September 1998, pp. 15–18. Based on the experiences of one survivor, Claire Innes, this article recounts the events of the Great Chicago Fire and the damage it caused. Her escape dramatizes the response of residents to the fire, and maps and picture help convey the extent of the damage.

Carnahan, Ira. "Who Gets the $20 Billion" Disbursing Money for Disaster Relief." *Forbes*, vol. 168, no. 10, October 15, 2001, pp. 62–63. This article discusses how FEMA distributed $7 billion in funds after the Northridge earthquake of 1994. It criticizes the spending as, in many cases, wasteful and unnecessary and suggests that relief for the September 11 attacks will similarly waste taxpayer funds.

Cheers, D. Michael. "Charleston, S.C., Rebounds from $2-Billion Destruction by Hugo; Jackson Tours State." *Jet*, vol. 77, October 9, 1989, pp. 5–6. Hurricane Hugo brought 135-mile-per-hour winds and 17-foot waves to coastal South Carolina. This article describes the damage and the difficulty in getting telephone, water, and electricity services restored, particularly in the rural areas of the state.

Dvorak, John. "San Francisco Then and Now." *American Heritage*, vol. 57, no. 2, April/May 2006, pp. 54–59. A burst of articles about the 1906 San Francisco earthquake has preceded the 100-year anniversary in 2006. This article describes the earthquake and its destruction (and includes pictures). It also uses the 1906 experience to forecast what might happen if a similar earthquake hits the city in the near future.

Fins, Antonio N., Stephanie Anderson Forest, and Bob Andelman. "In Hugo's Wake, a New Storm Kicks up to Curb Building on the Coast." *Business Week*, July 9, 1990, p. 78. The damage of Hurricane Hugo to the South Carolina coast led the state to restrict further development of coastal areas. This article reviews the disputes over these restrictions and the goal to protect areas prone to flooding and high winds from hurricanes.

"Flood, Sweat and Tears." *Time*, vol. 142, July 26, 1993, pp. 22–33. This cover story about the 1993 Great Midwest Flood describes the dramatic rise of the Mississippi, Missouri, and tributary rivers and the economic damage the consequent flooding caused. Despite the extensive flooding, only 26 people died, far fewer than the 2,100 killed by the Johnstown flood. The article praises the warning and evacuation plans that helped limit deaths.

Gordon, John Steele. "Forgotten Fury: 1871 Forest Fire Destroys Peshtigo, Wis." *American Heritage*, vol. 54, no. 2, April/May 2003, pp. 35–36. Although the nation's largest and most lethal fire seems to be forgotten, this recent article is a reminder of how it started and how much damage it caused. It further uses the facts about the fire to comment on managing the nation's forests and overcoming debates between environmentalists and the timber industry.

Gore, Rick. "Living with California's Faults." *National Geographic*, vol. 187, April 1995, pp. 2–35. In describing the Loma Prieta earthquake of 1989 and the Northridge earthquake of 1994, this article quotes the predictions of experts that an even greater California earthquake is overdue. It discusses the kind of damage that will occur but notes that it is nearly impossible to pinpoint the location.

Halverson, Jeff. "Queen of Rains: Hurricane Camille." *Weatherwise*, vol. 58, no. 6, November/December 2005, pp. 24–29. The danger from hurricanes and the need for preparedness and response extends beyond the coastal areas of the Atlantic and Gulf Coasts. This article describes how Hurricane Camille, which made landfall in Mississippi in 1969, unexpectedly moved with renewed force through the state of West Virginia. Leaving 25 inches of rainfall in five hours, Camille stripped mountain forests, led to mudslides, and killed 158 people in the state.

"Hugo: A Case Study. Successful Regional Disaster Response." *UN Chronicle*, vol. 28, June 1991, pp. 50–51. Despite winds of 150 miles per hour, Hurricane Hugo killed only 14 people on the islands of the eastern Caribbean. This article attributes the low death rate to the Pan-Caribbean Disaster Preparedness and Prevention Project. Launched in 1981, this project improved preparedness, mitigation, and response efforts in the region.

Jackson, Donald Dale. "When 20 Million Tons of Water Flooded Johnstown." *Smithsonian*, vol. 20, May 1989, pp. 50–54. Along with describing the cause of the flood—a break in a poorly constructed dam holding a lake—and the damage to the town, this article highlights issues of social inequality. The lake was a resort area of the wealthy, and the inadequate management of the lake and the dam led to the deaths of thousands of less wealthy residents living in the valley below the lake.

"Major Natural Disasters: America's Worst Hurricanes, Floods, Tornadoes, and Earthquakes." *Congressional Digest*, vol. 84, no. 9, November 2005, pp. 259, 288. As background for discussion of disaster policy after Katrina, this article describes other major disasters in the United States. Drawing on information from the National Oceanic and Atmospheric Administration and the National Weather Service, it focuses on the force of the natural hazards and the death and damage they cause rather than on the response. Still, the article furnishes a helpful background for understanding the danger of natural disasters.

Shacochis, Bob. "Written in the Big Wind." *Harper's*, vol. 283, September 1991, pp. 45–53. Concerns about development of fragile areas that are subject to hurricanes date back several decades. This 1991 article describes the destruction caused by Hurricanes Camille and Hugo but also criticizes the unwillingness of some local officials and business leaders to plan for pre-hurricane evacuation and the resistance of residents to recommendations or orders to leave. Problems also came from the dense development of areas prone to hurricanes and the difficulty of moving large numbers of people out of the areas.

Steinhauer, Jennifer. "For Californians, Deadly Heat Cut a Broad Swath." *New York Times*, August 11, 2006, pp. A1, A12. The recent heat wave in California, which lasted particularly long and gave little relief during nighttime, caused 140 deaths. This article describes victims from different areas of the state, social backgrounds, and age groups.

Stimpson, Dee Rivers. "Beehive and Me: Volunteers Help Rebuild Poor Town." *Mother Jones*, vol. 16, January/February 1991, pp. 39–41. Hurricane Hugo devastated many poor, rural towns in South Carolina, which nonetheless received less assistance than larger cities such as Charleston. The author helped residents of Beehive, South Carolina, rebuild and describes his dealings with the government bureaucracy. Most of the help ended up coming from volunteers and charities rather than the government.

Taylor, Cynthia Ramsay. "Building Disaster-Resistant Communities: Work of FEMA." *USA Today (Periodical)*, vol. 130, no. 2674, July 2001, pp. 32–34. This article traces the efforts of FEMA in the 1990s to change its strategy of responding to disasters by putting more funds and efforts into prevention. The agency aimed to limit disaster damage and save money by helping communities identify and mitigate risks before a disaster occurs.

Wagner, Betsy. "The Morgue That Overflowed: Fatalities from Heat in Chicago." *U.S. News & World Report*, vol. 119, July 31, 1995, p. 9. Due to heat-related deaths in 1995, hundreds of bodies piled up at the Cook County morgue. With temperatures in the city reaching 106 degrees, the sick, poor, and isolated were at particular risk. The criticism of the city for not doing more to prevent the deaths led Mayor Richard Daley to investigate the city's heat emergency plan. This article describes the disaster and plans of the city to try, belatedly, to respond better next time.

WEB DOCUMENTS

"The 1900 Storm: Galveston Island, Texas." Galveston County Daily News. Available online. URL: http://www.1900storm.com. Downloaded in July 2007. The web page includes stories about the terrible night of the hurricane, the survivors, the American Red Cross, and the rebuilding of the city. Complemented by pictures of the aftermath, these stories tell of the force of the hurricane and the terror it caused. The web page lauds the rebuilding of the city, calling it "Galveston's finest hour."

"The 1974 Tornado Super Outbreak Report." Risk Management Solutions. Available online. URL: http://www.rms.com/Publications/1974Super TornadoReport.pdf. Posted on April 2, 2004. This report on the most intense and widest tornado outbreak in recorded history details the meteorological traits of the outbreak and the damage the tornadoes caused. It also describes the likely damage if a similar outbreak occurred today.

"1989 Earthquake Reports and Photographs." The Virtual Museum of the City of San Francisco. Available online. URL: http://www.sfmuseum. org/1906/89.html. Downloaded in July 2007. The Loma Prieta earthquake in 1989 is well documented, and this page contains the usual kinds of information such as a time line, maps, oral histories, and damage estimates. More unusual are transcripts of 9-1-1 calls, a report on the earthquake from the San Francisco Police Department, and a debriefing on command center operations. The web page also has information on how residents of the Bay Area can prepare better for earthquakes.

"The 1993 Great Midwest Flood: Voices 10 Years Later." FEMA. Available online. URL: http://www.fema.gov/business/nfip/voices.shtm. Updated on April 6, 2006. FEMA presents stories about the flood as a reminder of its success in mitigating future disasters. It tells not only of the flooding experienced by landowners near the Mississippi River and its tributaries but also of efforts to relocate people away from flood-prone areas with help from federal programs. The web page states its hopes that these stories will be a source of inspiration to individuals and communities needing to reduce their risks from flooding.

"American Experience: Fatal Flood." American Experience, PBS Online. Available online. URL: http://www.pbs.org/wgbh/amex/flood/timeline/ timeline2.html. Downloaded in July 2007. This time line of the Great Mississippi Flood of 1927 lists major events and includes a few pictures. It also highlights the impact of racism on the response to the flood.

"Effects of Catastrophic Events on Transportation System Management and Operations," U.S. Department of Transportation. Available online. URL: http://www.its.dot.gov/JPODOCS/REPTS_TE/13775.html. Posted on April 22, 2002. This report summarizes the response and recovery efforts of the Department of Transportation to damage of roads and highways caused by the 1994 Northridge earthquake. It includes statistics, maps, and pictures to help understand the damage and describes federal actions taken to deal with the disaster.

"FEMA History." FEMA. Available online. URL: http://www.fema.gov/ about/history.shtm. Downloaded in July 2007. A history of an agency written by the agency itself will invariably present a positive view of its accomplishments. Although true of this short web page, it still gives a helpful overview of how disaster policy has changed in the United States.

"The Galveston Hurricane." American Experience, PBS Online. Available online. URL: http://www.pbs.org/wgbh/amex/1900/peopleevents/pande27.html. Downloaded in July 2007. Based on a series about what it was like to live in the United States in 1900, this web page from the Public Broadcasting System includes a helpful timeline of events, maps, and stories about people involved in the hurricane, during relief, and in the rebuilding process.

"The Great 1906 San Francisco Earthquake." USGS Earthquake Hazards Program—Northern California. Available online. URL: http://quake.usgs.gov/info/1906. Updated on November 21, 2001. Along with the striking pictures of the damage caused by the earthquake, this web page gives background information on earthquake science, describes casualties and damage, and includes eyewitness accounts.

"The Great Chicago Fire and the Web of Memory." Chicago Historical Society. Available online. URL: http://www.chicagohs.org/fire/intro. Updated on October 8, 1996. Both history and exhibition, this web page tells the story of the Great Chicago Fire and includes galleries of pictures and maps. It also includes many eyewitness accounts and some background information on the history of Chicago.

"The Great Tri-State Tornado of 1925." GeoCities. Available online. URL: http://www.geocities.com/heartland/7847/tornado2.htm. Updated on May 11, 1999. This short web page maps the path of the most devastating and powerful tornado in recorded U.S. history. It also identifies the locations of the most damage and lists the basic facts about the tornado.

Hipke, Deana C. "The Great Peshtigo Fire of 1871." Available online. URL: http://www.peshtigofire.info. Downloaded in July 2007. An amateur historian who grew up near Peshtigo, Wisconsin, has gathered and organized information on the fire. The web page includes sections on the causes, the victims, a bibliography, and pictures. The text is short but interesting and informative.

"History of the Johnstown Flood." Johnstown Area Heritage Association. Available online. URL: http://www.jaha.org/FloodMuseum/history.html. Downloaded in July 2007. This brief history of the flood quotes several witnesses and has links to survivor stories. It also gives statistics on the flood and its damage and tells about the relief efforts (including the role of the American Red Cross).

"Hurricane Agnes 1972." Commonwealth of Pennsylvania, Department of Environmental Protection. Available online. URL: http://www.depweb.

state.pa.us/heritage/cwp/view.asp?a=3&q=444559. Downloaded in July 2007. Pennsylvania suffered greatly from rains and floods brought by Hurricane Agnes. This web page includes links to information on the movement of the hurricane, the flooding of several rivers in the state, and the efforts to forecast and warn residents of the coming floods.

"Hurricane Andrew." National Oceanic and Atmospheric Administration. Available online. URL: http://www.noaa.gov/hurricaneandrew.html. Updated on August 22, 2002. As one of the few Category 5 hurricanes to reach land in the United States, Hurricane Andrew attracts much attention for its meteorological characteristics. This web page from NOAA emphasizes meteorology rather than disaster response. Still, the force of the hurricane is a reminder of the risks faced by states on the Atlantic and Gulf coasts and the need for preparation for another major hurricane.

"Hurricane Andrew: After the Storm, Ten Years Later." St. Petersburg Times Special Report. Available online. URL: http://www.sptimes.com/2002/webspecials02/andrew. Downloaded in July 2007. The stories linked to this web page cover the storm itself, the harm it caused to the insurance industry, the poor construction of buildings left most damaged, and the people who helped with the response.

"Hurricane Hugo 10th Anniversary." Clemson University. Available online. URL: http://www.clemson.edu/special/hugo/summary.htm. Updated on July 17, 2006. Along with a description of Hurricane Hugo and the harm it brought to South Carolina, this web page advises homeowners about what they can do to protect themselves from another hurricane.

Koser, Kevin R. "Disaster Response and Appointment of a Recovery Czar: The Executive Branch's Response to the Flood of 1927." Congressional Research Service Available online. URL: http://www.fas.org/sgp/crs/misc/RL33126.pdf. Posted on October 25, 2005. This report describes the federal government response to the Great Mississippi Flood of 1927, the most extensive such response to that time. The appointment of Herbert Hoover as the recovery czar greatly aided the response, suggesting that an appointment of someone to a similar position today might improve disaster response.

Mandia, Scott A. "The Long Island Express: The Great Hurricane of 1938." SUNY-Suffolk. Available online. URL: http://www2.sunysuffolk.edu/mandias/38hurricane. Updated on May 15, 2006. A professor of physical sciences describes how this hurricane damaged Long Island, New York, and changed the geography of the island. He also considers the likelihood of another storm of similar power reaching Long Island in the next several decades: "History has shown that these powerful storms are rare but do in fact occur with long-term frequency. Case studies have shown that the next time a storm like the Long Island Express roars through, it might be the greatest disaster in U.S. history."

"Oklahoma City—Seven Years Later." National Memorial Institute for the Prevention of Terrorism. Available online. URL: http://www.mipt.org/okc7toc.asp. Downloaded in July 2007. This web page offers advice to schools, clergy, first responders, city officials, and volunteers on responding to and recovering from a terrorist attack such as occurred in Oklahoma City.

"The Oklahoma Department of Civil Emergency Management after Action Report: Alfred P. Murrah Federal Building Bombing, 19 April 1995 in Oklahoma City, Oklahoma." Oklahoma Department of Civil Emergency Management. Available online. URL: http://www.ok.gov/OEM/documents/Bombing%20After%20Action%20Report.pdf. Downloaded in July 2007. This report details the actions taken after the 1995 Oklahoma City bombing. In evaluating the response, it finds that the operations ran smoothly and offers reasons for the effective response. It also relays lessons learned on how future terrorist response can improve. Thorough and detailed, the report includes maps, statistics, and diagrams of the bombed building.

Pielke, Roger A., Jr., Chantal Simonpietri, and Jennifer Oxelson. "Thirty Years after Hurricane Camille: Lessons Learned, Lessons Lost." Center for Science and Technology Policy Research. Available online. URL: http://sciencepolicy.colorado.edu/about_us/meet_us/roger_pielke/camille. Posted on July 12, 1999. This thorough report on the hurricane and its destruction describes the federal relief efforts that followed and led to a greater role of the federal government in future disaster response. It also criticizes the continued failure of the country to prepare adequately for major hurricanes.

"Storms of the Century: #7—1925 Tri-State Tornado." The Weather Channel. Available online. URL: http://www.weather.com/newscenter/specialreports/sotc/storm7/page1.html. Downloaded in July 2007. Told as a drama, this story follows the tornado from its start ("A Monster Storm Develops") to its destructive end ("A War Zone").

"Timeline of the San Francisco Earthquake, April 18–23, 1906." The Virtual Museum of the City of San Francisco. Available online. URL: http://www.sfmuseum.org/hist10/06timeline.html. Downloaded in July 2007. This timeline lists events that followed the earthquake, particularly the spread of fire and efforts to control it. It also lists efforts in the days following the earthquake to provide relief to the city.

"USGS Response to an Urban Earthquake: Northridge '94." U.S. Geological Survey. Available online. URL: http://pubs.usgs.gov/of/1996/ofr-96-0263. Updated on November 16, 2005. Although focused on the activities of one government agency, the U.S. Geological Survey, this web page also contains background information on the earthquake and the damage it caused. Of particular value, the section on communicating and applying lessons learned gives insight on how to improve the response to earthquakes.

White, Horace. "The Great Chicago Fire." National Center for Public Policy Research. Available online. URL: http://www.nationalcenter.org/ChicagoFire.html. Downloaded in July 2007. This reprint of a story written on October 14, 1871, by the editor in chief of the *Chicago Tribune* gives a firsthand account of the destruction of the fire and the largely futile efforts to control it.

RESPONSE TO THE 9/11 TERRORIST ATTACKS

BOOKS

Brill, Steven. *After: How America Confronted the September 12th Era*. New York: Simon and Schuster, 2003. Offering a nearly day-by-day account of what followed the September 11 terrorist attacks, this thoroughly detailed book covers efforts to protect the borders and airports, provide help to victims, plan for rebuilding on Ground Zero, and reorganize the government for the new goal of protecting homeland security. The book is strongest in describing the players and interests involved in the new homeland security effort, but it gives some attention to issues of disaster response.

Clarke, Lee, ed. *Terrorism and Disaster: New Threats, New Ideas*. Kidlington, UK: Elsevier, 2003. This volume presents analyses by disaster scholars of the 9/11 events and of terrorism more generally. The scholars bring knowledge gained from studying natural disasters to this relatively new form of disaster. Some claims made in the book are that the disaster showed how people remain resilient rather than panic in the face of catastrophe, that infrastructure remains vulnerable to attack, and that Americans are no safer now than at the time of the attacks. The authors are generally critical of the government's preparation for terrorist attacks and its antiterrorism policy.

Dalton, Dennis R. *Rethinking Corporate Security in the Post 9-11 Era: Issues and Strategies for Today's Global Business Community*. Amsterdam: Elsevier, 2003. This book makes the case that corporations, like the nation more generally, are vulnerable to terrorist threats. It accordingly focuses on what security managers can do to convince others of the importance of protecting the corporation and what changes they can make to increase security. Although concerned with prevention, the book also discusses how corporations can respond to terrorist disasters after they occur.

Danieli, Yael, and Robert L. Dingman, eds. *On the Ground after September 11: Mental Health Responses and Practical Knowledge Gained.* Binghamton, N.Y.: Hawthorne Press, 2005. With some 100 chapters by mental health scholars who helped in the response to the 9/11 attacks, this volume describes the psychological consequences experienced by the victims and the programs set up to meet their needs. It includes many personal accounts of what survivors went through after the attacks. The book will most interest mental health counselors who work with disaster victims.

Dixon, Lloyd. *Compensation for Losses from 9/11 Attacks.* Santa Monica, Calif.: RAND, 2004. In describing the benefits received by those killed or seriously injured by the World Trade Center terrorist attacks, this study evaluates the U.S. disaster compensation system. Each of the four compensation mechanisms—insurance, the tort system, government programs, and charity—receives attention. The book also compares compensation systems for this terrorist disaster with those for natural disasters. The goal of the book is to make policy recommendations and improve efforts to help victims of disasters.

General Accounting Office. *Major Management Challenges and Program Risks: Federal Emergency Management Agency.* Washington, D.C.: General Accounting Office, 2003. Also available online. URL: http://purl.access. gpo.gov/GPO/LPS32158. Downloaded in July 2007. This evaluation of DHS, conducted soon after its creation, argues that the department must do more to integrate its agencies and the activities it oversees. Having to combine 170,000 employees and 22 agencies is a daunting task, yet failing to carry out this mission will expose the nation to serious harm. Although focused on terrorism, the report's concerns also apply to the response to natural disasters, which now falls under DHS.

Hecker, JayEtta Z. *Federal Aid to the New York City Area Following the Attacks of September 11th and Challenges Confronting FEMA.* Washington, D.C.: General Accounting Office, 2003. Also available online. URL: http:// purl.access.gpo.gov/GPO/LPS38097. Downloaded in July 2007. This statement from the GAO lists the billions in aid provided by the federal government to those in the New York City area and the actions of FEMA and other agencies to help in search and rescue, debris removal, provision of emergency transportation, and emergency utility service. It also discusses the challenges faced by FEMA in moving to the Department of Homeland Security (DHS).

Jacobson, Sid, and Ernie Colon. *The 9/11 Report: A Graphic Adaptation.* New York: Hill and Wang, 2006. The authors combine the material from *The*

9/11 Report with pictures to create an accessible—and indeed gripping—
account of the attacks. It contains little new information but makes it
easier to learn about the events without going through the detail of the
original report.

Kayyem, Juliette N., and Robyn L. Pangi, eds. *First to Arrive: State and Local
Responses to Terrorism.* Cambridge, Mass.: MIT Press, 2003. Papers in this
volume argue that the response to the 9/11 attacks was too centralized
and focused on federal government policy. Less attention has gone to
state and local preparedness for terrorist events. Yet those working on the
ground in cities and towns can help guide decisions at the top. The contributions come from a series of discussions held at Harvard University
and will most interest academics.

National Commission on Terrorist Attacks. *The 9/11 Commission Report:
Final Report of the National Commission on Terrorist Attacks upon the United
States.* New York: W. W. Norton, 2004. The bipartisan commission appointed to investigate the terrorist attacks gives most attention to the
intelligence failure in preventing the attacks. However, several chapters
review the response to the attacks in New York City and Washington,
D.C. The chapters use massive amounts of information from interviews,
documents, and testimony to present a readable summary of the events
that followed the plane crashes, the problems faced by responders, and
recommendations for changes in future response. This may be the most
comprehensive and valuable resource on the events of September 11.

Natural Hazards Research and Applications Information Center, Public
Entity Risk Institute, and Institute for Civil Infrastructure Systems. *Beyond September 11th: An Account of Postdisaster Research.* Special Publication
Number 39. Boulder: Natural Hazards Research and Applications Information Center, University of Colorado, 2003. Immediately after the 9/11
attacks, the Natural Hazards Center at the University of Colorado provided funds under its Quick Response Program for researchers to conduct field investigations in New York City, Pennsylvania, and Washington,
D.C. The two-dozen chapters in this volume present the findings of these
investigations. The chapters cover topics such as victim management and
identification, use of geographic technology, creativity in emergency response, volunteer behavior, lessons learned for building structures, experiences of Muslim students after the attacks, the business response, and
newspaper representation of the attacks.

ARTICLES

"9/11 by the Numbers." *New York*, vol. 35, no. 31, September 16, 2002,
p. 54. A listing of statistics on the deaths and damage from the attacks—

without comment or discussion—gives a sad and gruesome summary of this disaster.

Adler, Jerry. "Ground Zero." *Newsweek*, vol. 138, no. 13, September 24, 2001, pp. 72–85. This story came out soon after the September 11 attacks and notes some of the problems in the response. One in particular was establishing the fire command post at the base of the World Trade Center towers, which resulted in the deaths of hundreds of police and firefighters when the towers collapsed.

Alter, Jonathan, and Geoffrey Gagnon. "The Future of New York. M. Bloomberg and Fellow New Yorkers Feel Fall-Out from Sept. 11." *Newsweek*, vol. 140, no. 11, September 11, 2002, pp. 50–55. At the one-year anniversary of the terrorist attacks, New York City under newly elected Mayor Michael Bloomberg has developed a strategy for future attacks. According to this article, the city has gone through disaster simulations of a bioterrorism attack and has the hospital system well prepared to handle large casualties.

Argenti, Paul. "Crisis Communication: Lessons from 9/11." *Harvard Business Review*, vol. 80, no. 12, December 2002, pp. 103–109. Given the difficulties of communication after the terrorist attacks, corporations and managers need plans for crisis communication. This article reports on how executives in a range of industries are developing such plans and how businesses near Ground Zero have worked to restore operations and morale after the attacks.

Baker, Al, and James Glanz. "911 Tapes Echo Grim Struggle in Towers: Disaster Defied Operators' Training." *New York Times*, April 1, 2006, pp. A1, B7. Many workers in the World Trade Center called 911 after the first plane hit the north tower. The 911 operators, not having been informed of decisions by police and fire commanders at Ground Zero to evacuate, told callers to stay put. The article highlights the importance of communication in a disaster and the need for proper training and good communication among those involved in the response.

Blakeley, Kiri. "Tracking the Disaster Relief Charities: World Trade Center Terrorist Attacks." *Forbes*, vol. 168, no. 11, October 29, 2001, p. 64. With charities having received by the date of this article some $700 million in donations, the author describes the difficulties in administering the large amounts. For charities with little disaster relief experience, distributing these funds has been a challenge.

Chen, David W. "After Criticism, U.S. Broadens 9/11 Aid Pool." *New York Times*, June 29, 2002, pp. A1, B3. This news story reports on the announcement from FEMA that it will extend aid to those working and living outside the Ground Zero area. Anyone working or living in Manhattan who suffered financially from the World Trade Center attacks may receive assistance to prevent eviction from their homes. Others working in surrounding boroughs of New York City may receive assistance if their business was economically dependent on activity in lower Manhattan.

Chivers, C. J. "Ground Zero Diary: 12 Days of Fire and Grit." *New York Times*, September 30, 2001, pp. A1, B9. A description of the rescue efforts that took place at Ground Zero after the terrorist attacks on the World Trade Center.

"Disaster Planning Still Lacking." *USA Today (Periodical)*, vol. 133, June 2005, p. 13. Despite calls from the *9/11 Commission Report* for a comprehensive state, regional, and national disaster response plan for terrorist events, this article suggests that even four years after the terrorist attack, the nation is not well prepared for another. It makes this case by reviewing the response to a 2003 explosion in a pharmaceutical plant in Kinston, North Carolina, that resembled a terrorist bombing in some ways. The response was plagued by communication problems and inadequate medical services to deal with the injuries.

France, David. "$75 Million of Stuff." *Newsweek*, vol. 139, no. 7, February 18, 2002, pp. 62–63. FEMA estimates that goods contributed to New York City after the terrorist attacks totaled about $75 million. Although demonstrating the generosity of Americans, the goods included many items such as toothpaste, canned beans, and shovels that were not needed immediately after the response. Most of the goods now have been given to families of victims and survivors.

Goldberg, Jonah. "Canines to the Rescue." *National Review*, vol. 53, no. 21, November 5, 2001, pp. 34–36. Often victims of disasters, dogs instead played an active role in the rescue efforts after the collapse of the World Trade Center towers. This article describes the disaster work of the dogs and their handlers.

Griscom, Amanda. "Man behind the Mayor: R. Sheirer, Unsung Hero of the Hot Zone." *New York*, vol. 34, no. 39, October 15, 2001, pp. 78–82. Richard Sheirer, the New York City director of the Office of Emergency Management, helped lead the rescue and cleanup efforts after the terrorist attacks. This article reports on his efforts to coordinate the federal, state, local, and charitable organizations involved in the response.

Herlinger, Chris. "Emergency Spending." *Christian Century*, vol. 119, no. 8, April 10–17, 2002, pp. 19–20. Charitable organizations received unprecedented donations to help the victims of 9/11 but also faced new pressures to spend the funds quickly. The author discusses some of the difficulties faced by charitable organizations in meeting the demands of the public and responding to negative publicity.

Louie, Miriam Ching. "The 9/11 Disappeareds: Alternative Emergency Relief System for 9/11 Undocumented Immigrant Workers." *Nation*, vol. 273, no. 18, December 3, 2001, pp. 7–8. Undocumented immigrants affected by the terrorist attacks have not received the same amount of help as others. This article describes one Mexican community organization called Asociación Tepeyac that helped immigrant workers and their families with relief. The organization collaborated with the Red Cross to get more help for these sometimes invisible victims.

McDonald, Marci, Josh Fischman, and Mary Brophy Marcus. "Courage under Terrible Fire: Heroic Rescue Efforts of Firefighters and Others after Terrorist Attacks on United States." *U.S. News & World Report*, vol. 131, no. 12, September 24, 2001, pp. 40–43. The response to the September 11 terrorist attacks involved the rescue efforts of police, firefighters, and emergency medical personnel in New York City and Washington, D.C. This article tells the story of these efforts.

Sostek, Anya. "New York's State of Mind." *Governing*, vol. 18, supplement, October 2004, pp. 30–32. Since the September 11 attacks, the New York City Police Department has refashioned itself as a "world-class terror fighting machine." This article describes the efforts made with this transformation to prevent another disaster: posting detectives overseas, assigning 250 city officers to work on counterterrorism, and committing 20 times the manpower to counterterrorism than before the attack. Such efforts are part of a widened definition of disaster mitigation and prevention.

Starr, Douglas. "Bad Blood." *New Republic*, vol. 227, no. 5, July 29, 2002, pp. 13–16. Calls for blood donations after 9/11 and the goodwill of citizens in helping led the Red Cross and other organizations to collect massive amounts of blood—much more than needed. This article argues that the method of collection was wasteful and inefficient, and it suggests some other ways to collect blood donations after a disaster.

Tierney, Kathleen. "The 9/11 Commission and Disaster Management: Little Depth, Less Context, Not Much Guidance." *Contemporary Sociology*, vol. 34, no. 2, March 2005, pp. 115–120. This book review of the *9/11 Commission Report* by a sociologist places the problems of response identified by the commission (e.g., lack of coordination among responders) in the larger context of disaster response. The author argues that inadequate emergency preparedness, organizational rivalries, and poor training of responders predate 9/11 by many decades. She maintains that understanding the response to 9/11 requires more general understanding of the weaknesses of disaster response in the United States.

Walters, Jonathan. "Safety Is Still a Local Issue. Roles of Federal, State and Local Government in Aftermath of Sept. 11 Attacks and Defense against Future Terrorist Attacks." *Governing*, vol. 15, no. 2, November 2001, p. 12. The response to the New York City terrorist attacks relied on the leadership of Mayor Giuliani rather than the federal government. The author points out that the buck stops with states and localities in responding to disasters. He calls on leaders to remember that cities must rely primarily on their own resources after a disaster.

Wyatt, Edward, David W. Chen, and Charles V. Bagli. "After 9/11, Parcels of Money, and Dismay." *New York Times*, December 30, 2002, pp. A1, B4. Despite the transfer of some $5 billion from Washington, D.C., to New York City, city residents are confused and angry that this amount is less than a quarter of what the federal government promised. The article describes these concerns and efforts to meet expected relief goals after the terrorist attacks.

WEB DOCUMENTS

"9/11 First Responders Getting Sick and Dying: What the Investigators Found out about Dust from Ground Zero." 7online.com, ABC News. Available online. URL: http://abclocal.go.com/wabc/story?section=investi gators&id=4203468. Posted on May 24, 2006. Although official recognition has not come from the city, state, or federal government, first responders who helped after the terrorist attacks may have started to die from lung-related problems. According to this web article, many attribute the deaths to the dust created by the collapse of the towers. The article describes the victims and the claims made about the causes of their deaths.

"9/11 Response." Philanthropy News Digest. Available online. URL: http://foundationcenter.org/pnd/911/index.jhtml;jsessionid=D2HLYIZT0PBH RTQRSI4CGX D5AAAACI2F. Downloaded in July 2007. This paper contains links to two useful Web documents: "September 11: The Philanthropic Response" and "Giving in the Aftermath of September 11: Final Update on the Foundation and Corporate Response." The documents and summary press releases linked to the web page describe the charitable response to the terrorist attacks and the sources of more than $1.1 billion in grants awarded by foundations and corporations.

"Amid Heckles, Giuliani Defends 9/11 Response to Panel: Ex-Mayor, Interrupted by Protesters, Says Angry Reaction 'Understandable.'" NBC4. com, NBC News. Available online. URL: http://www.nbc4.com/news/ 3322275/detail.html. Posted on May 19, 2004. This article gives voice to critics of the New York City response to the terrorist attacks. Mayor Giuliani believes the city did well in responding to the enormous challenge created by the plane crashes. Although he expected up to 15,000 deaths from the collapse of the towers, he believes quick evacuation kept the deaths under 3,000. However, some who lost family members in the attacks believe that communication problems prevented many people from being saved.

Annotated Bibliography

"Analysis of 9/11 Pentagon Response Reveals Strengths, Weaknesses: Arlington County Creating Emergency Preparedness Blueprint from 9/11 After-Action Report Recommendations and First-hand Experience." Firehouse.com. Available online. URL: http://www.firehouse.com/news/2002/7/23_Ppentagon.html. Updated on July 23, 2002. The analysis summarized on this web page lists both strengths and weaknesses in the response to the terrorist attack on the Pentagon. Among the strengths were the willingness of multiple units and commanders to work together, reliance on a comprehensive emergency plan, and efforts to support first responders, victims, and families of those who died. Among the weaknesses were problems of communication due to the failure of cell phones, a shortage of space at the command control center, and a lack of emergency supplies.

"Command Performance? Response to the 9/11 Pentagon Disaster." Suburban Emergency Management Project. Available online. URL: http://www.semp.us/biots/biot_135.html. Posted on November 7, 2004. The Suburban Emergency Management Project promotes communication and training for local emergency response units. This web page summarizes one report on the emergency response on September 11, 2001, in Arlington, Virginia, and provides links to several other reports. The text explains the reasons given for the actions taken by the emergency responders at the time and some of the problems they faced.

"Disaster Assistance: Report on FEMA's Post 9/11 Public Assistance to the New York City Area." U.S. General Accounting Office. Available online. URL: http://www.gao.gov/new.items/d03926.pdf. Posted in August 2003. This report summarizes how FEMA's response to the New York City terrorist attacks differed from FEMA's typical response to natural disasters. Congress had requested the report to help it understand how well the usual forms of disaster assistance worked in responding to a terrorist event. New York officials say changes are needed to tailor FEMA's response to a terrorist event, while FEMA officials suggest their general programs worked well in New York City.

"EPA Response to September 11." Environmental Protection Agency. Available online. URL: http://www.epa.gov/wtc. Updated on September 20, 2006. The collapse of the World Trade Center towers and the disintegration of most of the objects inside the towers created dangerous air-quality problems in lower Manhattan. The EPA has monitored outdoor and indoor air quality in the area. An expert review panel will evaluate the air pollution harm resulting from the collapse of the towers and recommend further steps to minimize the harm. This web page contains information on the monitoring programs and the review panel.

"Heroism and Horror." The National Commission on Terrorist Attacks upon the United States. Available online. URL: http://www.9-11

commission.gov/report/911Report_Ch9.htm. Posted on September 20, 2004. This excerpt of chapter 9 from the *9/11 Commission Report* focuses directly on the disaster response to the terrorist attacks in New York City and Washington, D.C. It discusses the preparedness of the buildings and the first responders, response of police and fire officials at the sites, and problems encountered in evacuating the buildings. The material is remarkable in the detailed chronology of actions taken in response to the attacks. The commission also carefully and fairly draws lessons on what responders should do to prepare better for future disasters.

"A Partial Administration Timeline of Homeland Security Actions through May 29 of 2002." Department of Homeland Security. Available online. URL: http://www.dhs.gov/xabout/history/editorial_0114.shtm. Downloaded in September 2006. DHS presents its own history on this web page. The history begins with the events of September 11, 2001, that led to the creation of the department. In one sense, the new department is a response of the federal government to the terrorist attacks.

"Responding to the September 11 Terrorist Attacks." International Information Programs, USINFO.STATE.GOV. Available online. URL: http://usinfo.state.gov/is/Archive_Index/Responding_to_the_September_11_Terrorist_Attacks s.html. Posted on October 3, 2001. This fact sheet from the White House lists the funds provided in response to the terrorist attacks. For example, of the $40 billion emergency response program from the federal government, $2 billion went to FEMA to distribute for emergency assistance, $126.2 million went to the Department of Health and Human Services to distribute for health-related needs, and $100 million went to the Small Business Administration to distribute for loans.

"September 11, 2001 Attacks." Wikipedia: The Free Encyclopedia. Available online. URL: http://en.wikipedia.org/wiki/September_11,_2001_attacks. Downloaded in July 2007. As discussed in chapter 6, Wikipedia has both strengths and weaknesses. For a compilation of information on the 9/11 terrorist attacks and the response, the strengths outweigh the weaknesses. The comprehensive nature of the article and the links to more detail on specialized topics are helpful.

"September 11: Chronology of Terror." CNN.com. Available online. URL: http://archives.cnn.com/2001/US/09/11/chronology.attack. Posted on September 12, 2001. This timeline begins with the crash of the first hijacked plane into the north tower of the World Trade Center. It then lists the times of public announcements and media reports about the disaster response.

"September 11: More Effective Collaboration Could Enhance Charitable Organizations' Contributions in Disasters." U.S. General Accounting

Office. Available online. URL: http://www.gao.gov/cgi-bin/getrpt?GAO-03-259. Posted in December 2002. With as many as two-thirds of U.S. households donating to 9/11 relief, Congress asked the GAO to evaluate the use of the contributions. The report suggests that, in the future, FEMA should organize the major charitable organizations receiving the funds so that they can standardize applications, ease access to the funds, speed distribution, and prevent fraud. Implementing these recommendations will require more cooperation among charitable organizations than occurred in the past.

"September 11th Recovery Program, a Legacy of Compassion." American Red Cross. Available online. URL: http://www.redcross.org/article/0,1072,0_312_5646,00.html. Posted on September 11, 2006. The American Red Cross lauds its response and recovery efforts after the September 11 attacks. It describes their efforts to open shelters, staff food centers, and provide counseling. It also describes the distribution of the charitable funds it collected to victims and families of victims. A link to the full report summarized in the article appears at the bottom of the web page.

Tierney, Kathleen. "Recent Developments in U.S. Homeland Security Policies and Their Implications for the Management of Extreme Events." Available online. URL: http://training.fema.gov/EMIweb/downloads/Tierney2005japanfinal2.pdf. Posted in January 2005. In this paper presented at a conference in Japan, the author argues that changes in federal disaster policy after 9/11, particularly the creation of DHS, have weakened the government's ability to respond to natural disasters. The law enforcement and military strategies used for terrorism in the department will not work well for dealing with natural disasters. The response to Hurricane Katrina nine months later confirmed these claims.

"Victims of September 11—Benefits and Assistance." FirstGov.gov. Available online. URL: http://www.firstgov.gov/Topics/Usgresponse/Victims_Benefits.shtml. Downloaded in July 2007. The long list of benefits and assistance from the federal government on this page includes, for example, programs for victim compensation, federal and military personnel, workers and the unemployed, businesses, and mental health assistance. The page itself does not describe the programs but offers links to information on each one.

HURRICANE KATRINA RESPONSE

BOOKS

2005 Complete Guide to the Hurricane Katrina Disaster: Federal Reports, Government Response, Science Reports, Devastation to Louisiana, New Orleans,

Mississippi, Alabama. Washington, D.C.: Progressive Management, 2005. This electronic book on DVD-ROM contains a comprehensive collection of government documents on Katrina. Although not as readable as other books on Katrina (the DVD-ROM contains more than 38,000 pages), the collection can be searched to find information on a variety of topics.

Brasch, Walter M. *"Unacceptable": The Federal Government's Response to Hurricane Katrina.* Charleston, S.C.: BookSurge Publishing, 2006. Brasch, a journalism professor and columnist, examines the question of why the federal response to Katrina was so inefficient and inept. The book lays much of the blame on the policies of the George W. Bush administration, such as downgrading FEMA, emphasizing terrorism, and sending resources to the Iraq war.

Brinkley, Douglas. *The Great Deluge: Hurricane Katrina, New Orleans, and the Mississippi Gulf Coast.* New York: William Morrow, 2006. A history professor at Tulane University and well-known author, Brinkley presents a comprehensive and impressive account of the preparation for Hurricane Katrina, the day of the storm, the flooding of New Orleans, and the disaster response over the following week. Longer than other accounts, the book mixes stories of victims and responders with facts and explanation. Brinkley criticizes Mayor Ray Nagin, Governor Kathleen Blanco, FEMA Director Michael Brown, DHS Secretary Michael Chertoff, and President George W. Bush for their roles in the failed disaster response.

Childs, John Brown, ed. *Hurricane Katrina: Response and Responsibilities.* Santa Cruz, Calif.: New Pacific Press, 2006. The contributors to this edited volume use Katrina to look critically at the rifts in U.S. society brought to light by the disaster. The editor aims with the articles to include diverse perspectives on the topic and extend journalistic description to analysis of the causes and meaning of the event.

Cooper, Christopher, and Robert Block. *Disaster: Hurricane Katrina and the Failure of Homeland Security.* New York: Times Books, 2006. In this readable book, two *Wall Street Journal* reporters trace the breakdown of response after Hurricane Katrina to two main sources. The first was the failure of local officials and the Army Corps of Engineers to prepare the city for a severe hurricane, and the second was the merging of FEMA into the DHS. The authors call for an overhaul of the response system.

Daniels, Ronald J., Donald F. Kettl, and Howard Kunreuther. *On Risk and Disaster: Lessons from Hurricane Katrina.* Philadelphia: University of Pennsylvania Press, 2006. The edited volume presents papers from the National Symposium on Risk and Disasters held at the University of Pennsylvania. Using Katrina as a case study, the papers address questions of how the nation should manage risks. Some chapters describe the sources of the failed response (e.g., poor leadership, racism, human short-sightedness), while others consider how to change incentives for effective disaster preparedness and response.

Dyson, Michael Eric. *Come Hell or High Water: Hurricane Katrina and the Color of Disaster.* New York: Basic Civitas, 2006. Dyson, a professor at the University of Pennsylvania, lays the blame for the mishandled Katrina response not just on the performance of FEMA and politicians but on the inevitable result of race and class inequality in the United States. He accuses leaders of a "passive indifference" to the problems of the poor and blacks in New Orleans. The book includes a description of how these groups suffered more than others during Katrina and how larger society has failed to protect all its citizens. In comparison to other books on Katrina, it emphasizes interpretation and theory about American culture and racism.

Horne, Jed. *Breach of Faith: Hurricane Katrina and the Near Death of a Great American City.* New York: Random House, 2006. The metro editor of the *New Orleans Times-Picayune* tells the stories of people who died and people who lived through the flooding of New Orleans after Hurricane Katrina. While keeping the focus on New Orleans rather than Washington, D.C., the author also describes the bumbling response of the federal government. The stories cover patients trapped in hospitals, life in overcrowded shelters, the actions of the mayor and governor, and dealings with the Army Corps of Engineers.

McQuaid, John, and Mark Schleifstein. *Path of Destruction: The Devastation of New Orleans and the Coming Age of Superstorms.* New York: Little, Brown, 1996. This book by two journalists gives more attention than other books on Katrina to the history of the city, its vulnerability to hurricanes, and the building of the levees. The history stresses the inevitability of a disaster and the failed efforts of engineers to devise a way to prevent damage from a major disaster. The book also discusses the possible links of the hurricane to global warming and the likelihood of more severe weather events to come.

Olasky, Marvin. *The Politics of Disaster: Katrina, Big Government, and a New Strategy for Future Crises.* Nashville, Tenn.: W Publishing Group, 2006. Concluding that big government did not work in meeting human needs after Hurricane Katrina, Olasky suggests new and better ways to respond to national crises. For example, private and faith-based organizations can fill in where the government fails. Hurricane Katrina serves as a case study for presenting the author's criticisms of current policy and ideas for changes.

Select Bipartisan Committee to Investigate the Preparation for and Response to Hurricane Katrina. *A Failure of Initiative: The Final Report of the*

Select Bipartisan Committee to Investigate the Preparation for and Response to Hurricane Katrina. Washington, D.C.: U.S. House of Representatives, 2006. Also available online. URL: http://katrina.house.gov/full_katrina_ report.htm. Posted on February 15, 2006. This report reaches its conclusion in the first sentence: "The Select Committee identified failures at all levels of government that significantly undermined and detracted from the heroic efforts of first responders, private individuals and organizations, faith-based groups and others." The volume describes these failures and offers recommendations for change. The executive summary nicely reviews the key points of the long report.

Time Magazine. *Hurricane Katrina: The Storm That Changed America.* New York: Time, 2006. With most of the books on Katrina focusing on issues of policy, government response, and inequality, this one does something different. It presents vivid pictures of the disaster and tells the personal stories of those who survived the storm.

Troutt, David Dante, ed. *After the Storm: Black Intellectuals Explore the Meaning of Hurricane Katrina.* New York: New Press, 2006. The death and devastation that Hurricane Katrina brought to African Americans raise larger issues about racial inequality in poverty, housing, and treatment by the government. The 10 chapters in this volume explore these issues in some detail. They pay less attention to the experience of Katrina than to the social and historical background of race and disasters. For example, one chapter examines how disasters have in the past led to black out-migration from the South, and another chapter examines the perceptions of the public about crime and looting by New Orleans residents.

U.S. Government Accountability Office. *Statement by Comptroller David M. Walker on GAO's Preliminary Observations Regarding Preparedness and Response to Hurricane Katrina.* Washington, D.C.: U.S. Government Accountability Office, 2006. Much shorter than other government reports on Katrina, this nine-page document highlights three key themes: the lack of clear and decisive leadership; inadequate advance planning, training, and exercise programs; and the failure to develop capabilities for a catastrophic event. The nonpartisan approach of the Government Accountability Office shows clearly in this evenhanded report.

U.S. House of Representatives. *Back to the Drawing Board: A First Look at Lessons Learned from Katrina.* Hearing before the Committee on Government Reform, House of Representatives, One Hundred Ninth Congress, First Session, September 15, 2005. Washington, D.C.: U.S. Government Printing Office, 2006. Also available online. URL: http://a257.g. akamaitech.net/7/257/2422/08dec20051200/www.access.gpo.gov/ congress/house/pdf/109hrg/24205.pdf. Downloaded in July 2007. Published reports on Hurricane Katrina from the House Select Committee and the White House describe the problems in the response and make recommendations for improvements. This hearing followed soon after the hurricane and preceded these reports. Those testifying at the hearing included professors, national-security experts, FEMA professionals, state legislators, emergency responders, and disaster victims. Along with prepared statements from experts, the hearings included questions from house members and statements of their views on the problem.

White House. *The Federal Response to Hurricane Katrina: Lessons Learned.* Washington, D.C.: White House, 2006. Also available online. URL: http://purl. access.gpo.gov/GPO/LPS67263. Posted in February 2006. This report reviews what happened before, during, and after Hurricane Katrina and, in so doing, describes federal disaster response and its limitations. It is less concerned with assigning blame than in developing recommendations or lessons to guide future disaster response. The 125 recommendations for policymakers and managers are detailed and thorough.

ARTICLES

Abrahms, Sally. "Shelter from the Storm: Help for Victims of Hurricane Katrina and Hurricane Rita; Work of AARP Foundation." *AARP the Magazine,* vol. 49, no. 4C, July/August 2006, pp. 78–79. The foundation of the American Association of Retired Persons has a Disaster Relief and Recovery Fund that it used to help older persons harmed by Hurricane Katrina. This article describes how the funding of local groups in Mississippi, Louisiana, and Alabama aided rebuilding.

Bacon, Jacqueline. "Saying What They've Been Thinking." *Extra!,* vol. 18, no. 6, December 2005, pp. 13–15. The author criticizes several media commentators who relied on stereotypes of black Americans in criticizing residents of New Orleans for not doing more to help themselves after Hurricane Katrina. According to the article, victims of the disaster were wrongly portrayed as selfish, criminal, and unwilling to work hard.

Bailey, Ronald. "Unnatural Disasters." *Reason,* vol. 37, no. 7, December 2005, pp. 32–33. This article on how to reform FEMA fits the limited government and free-market philosophy of the magazine. It recommends that the federal government stop offering flood insurance, which encourages people to live in areas prone to disaster. It also suggests that local citizens assume more responsibility for protecting themselves from disasters rather than expecting the federal government to cover disaster losses. Last, it suggests that the federal government allow private charities to take a larger role in disaster response and relief.

Ballard, Scotty. "Blacks among Major Victims of Deadly Hurricane Katrina." *Jet,* vol. 108, no. 12, September 19, 2005, pp. 6–10, 12–14, 16–17,

51–53. This article describes the hurricane and the response from the perspective of African Americans in Louisiana, Alabama, Mississippi, and Florida.

Beinner, Ron, and David Halberstam. *Vanity Fair,* no. 543, November 2005, pp. 359–385. The authors place most blame for the slow federal response to Hurricane Katrina on President Bush. Although not directly responsible for bureaucratic incompetence, the president's slow recognition of the seriousness of the disaster and the initial praise he gave to FEMA Director Michael Brown for doing "a heck of a job" showed poor understanding of the situation.

Chappell, Kevin. "The Devastation, the Hope, the Recovery." *Ebony,* vol. 61, no. 11, September 2006, pp. 118–121. Giving particular attention to the African-American wards in New Orleans, this article describes some of the progress made in the recovery after Hurricane Katrina. It also recognizes the vast amount of work remaining to be done—repairing damaged homes, cleaning out junked cars, making the drinking water safe, and providing reliable electricity. It concludes optimistically, saying that residents have the strength and steadiness to return the city to its former glory.

Clarke, Richard A. "Things Left Undone: Disaster Response and Homeland Security." *Atlantic Monthly,* vol. 296, no. 4, November 2005, pp. 37–38. The author blames the response problems after Hurricane Katrina on the shift of FEMA to the DHS. The shift led to reductions in staff and budget in FEMA as more resources went instead to antiterrorism efforts. The article concludes that a strong DHS does not serve the nation's interest.

DeWan, Shaila, and Janet Roberts. "Louisiana's Deadly Storm Took Strong as Well as the Helpless." *New York Times,* December 18, 2005, pp. 1, 46. Also available online. URL: http://www.nytimes.com/2005/12/18/national/nationalspecial/18victims.html?ex=1292562000&en=6df5ae74349cf92b&ei=5088&partner=rssnyt&emc=rss. Posted on December 18, 2005. This story reports on an investigation into the death of 260 Louisianans during or after Hurricane Katrina. The major findings were that almost all deaths came after rather than during the storm, and most deaths occurred among the elderly, disabled, or ill. Such information should help identify groups that need special protection and attention during a disaster.

Elliott, James R., and Jeremy Pais. "Race, Class, and Hurricane Katrina: Social Differences in Human Responses to Disaster." *Social Science Research,* vol. 35, no. 2, June 2006, pp. 295–321. The authors report on a survey of 1,200 Hurricane Katrina survivors about their experiences with the disaster and the response. The results show differences across races and income groups. Low-income black homeowners from New Orleans suffered the most damage and, based on the survey results, need the most assistance.

Helyar, John. "The Washington That FEMA Forgot: After Katrina; Washington Parish, La." *Fortune*, vol. 152, no. 7, October 3, 2005, pp. 92–93, 95. This story recounts the experiences of residents of Washington Parish after Hurricane Katrina. No federal assistance came to the parish until a week after the hurricane, and the first FEMA relief team arrived 18 days after the hurricane. Parish leaders found, however, that private relief donations came in quickly and helped the parish take action in the absence of federal help. A sidebar to the article suggests five proposals to reform FEMA: involve the military in major catastrophes, strengthen ties to state and local disaster officials, end political appointments, separate FEMA from the DHS, and involve the private sector in new ways to help with disaster response.

Hoffman, Carl. "The Kindness of Strangers." *Popular Mechanics*, vol. 182, no. 12, December 2005, pp. 86–91. The author tells of his experiences and those of other volunteers who brought their own boats to New Orleans to help with the rescue. According to the author, ordinary citizens saved thousands of trapped residents.

Lawton, Kim A. "Responses to Hurricane Boost Hopes for Faith-Based Funding." *Christian Century*, vol. 123, no. 6, March 21, 2006, p. 14. Unlike the federal, state, and local governments, faith-based organizations have received praise for their response to Hurricane Katrina. Consequently, they may come to play larger roles in future disasters. As this article notes, however, many faith-based organizations are hesitant to accept government funds or become too closely involved with government response. They prefer to remain independent in their relief efforts.

Lipton, Eric. "$11 Million a Day Spent on Hotels for Storm Relief." *New York Times*, October 13, 2005, pp. A1, A20. As described in this news story, the cost of moving some 600,000 evacuees from shelters into hotels is enormous. In response to criticism of the expense, local officials say that FEMA was slow to deliver trailers and find apartments for victims.

MacDonald, Elizabeth, and Megha Bahree. "The Big Sleazy." *Forbes*, vol. 177, no. 12, June 5, 2006, pp. 40–42. This article describes the fraud and corruption in the relief and rebuilding efforts in New Orleans after Hurricane Katrina. The authors attribute the problems to the rush to begin reconstruction, which led to no-bid contracts and lack of oversight. They also describe the government investigations designed to find and end fraud in spending government funds.

Marek, Angie C. "A Crisis Agency in Crisis: FEMA's Woes." *U.S. News & World Report*, vol. 139, no. 10, September 19, 2005, pp. 36–38. This post-Katrina report on FEMA describes the problems in the agency that led to the failed disaster response. It suggests that the problems go well beyond the leadership of former director Michael Brown and concludes that addressing them will require major changes in the agency.

Mitchell, James K. "The Primacy of Partnership: Scoping a New National Disaster Recovery Policy." *Annals of the American Academy of Political and Social Science*, vol. 604, March 2006, pp. 228–255. The key to improving disaster response is to strengthen the partnership among all groups with a stake in the outcome, according to the author of this article. Too often, strategies instead involve giving one group or another more power. The author recommends policy changes to overcome this problem.

Nossiter, Adam. "Wearying Wait for Federal Aid in New Orleans." *New York Times*, December 3, 2005, pp. A1, A15. This report describes the frustration and anger felt by Hurricane Katrina victims in New Orleans over the delay in obtaining government aid. More than three months after the hurricane, many victims have found that getting trailers, loans, and other help involves excessive paperwork, slow action, and rules that few understand.

Peters, Charles. "Tilting at Windmills." *Washington Monthly*, vol. 37, no. 10/11, October/November 2005, pp. 8–17. In criticizing the federal government's response to Hurricane Katrina, the author offers an accurate and telling metaphor about the lack of leadership. He says that "the chain of command in Washington seemed to go in a circle." He also argues that experienced members of the Bush administration should have made sure things were handled better.

Ripley, Amanda, Karen Tumulty, and Mark Thompson. "Four Places Where the System Broke Down." *Time*, vol. 166, no. 12, September 19, 2005, pp. 34–41. Recognizing that the breakdown in response to Katrina involved all levels of government, this article describes the failures of each of the major leaders: New Orleans mayor Ray Nagin, Louisiana governor Kathleen Blanco, FEMA Director Michael Brown, and DHS Secretary Michael Chertoff.

Roberts, Patrick S. "FEMA after Katrina." *Policy Review*, no. 137, June/July 2006, pp. 15–33. The author argues that FEMA is too small in size to take on the many tasks it is assigned. To repeat its 1990s success, FEMA should concentrate its resources on natural disasters and delegate more authority to states and localities. He believes that decentralization is the best strategy to deal with the increasingly diverse and complex set of disasters the nation faces.

Song, John. "Dome away from Home: Astrodome, Emergency Shelter for Hurricane Katrina Victims." *Texas Monthly*, vol. 33, no. 11, November 2005, pp. 154–159, 261–266, 268. After the flooding of New Orleans, "the Astrodome in Houston became the biggest shelter ever organized by the American Red Cross—a temporary home to 17,500 people." The article describes the experiences of those who stayed in the Astrodome. Help and provisions from the Red Cross; FEMA; state, county, and local officials; area churches; and concerned citizens of Houston made conditions in the Astrodome vastly better than those in the New Orleans Superdome.

Starks, Tim. "Brown Explains FEMA's Flaws." *CQ Weekly*, vol. 63, no. 38, October 3, 2005, p. 2661. This article summarizes the testimony before Congress of Michael Brown, the former director of FEMA, about the response to Katrina and the criticism and pointed questions of the legislators during the testimony. Legislators greeted with skepticism and hostility Brown's claim that he was not at fault for the slow response but also agreed that Brown gave helpful insight into the source of the problem.

———. "Katrina Panel Indicts Response." *CQ Weekly*, vol. 64, no. 8, February 20, 2006, pp. 488–489. This article summarizes the conclusions of the report from the House Select Panel on Hurricane Katrina and the reaction of others in Congress to the report. According to the article, the report has triggered "partisan bickering that could hinder cooperation on major issues in 2006." Although the bickering did not last, it illustrates the intensity of political debates about Katrina and disaster policy.

Steinhauer, Jennifer, and Eric Lipton. "FEMA, Slow to the Rescue, Now Stumbles in Aid Effort." *New York Times*, September 17, 2005, pp. A1, A13. Following the late arrival of federal workers in New Orleans after the hurricane, lack of coordination in relief efforts slowed getting assistance to victims. This story describes how entrenched bureaucracies made it hard to set up help centers and get food, shelter, and money to victims.

Strom, Stephanie. "Red Cross Sifting Internal Charges over Katrina Aid." *New York Times*, March 24, 2006, pp. A1, A14. The Red Cross faced not only criticism for its slow response after Hurricane Katrina but also claims that its volunteers misused millions in cash and supplies set aside for Katrina victims. This article notes that investigators have filed no criminal charges. Even so, the allegations of fraud indicate problems within the organization.

Taylor, Stuart, Jr. "Catastrophe Management: Interview with M. Chertoff." *Atlantic Monthly*, vol. 298, no. 2, September 2006, pp. 42, 44. In this interview, the DHS secretary discusses the mishandled response to Hurricane Katrina and defends the performance of his department. He denies that moving FEMA to the DHS harmed disaster response. He does admit, however, that Katrina provided lessons for how to react better to both terrorist and natural disasters.

Thomas, Evan. "What the Hell Is Going On?" *Newsweek*, vol. 146, no. 26/vo. 147, no. 1, December 26, 2005/January 2, 2006, pp. 54–55. The author identifies the problems at FEMA and the DHS that led to the failed response to Hurricane Katrina. These problems include a focus at the DHS on bioterrorism, lack of preparation for a catastrophe the size of Katrina, bureaucratic infighting between FEMA and the DHS, and tensions between state and federal officials.

Walker, Jesse, Dave Kopel, Kerry Howley, Ronald Bailey, Jeff A. Taylor, and Jacob Sullum. "After the Storm: Hurricane Katrina and the Failure of Public Policy." *Reason*, vol. 37, no. 7, December 2005, pp. 26–35. Also available online. URL: http://www.reason.com/0512/fe.jw.after.shtml. Posted in December 2005. Pieces by each of the authors present viewpoints from a libertarian philosophy of limited government and free markets. The authors blame the failed response on the excessive reliance of the public on big government and criticize those who demand still more government to fix the failure. The authors thus present an intriguing but minority perspective on disaster policy.

Walters, Jonathan, and Donald Kettl. "The Katrina Breakdown." *Governing*, vol. 19, no. 3, December 2005, pp. 20–22, 24–25. Concentrating on problems of communication between federal, state, and local governments, this article argues that these problems must be corrected to produce effective disaster response. A start toward this goal would come from more clearly defining the roles of each level of government.

"When Government Fails." *Economist*, vol. 376, September 10, 2005, pp. 26–28. This article considers several explanations offered soon after Katrina for the slow response and government bumbling: war in Iraq, lack of concern with the natural environment, and racism and discrimination in dealing with the poor and minorities.

Wilkinson, Peter. "Welcome to Nowhere: Pop. 1,062." *Rolling Stone*, no. 987, November 17, 2005, pp. 58–62, 64. "FEMAville" refers in this article to a makeshift mobile-home park in Punta Gorda, Florida, that still houses victims 13 months after Hurricane Charley. The author notes that the size of this trailer park will likely be surpassed as the 200,000-plus people displaced by Hurricane Katrina start to move into a series of FEMA trailer parks across Louisiana and Mississippi. He believes that these makeshift towns will have "no essential services, high crime, isolation from even their nearest neighbors, and a pervasive air of despair due to the difficulty of locating permanent housing."

Wise, Charles R. "Organizing for Homeland Security after Katrina: Is Adaptive Management What's Missing?" *Public Administration Review*, vol. 66, no. 3, May/June 2006, pp. 302–318. After examining organizational changes in disaster response brought about by the creation of the

DHS, the author makes recommendations for changes. A new organizational strategy based on the idea of adaptive management would deal with several of the problems that became apparent in the response to Hurricane Katrina. The article defines and illustrates adaptive management in the area of disaster response.

WEB DOCUMENTS

"Hurricane Katrina Advisory Archive." National Weather Service, National Hurricane Center, Tropical Prediction Center. Available online. URL: http://www.nhc.noaa.gov/archive/2005/KATRINA.shtml. Updated on August 30, 2005. Readers can see the advisories issues by the National Weather Service for Katrina. The advisories began with a storm warning for the Bahamas nearly a week before Katrina made landfall near New Orleans. They progressed to a hurricane warning the day before landfall, when advisories said that preparations to protect life and property should be rushed to completion.

"Hurricane Katrina Disaster." Jurist Legal News and Research. Available online. URL: http://jurist.law.pitt.edu/currentawareness/katrinadisaster. php. Downloaded in July 2007. Legal-related stories about Hurricane Katrina on this web page cover criminal behaviors after the storm, court decisions involving payment of insurance, and indictments of nursing-home owners for deaths of residents during the storm. The web page also includes links to organizations, such as the U.S. Department of Justice, the University of California at Berkeley, and the American Bar Association, that give legal assistance to disaster victims.

"Hurricane Katrina Disaster Shows the Failure of the Profit System." World Socialist Web Site. Available online. URL: http://www.wsws.org/ articles/2005/sep2005/stat-s06.shtml. Posted on September 6, 2006. For a radical perspective on the failed response to Hurricane Katrina, see this web page from an international socialist organization. It blames the disaster in New Orleans not on failed levees or incompetence of officials but on capitalism. It says that the real cause comes from poverty among millions of citizens and inequitable distribution of income in the country.

"Hurricane Katrina Document Analysis: The E-mails of Michael Brown." Staff Report for Representative Charles Melacon, CNN. Available online. URL: http://i.a.cnn.net/cnn/2005/images/11/03/brown.emails.analysis.pdf. Posted on November 2, 2005. The analysis done of e-mails sent by FEMA Director Michael Brown during the period from shortly before to soon after Hurricane Katrina reveals a failure to make decisions, misinformation about the break in the levees, and concern about appearance and reputation. The report suggests that Brown failed to provide effective leadership during the Katrina response.

"Hurricane Katrina Information." FEMA. Available online. URL: http://www.fema.gov/hazard/hurricane/2005katrina/index.shtm. Downloaded in July 2007. This web page contains the disaster declarations made by President Bush for Florida, Alabama, Mississippi, and Louisiana and lists the assistance given by FEMA to the hurricane victims. For example, the figures show FEMA paid $15.4 billion in flood insurance claims, which averages to $99,721 per paid claim. Payments for individual and public assistance are lower but still substantial.

"Hurricane Katrina Mississippi Recovery Update: Week 57." FEMA. Available online. URL: http://www.fema.gov/news/newsrelease.fema?id=30380. Posted on September 29, 2006. The Katrina response and recovery has gone better in Mississippi than in New Orleans. As a result, the Mississippi success gets less attention than the New Orleans failure. This press release from FEMA states that the agency has paid or agreed to pay $9.1 billion for disaster assistance to the state. It further lists the payments made by individual programs for public buildings, individual assistance, and small businesses.

"Hurricane Katrina: One Year Later." FEMA. Available online. URL: http://www.fema.gov/hazard/hurricane/2005katrina/anniversary.shtm. Updated on August 30, 2006. This FEMA web page offers much information on the damage caused by Katrina and on the help the agency has provided. Links on the page give information on recovery efforts in Alabama, Mississippi, and Louisiana; frequently cited statistics; lessons learned from Katrina; and preparations for the 2006 hurricane season. Although FEMA presents a more flattering picture of its efforts than others would, the facts listed on the web page prove helpful.

"Hurricane Katrina Timeline." The Brookings Institution. Available online. URL: http://www.brookings.edu/fp/projects/homeland/katrinatimeline.pdf. Downloaded in September 2006. Many web pages have timelines for Hurricane Katrina, but this one from a Washington think tank is one of the most detailed and precise. It lists events and, when possible, the time of day the events occurred.

"Hurricane Katrina: What the Government Is Doing." Department of Homeland Security, Emergencies and Disasters. Available online. URL: http://www.dhs.gov/xprepresp/programs/gc_1157649340100.shtm. Downloaded in July 2007. The list of actions taken by the federal government after Katrina is a long one. This web page summarizes the contributions made by the DHS and FEMA in meeting long-term housing needs, restoring energy and water, stimulating business, developing the workforce, paying out insurance, removing debris, and rebuilding roads, public buildings, and ports. The efforts appear impressive but must be balanced by stories from victims that the government has been slow to help and by the slow progress in rebuilding in New Orleans.

"Hurricane Pam Exercise Concludes." FEMA. Available online. URL: http://www.fema.gov/news/newsrelease.fema?id=13051. Posted on July 23, 2004. This press release describes a simulation exercise done long before Katrina to develop a response to a major hurricane hitting New Orleans. The release emphasizes the progress made in preparing for such an event and demonstrates that officials knew of the damage a hurricane could do to the city. However, the exercise failed to address a number of problems involving evacuation, medical care, and communication that would develop when the real thing occurred. Officials quoted in the press release promise that planning for the response would continue, but they obviously did not do enough.

"Hurricane Recovery." FirstGov.gov. Available online. URL: http://www.firstgov.gov/Citizen/Topics/PublicSafety/Hurricane_Katrina_Recovery.shtml. Downloaded in July 2007. This resource for victims of Katrina and other hurricanes has links on how to find missing family members and children, get government help, and locate emergency shelter and housing. It also gives tips on how to prevent injury and illness during a hurricane, keep food and water safe, and find mental health resources. Like several other web pages from FirstGov.gov, this one comes from an effort of the U.S. government to make its information available to the public via the Internet.

"Hurricane Rita One Year Later—From Disaster to Recovery—by the Numbers." FEMA. Available online. URL: http://www.fema.gov/news/newsrelease.fema?id=29987. Posted on September 16, 2006. Hurricane Rita damaged parts of Louisiana but did not cause the severe flooding that Hurricane Katrina did. Nonetheless, the federal government devoted considerable resources to the Rita response and recovery. To back up that point, this press release lists statistics on the disaster and response. The smallest number, 23, refers to the parishes in Louisiana that were designated as disaster areas; the largest number, $431 million, refers to the amount of loans approved by the Small Business Administration for homeowners and renters suffering financial damage from Rita.

"Katrina Photos." WWLTV.com. Available online. URL: http://www.wwltv.com/Katrina/index.html. Downloaded in July 2007. Most Americans saw pictures of the devastation Katrina caused New Orleans, but the pictures on this web page are reminders of the damage.

"New Bush-Clinton Katrina Fund Grants Highlight Ongoing Recovery Effort." Bush-Clinton Katrina Fund. Available online. URL: http://www.bushclintonkatrinafund.org. Downloaded in September 2006. Former presidents George H. W. Bush and Bill Clinton led an effort to collect donations for relief and recovery from Hurricane Katrina. This web page describes how the fund has supported faith-based organizations, rehabilitated housing, and contributed to higher education.

"New Orleans: Survivor Stories." City Pages. Available online. URL: http://citypages.com/databank/26/1294/article13694.asp. Posted on September 20, 2005. Some dozens of stories on this page express the fear, suffering, and effort to survive that followed Hurricane Katrina. For example, Denise Moore tells of death and gunfire at the New Orleans convention center, Katy Reckdahl tells of going into labor soon before the hurricane and enduring a hospital stay without electricity and water, and Sidney Smith tells of how floodwaters rose to five feet in his house.

"Prepare Now for the 2006 Hurricane Season." Katrina Recovery. Available online. URL: http://www.katrinarecovery.disasterhelp.gov. Downloaded in July 2007. The victims of Hurricane Katrina who remain in the Gulf Coast area are vulnerable to another hurricane. This government web page gives advice on how to prepare for one and offers information for Katrina victims on how to apply for disaster assistance.

"Race an Issue in Katrina Response." CBS News. Available online. URL: http://www.cbsnews.com/stories/2005/09/03/katrina/main814623.shtml. Posted on September 3, 2005. This story describes concerns of the Black Congressional Caucus that the response to Katrina was affected by racism, but it also reports denials from the administration.

Reynolds, Paul. "Multiple Failures Caused Relief Crisis." BBC News. Available online. URL: http://news.bbc.co.uk/2/hi/americas/4216508.stm. Updated on September 7, 2005. This analysis nicely summarizes the major causes of the failed response to Katrina: poor planning, inadequate evacuation, slow action in the DHS, and delayed recognition of the seriousness of the disaster by the president. Perhaps the most serious failure identified by the article came from the gamble that the New Orleans levees could withstand a major hurricane.

Smith, Martin. "The Storm." Frontline, PBS Online. Available online. URL: http://www.pbs.org/wgbh/pages/frontline/storm. Downloaded in July 2007. Excellent reporting and careful analysis from this PBS television series make this web page one of the best on Hurricane Katrina. Along with a timeline, a history of FEMA, and an analysis of the breakdown in communication, the web page contains interviews with nearly all the major participants. Mayor Ray Nagin, Governor Kathleen Blanco, former FEMA Director Michael Brown, former DHS Secretary Tom Ridge, FEMA workers, and others answer questions on the Katrina response. Smith, the producer of the show and web page, aims to answer the question "What has America learned from the failures of preparedness, communication, and leadership?"

"A Timeline of Government Response to Hurricane Katrina." A USC An-
nenberg Online Journalism Review. Available online. URL: http://www.
ojr.org/ojr/wiki/Katrina_Timeline. Downloaded in July 2007. This timeline focuses on events involving government response rather than the
hurricane itself. It lists public statements made by officials about the response and provides links to sources of the quotes. Although based on
contributions of readers of the Online Journalism Review, the page gives
sources to ensure accuracy.

"A Year of Healing: A Red Cross Report on Katrina, Rita, and Wilma."
American Red Cross. Available online. URL: http://www.redcross.org/
images/pdfs/Katrina_OneYearReport.pdf. Downloaded in July 2007. According to the statistics presented in this report, the American Red Cross
has collected more than $2.1 billion for relief from the harm of these
three hurricanes. The funds have been spent or set aside for emergency
assistance ($1.5 billion), food and shelter ($229 million), physical and
mental services ($4 million), hurricane recovery ($198 million), fund-raising and administration ($70 million), and other forms of aid. Along with
the statistics, the report contains stories on volunteers who helped the
Red Cross and victims who received help.

FEMA AND FEDERAL
DISASTER POLICY

BOOKS

*21st Century Complete Guide to FEMA—Federal Emergency Management
Agency—Comprehensive Coverage of Natural Hazards, Floods, Storms, Earthquakes, Nuclear, Incidents, Hazardous Materials.* Washington, D.C.: Progressive Management, 2005. This electronic book on DVD-ROM contains an
enormous amount of material, 62,000 pages in total. The government
documents in the collection are available elsewhere, but having them in
one place makes it easy to sort through all the information. The documents include descriptions of programs to protect the public from and
respond to dozens of different hazards, materials from the Emergency
Management Institute for independent study courses, and training manuals on special events, nuclear hazards, and hazardous material.

*21st Century Emergencies and Disasters: Department of Homeland Security Na-
tional Response Plan and FEMA Training Course Manuals Collection on Disaster Management, Terrorism Response.* Washington, D.C.: Progressive
Management, 2005. Like other compilations of documents from the pub-
lisher, this electronic book on CD-ROM puts information together in
one source that could be obtained elsewhere. The FEMA course materi-

als in this collection overlap with other similar collections, but the documents from the DHS generally do not.

Alexander, David. *Principles of Emergency Planning and Management.* New York: Oxford University Press, 2002. This book by a professor of geography at the University of Massachusetts, Amherst, is more advanced in its approach and methods than other books on the topic (such as the one by Haddow and Bullock below). Its attention to mathematical models and sophisticated mapping techniques will most interest advanced undergraduates, graduate students, and academicians who study emergency planning. That said, the book contains a wealth of information and detail on developing and using emergency plans.

Bea, Keith, ed. *Federal Disaster Policies after Terrorists Strike: Issues and Options.* Hauppauge, N.Y.: Nova Publishers, 2003. Some chapters in this volume summarize the federal policies that would be followed in the event of another terrorist attack. Others consider whether the policies and response actions need to be changed and suggest policies that may improve the response. Because Hurricane Katrina has changed the issues that confront policymakers today, this book proves more useful in understanding policies for terrorist disasters than for natural disasters.

Binns, Tristan Boyer. *FEMA: Federal Emergency Management Agency.* Chicago: Heinemann Library, 2003. One of a series of books for children ages 8–10 on government agencies, this 48-page book gives a short introduction to FEMA. It offers an inside look at FEMA by following its workers as they prepare for a hurricane, respond to an earthquake, and offer advice to families on protecting themselves from fire. The stories make FEMA's duties more concrete than the abstract discussion of FEMA contained in other sources.

Bullock, Jane A., George D. Haddow, Damon Cappola, Erdem Ergin, Lissa Westerman, and Sarp Yeletaysi. *Introduction to Homeland Security. Second Edition.* Burlington, Mass.: Elsevier Butterworth-Heinemann, 2006. Given the need for secrecy in fighting terrorism, information on the DHS and federal government security efforts can be hard to obtain. This book provides an overview of the agency and homeland security efforts. It includes chapters on terrorist-related hazards, mitigation and preparation, and response and recovery.

Burns, Linda, ed. *FEMA Federal Emergency Management Agency: An Organization in the Crosshairs.* Hauppauge, N.Y.: Nova Publishers, 2006. According to a publicity blurb, "This book summarizes principal federal disaster assistance programs, specifically FEMA, for possible use by Members of Congress and staff in helping address the needs of constituents." The chapters cover the historical development of FEMA and the DHS, FEMA's hazard map modernization initiative, federal disaster recovery programs, and the Stafford Act. Researchers as well as legislators may benefit from the summary and overview of a complex federal system.

Cahill, Kevin M., ed. *Emergency Relief Operations.* New York: Fordham University Press, 2003. Each chapter in this volume addresses a specific kind of problem faced by humanitarian organizations responding to emergencies and disasters. The problems may be political, medical, diplomatic, or organizational, and the book presents case studies and recommendations for dealing with each kind of problem. The book is designed for "students, teachers, practitioners, policy-makers, journalists, and other professionals."

Deal, Tim, Michael de Bettercourt, Vickie Huyck, Gary Merrick, and Chuck Mills. *Beyond Initial Response: Using the National Incident Management System's Incident Command System.* Bloomington, Ind.: AuthorHouse, 2006. This book aims to help train emergency responders in the National Incident Management System and prepare them to take command after an incident. For example, it describes the planning process, duties of the incident commander, makeup of the unified command, and roles of the command staff. The incident command system is complex, and this book can help those wanting to know more about how it works.

Emergency Management Institute. *A Citizen's Guide to Disaster Assistance.* Washington, D.C.: Department of Homeland Security, FEMA, 2003. Also available online. URL: http://purl.access.gpo.gov/GPO/LPS60473. Downloaded in July 2007. This volume published by FEMA takes the form of an independent study course. The five sections cover the basics of disaster assistance, local community response to disasters, the federal government role in disaster assistance, federal disaster assistance in action, and citizen roles in disaster preparedness. Each section ends with a short multiple-choice test to check the reader's understanding of the material. This clearly written book helps cut through the complexity of government programs to clearly explain the organization of disaster assistance.

Erikson, Paul A. *Emergency Response Planning for Corporate and Municipal Managers. Second Edition.* Amsterdam: Elsevier, 2006. Effective disaster response requires effective planning. This book covers the fundamental principles of emergency planning and developing a comprehensive response plan. The book considers a variety of disasters that leaders may face—hurricanes, earthquakes, terrorist attacks, chemical spills—and how the planning process can be adapted for the particular risks of a community or business. However, key goals of planning for all disasters include involving the public and forming strong partnerships across all levels of government.

Faggiano, Vincent F., and Thomas T. Gillespie. *Critical Incident Management: An On Scene Guide for Law Enforcement Supervisors.* Tulsa, Okla.: K&M Publishers, 2004. As first responders, law enforcement officials have central duties in disaster response. To help them in these duties, this book suggests strategies for a successful response. For example, it explains the background of the Incident Command System and the National Incident Management System. Unlike many guides, however, this one focuses on what happens at the scene of an emergency rather than on abstract principles.

FEMA. *Disaster Assistance: A Guide to Recovery Programs.* Washington, D.C.: FEMA, 2005. This volume lists nearly 100 disaster assistance programs for work, housing, health, transportation, community development, conservation, and other needs. It is intended as a resource for individuals, businesses, and public organizations looking for help after a disaster. Most of those wanting aid will qualify for only a few of the programs, but having them listed in one place can help in identifying those of most value. For researchers, the volume illustrates the variety of programs the federal government offers for disaster assistance and the complexity of the system.

Godschalk, David, Timothy Beatley, Philip Berke, and David Brower. *Natural Hazard Mitigation: Recasting Disaster Policy and Planning.* Washington, D.C.: Island Press, 1999. This book begins with a key point: Although natural hazards cannot be prevented, humans can do much to minimize their impact. Drawing out this point, the book describes and evaluates disaster programs in the United States in the 1990s and suggests policy changes to improve mitigation. Although dated, it gives a more detailed description of the Robert T. Stafford Disaster Relief and Emergency Assistance Act and its implementation than most other sources.

Haddow, George D., and Jane A. Bullock. *Introduction to Emergency Management.* Boston: Butterworth-Heinemann, 2003. The authors, former high-level FEMA officials, wrote this book for those wanting a career in emergency management. The book has chapters on the four components of the disaster cycle—mitigation, response, recovery, and preparedness—and on special topics of communication, terrorism, and international response. It complements the detailed description of programs and policies with many case studies of disasters and their management.

Miskel, James F. *U.S. Disaster Policy and Management in an Era of Homeland Security: What Works, What Doesn't.* Westport, Conn.: Praeger, 2006. A former deputy assistant associate director of FEMA, Miskel describes the problems in response that occurred after hurricanes such as Andrew, Hugo, and Katrina, and he offers recommendations for improving the disaster system. He also links the discussion to the 9/11 attacks and the need to respond to terrorist events as well as natural disasters.

Natural Hazards Center. *Holistic Disaster Recovery: Ideas for Building Local Sustainability after a Natural Disaster.* Boulder, Colo.: Natural Hazards

Center, 2005. This book links the environmental movement to disaster preparedness and recovery. Holistic disaster recovery refers to use of sustainability principles such as creating consensus for recovery decisions, promoting equity, and protecting environmental quality. Each chapter discusses one sustainability principle and how communities can apply the principle to disaster recovery. The book is written for local government officials, emergency professionals, disaster recovery experts, and others who help a community during disaster recovery.

Sylves, Richard T., and William L. Waugh, eds. *Disaster Management in the U.S. and Canada: The Politics, Policymaking, Administration and Analysis of Emergency Management.* Springfield, Ill.: Charles C. Thomas, 1996. This edited volume is most useful for the case studies it presents of the responses to the Great Midwest Flood of 1993 and Hurricane Andrew in 1992. It also contrasts U.S. disaster policy with that of Canada.

U.S. House of Representatives. *Funding for First Responders.* Hearing before the Committee on Homeland Security, House of Representatives, One Hundred Eighth Congress, First Session, October 16, 2001. Washington, D.C.: U.S. Government Printing Office, 2001. The help provided by first responders after the 9/11 terrorist attacks demonstrated their importance more generally to disaster response. Congress reacted with more funding for state and local first responders—police officers, firefighters, emergency medical technologists. This hearing considers how federal funding can help first responders do still more to protect the nation from terrorist threats and natural hazards.

———. *The National Preparedness System: What Are We Preparing For?* Hearing before the Subcommittee on Economic Development, Public Buildings and Emergency Management of the Committee on Transportation and Infrastructure, House of Representatives, One Hundred Ninth Congress, First Session, April 14, 2005. Washington, D.C.: U.S. Government Printing Office, 2005. After 9/11, the George W. Bush administration emphasized the importance of preventing and responding to terrorist attacks by, among other things, transferring FEMA to the DHS. This led to a hearing on how to integrate preparation for terrorist disasters with preparation for natural disasters. The views of witnesses testifying about the need to give more attention to natural disasters were confirmed four to five months later when Hurricane Katrina struck. The document highlights the tension between the goals of terrorist and natural disaster response.

U.S. Senate. *FEMA's Response to the 2004 Florida Hurricanes.* Hearing before the Committee on Homeland Security and Governmental Affairs, United States Senate, One Hundred Ninth Congress, First Session, May 18, 2005. Washington, D.C.: U.S. Government Printing Office, 2006. Concerns about problems of disaster response at FEMA predate Katrina. This hearing examines FEMA assistance given to those affected by four Florida hurricanes in 2004. The concerns do not include slowness in response but instead relate to widespread fraud in receipt of disaster assistance. The hearing describes the wasted funds spent by FEMA and the lack of controls to prevent fraud. Testimony from then-director Michael Brown defends FEMA's performance, but the same problems would emerge several months later after Katrina.

————. *Response of the Technology Sector in Times of Crisis.* Hearing before the Subcommittee on Science, Technology, and Space of the Committee on Commerce, Science, and Transportation, United States Senate, One Hundred Seventh Congress, First Session, December 5, 2001. Washington, D.C.: U.S. Government Printing Office, 2001. The 9/11 attacks and the new role of intelligence in preventing terrorism has made technology increasingly important in disaster prevention and response. Problems of communication after the explosion at the World Trade Center hampered the response and the work of emergency workers. Most of those testifying at these hearings come from the private sector and describe the technology their companies developed to help in disaster response. Also, then-director Joseph Allbaugh describes FEMA's plans to use new technology in disaster response.

ARTICLES

"After Hurricane Rita: Chaos on the Coast and on the Hill." *Economist,* vol. 377, October 1, 2005, p. 32. This story on the response to Hurricane Rita, which followed soon after the fiasco of Hurricane Katrina, finds that officials at every level were better prepared. Some problems did occur, however. For example, when gas stations in the Houston, Texas, area ran out of gas, many evacuating the city had to abandon their cars. Still, leaders learned from the problems of Katrina.

Borrus, Amy. "Up to His Neck in the Risk Pool." *Business Week,* no. 3936, June 6, 2005, pp. 109–111. According to a Washington think tank, the Center on Federal Financial Institutions, Congress has set up insurance programs that could amount to more than $6 trillion in potential claims. Massive claims would result from the simultaneous occurrence of several disasters involving natural hazards, bank failures, and nuclear reactor meltdowns. This article argues that, even if unlikely to pay out that much money at once, Congress should understand the risks they take on with federal insurance.

Briechle, Kendra. "Heavy Hurricane Season Expected: Time to Review Response and Recovery Plans." *Public Management,* vol. 82, no. 8, August 2000, pp. 24–25. Noting that communities tend to underestimate their vulnerability to natural hazards, particularly hurricanes, this article reminds leaders to review their response plans. It also summarizes FEMA's recommendations for how communities should prepare for a natural disaster.

Chertoff, Michael. "Strengthening FEMA to Maximize Mission Performance." *Vital Speeches of the Day*, vol. 72, no. 10, March 1, 2006, pp. 290–296. The DHS secretary lays out his post-Katrina views on the potential effectiveness of FEMA in responding to disasters. He emphasizes the importance of preparedness and partnerships with state and local officials in responding to both natural disasters and terrorism.

Congressional Research Service. "Federal Disaster Programs." *Congressional Digest*, vol. 84, no. 9, November 2005, pp. 260–262. In this article, the Congressional Research Service describes disaster assistance programs for individuals and families; small businesses; and state, local, and tribal governments. The shortness of the article makes it easy to see the outlines of disaster assistance without getting overwhelmed by details.

Franklin, Daniel. "The FEMA Phoenix." *Washington Monthly*, vol. 27, July/August 1995, pp. 38–42. This article describes the transformation of FEMA from one of the worst federal agencies into one of the best and suggests the transformation be used as a blueprint for improving government. It begins with the failures of the agency up to 1992 and follows with the improvements made after 1992 by Director James Witt. From a perspective of a decade later, it appears that the problems of FEMA have returned and the model of transformation in 1992 could profitably be adapted today.

Garrett, Thomas A., and Russell S. Sobel. "The Political Economy of FEMA Disaster Payments." *Economic Inquiry*, vol. 41, no. 3, July 2003, pp. 496–509. Most readers may not want to wade through the statistical complexities of this article, but the conclusions are disconcerting. States important politically to the president and having representatives on FEMA congressional oversight committees receive more presidential disaster declarations and more disaster benefits. The authors conclude that disaster relief is motivated more by politics than need.

Gentile, Annie. "The Federal Emergency Management Agency (FEMA) Is Implementing the Hazard Mitigation Planning Sections of the Disaster Mitigation Act of 2000." *American City and County*, vol. 120, no. 3, March 2005, pp. 28–30, 32. This article discusses how FEMA has implemented the Disaster Mitigation Act of 2000. The law requires state, local, and tribal governments to submit hazard mitigation plans to FEMA if they want to remain eligible for grant funds. The legislators and FEMA hope to reduce the costs of disaster response through mitigation.

Goodnough, Abby. "After 4 Hurricanes, Trailers and Homelessness." *New York Times*, November 25, 2004, pp. A1, A32. Before Katrina, FEMA and the state of Florida responded to a series of four hurricanes in 2004. This article finds that FEMA Director Michael Brown and Florida governor Jeb Bush did not meet their goal to quickly provide trailers for victims of the hurricanes. As in New Orleans, response to the massive damage of the Florida hurricanes moved slowly.

Harrington, Scott E. "Rethinking Disaster Policy." *Regulation*, vol. 23, no. 1, 2000, pp. 40–46. Also available online. URL: http://www.cato.org/pubs/regulation/regv23n1/harrington.pdf. Downloaded in September 2006. In reviewing federal disaster insurance programs, the author concludes that federal assistance reduces the willingness of the public to purchase insurance to protect themselves. He concludes that dealing with disaster risk in this way creates unnecessary expense and inefficiency and calls for greater reliance on private insurance.

"History of Federal Disaster Mitigation." *Congressional Digest*, vol. 84, no. 9, November 2005, pp. 258, 288. This review of disaster response efforts since 1803 ends with the shift of FEMA to the DHS. The article is part of a special issue on disaster response and Hurricane Katrina.

Hood, John. "Who Insures against Floods, and Why." *Consumers' Research Magazine*, vol. 83, no. 10, October 2000, pp. 16–20. This article describes the failures of the National Flood Insurance Program administered by FEMA. It cites a statistic that only one-quarter to one-third of homes and businesses in areas prone to floods purchase the insurance. The author recommends that the government try new strategies to get Americans the flood protection they need.

Hsu, Spencer S. "Caution Flag for Evacuation Plans: Road-User Group Gives Failing Grades to Majority of Urban Areas." *Washington Post*, October 26, 2006, p. A23. After problems evacuating New Orleans before Hurricane Katrina, the federal government has recently given funds to the DHS to improve evacuation plans for major cities. In an evaluation of the ability of major metropolitan areas to evacuate residents, a trade association for highway builders, the American Highway Users Alliance, offers reasons for concern. This article summarizes the evaluation, noting that only Kansas City received a top grade and that San Francisco, Miami, New York, Chicago, and Los Angeles ranked lowest. The article also cites experts who say that few cities can or need to evacuate residents as New Orleans did. These experts believe funds should go for other purposes.

Johnson, Dan. "Disaster-Resistant Communities: Federal Emergency Management Agency's Project Impact Encourages Preparation for Natural Disasters." *Futurist*, vol. 33, no. 7, August/September 1999, p. 14. As described in this article, Project Impact partnered FEMA with 118 communities to make them more resistant to damage and to minimize the costs of disaster response.

Lawson, R. Scott. "FEMA-Based Modeling Program Helps Assess Threats Accurately." *Public Management*, vol. 86, no. 5, June 2004, pp. 39–40. As described in this article, FEMA aims to better use computer technology to prepare for and respond to disasters. Some computer programs help predict the location of the worst damage and others estimate the costs of the damage. As shown by Katrina, technology will not make up for poor leadership, but it can help in disaster response.

Lehrer, Eli. "The Homeland Security Bureaucracy." *Public Interest*, no. 156, Summer 2004, pp. 71–85. The author criticizes the DHS for building a large bureaucracy to protect the public from terrorist threats and natural disasters. He argues that the department should instead aim to be flexible, speedy, and focused.

Liddy, Edward M. "Curing Catastrophe Amnesia." *Vital Speeches of the Day*, vol. 72, no. 10, March 1, 2006, pp. 296–299. The chairman and CEO of the Allstate Corporation wants to make disaster preparedness a national priority. In this speech, he urges better disaster education for consumers and municipalities and more pre-funding for unpredictable, catastrophic events. If states build reserves or pools of capital and a federal pool in turn reinsures the state pools, it would fully protect citizens from a catastrophe.

McGray, Douglas. "After Shock: Disaster Preparation." *New Republic*, vol. 233, no. 13, September 26, 2005, pp. 19–21. A major earthquake in San Francisco is likely in the next years or decades. According to this article, first responders are well prepared for an earthquake, but other problems remain. Building on high-risk land will increase the damage of an earthquake, and poor neighborhoods will suffer disproportionately.

"Mitigation Emerges as Major Strategy for Reducing Losses Caused by Natural Disasters." *Science*, vol. 284, no. 5422, June 18, 1999, pp. 1,943–1,947. The United Nations declared the 1990s the International Decade for Natural Disaster Reduction. The United States has likewise emphasized the wisdom of preventing rather than responding to disaster damage. This article describes mitigation programs in FEMA and other federal government agencies.

Monastersky, Richard. "Natural-Disaster Policies Need Shaking Up." *Science News*, vol. 155, no. 22, May 29, 1999, p. 341. As summarized in this short article, a comprehensive five-year study by 132 academics and officials "reports that natural disasters between 1975 and 1994 resulted in the deaths of an estimated 24,000 people, injuries to four times that figure, and direct damage costs of $500 billion." According to the study, the increasing damage comes from locating people in areas of high risk and expecting technology to eliminate disasters. It calls instead for policies that will prevent or mitigate damage from disasters.

Preston, Meredith. "Rethinking Readiness: Changes in Disaster Plans and Relief Efforts Are Sure to Come." *American City and County*, vol. 120, no. 12, November 2005, p. 32. Governors, mayors, and county commissions, much like federal government leaders, have opinions on how best to reform FEMA. As described in this article, many state and local leaders want to take more responsibility for disaster response and give less responsibility to FEMA. Florida governor Jeb Bush has taken a lead role in calling for such changes.

Roberts, Patrick. "The Master of Disaster as Bureaucratic Entrepreneur." *PS, Political Science and Politics*, vol. 38, no. 2, April 2005, p. 331. This article describes the strategies used by former FEMA director James Witt to make FEMA a respected and popular agency within the federal government. It calls Witt a bureaucratic entrepreneur and highlights how bureaucratic entrepreneurs in other agencies can follow his lead. For example, improving relations with Congress and the public and giving priority to fewer tasks can help make government agencies more successful.

Solomon, John. "Flirting with Disaster." *Washington Monthly*, vol. 28, October 1996, pp. 9–11. The author criticizes disaster relief used as a political tool to favor the rich and populous states of California and Florida. He says that, in part because of its political goals, disaster relief has become an increasingly expensive and unnecessary part of the federal budget. Disaster spending may even lead some Americans to choose to live, underinsured, in hazardous areas because they expect the government to compensate them for damage from a disaster.

Starks, Tim. "House Panels Take Differing Approaches to 'Fixing' FEMA." *CQ Weekly*, vol. 64, no. 21, May 22, 2006, p. 1,412. This article describes two competing bills proposed by different house committees. One would turn FEMA into an independent cabinet-level agency; the other would keep FEMA in the DHS but allow it to report directly to the president during an emergency. President Bush opposes such changes in FEMA, which makes it unlikely that either bill will become law.

Stossel, John. "Ocean View, Thanks to You: National Flood Insurance." *Reader's Digest*, vol. 148, January 1996, pp. 181–182. According to this story by the host of the television show *20/20*, the National Flood Insurance Program commits the federal government to paying up to $350,000 to replace a property damaged by the ocean. The program originally aimed to balance the lure of government insurance for floods with stricter building regulations. In fact, the program led more people to build in flood zones. According to the article, "the government now guarantees property worth $300 billion in these areas."

Sylves, Richard, and William R. Cumming. "FEMA's Path to Homeland Security: 1979–2003." *Journal of Homeland Security and Emergency Man-*

agement, vol. 1, no. 2, 2004, article 11. This article in an electronic journal traces the actions of presidents, bureaucratic turf wars, and experiences with disasters that led FEMA to become part of homeland security.

WEB DOCUMENTS

"2006 Federal Disaster Declaration." FEMA. Available online. URL: http://www.fema.gov/news/disasters.fema. Downloaded in July 2007. Those learning about federal disaster policy may be surprised to find out how commonly the president declares a major disaster. This web page lists about 40 declarations made between January 1, 2006, and September 22, 2006—more than four a month on average. The list summarizes the cause of each disaster declaration (e.g., severe storms and flooding, severe winter storm, extreme wildfire threat) and names the counties falling under the declaration. The web page also lists emergency declaration and fire management assistance declarations. Examining the declarations illustrates the disasters with which federal, state, and local governments routinely deal.

"About CERT." Community Emergency Response Team. Available online. URL: https://www.citizencorps.gov/cert/about.shtm. Downloaded in July 2007. The CERT program aims to train community members so they can help first responders in the event of an emergency. Volunteers can take courses, start their own community response team, and help prepare their community for a disaster. This web page describes the CERT program and how to get involved.

"Animal Emergency Services." American Humane. Available online. URL: http://www.americanhumane.org/site/PageServer?pagename=pa_disaster_relief&JServSessionIdr007=l4xk7nxfw1.app20a. Downloaded in July 2007. This web page highlights the importance of planning for evacuation of animals before or during a disaster. It also describes its animal emergency services to help care for animals during disasters, unite them with their owners, and distribute pet food and supplies.

"Apply for Assistance." FEMA. Available online. URL: http://www.fema.gov/assistance/index.shtm. Downloaded in July 2007. Information on this web page explains who is eligible for assistance, what information needs to be provided to get assistance, and how applications can be completed and submitted. For those wanting to know more about the application process but not wanting to apply, the page shows what others must do. The process appears straightforward, but disaster victims sometimes complain about the difficulty of dealing with the bureaucracy.

Bea, Keith. "Disaster Evacuation and Displacement Policy: Issues for Congress." CRS Report for Congress. Available online. URL: http://

www.fas.org/sgp/crs/misc/RS22235.pdf. Posted on September 2, 2006. Hurricane Katrina created new interest in disaster policy in Congress. This briefing report describes current policies, the laws on which the policies are based, and some issues for Congress to address. The briefing may also interest researchers wanting to learn about the legal basis of federal disaster policy.

"Before and after Disasters: Federal Funding for Cultural Institutions." FEMA and Heritage Preservation, National Endowment for the Arts. Available online. URL: http://www.heritagepreservation.org/PDFS/ Disaster.pdf. Posted in September 2005. This 36-page document describes 15 federal loan and grant programs for libraries, museums, historic sites, and other cultural institutions damaged by disasters. The guide helps the institutions plan for and recover from damage.

"The Earthquake Preparedness Handbook." Los Angeles Fire Department. Available online. URL: http://www.lafd.org/eqindex.htm. Downloaded in July 2007. This web page offers extensive advice for those living in earthquake-prone areas of California. Sections cover planning for home and office, emergency supplies to have on hand, and securing heavy furnishings. The Los Angeles Fire Department urges all residents of the city to make earthquake preparedness a way of life.

"Emergency Managers: National Situation Update." FEMA. Available online. URL: http://www.fema.gov/emergency/reports/index.shtm. Downloaded in July 2007. Daily updates on this web page list the homeland security threat level, summarize the outlook for weather problems across the nation, and list disaster declarations. Although meant for emergency managers, the web page and its situation updates may interest others wanting to know about the daily disaster threats faced by the nation.

"Executive Order: Equal Protection of the Laws for Faith-Based and Community Organizations." The White House, President George Bush. Available online. URL: http://www.whitehouse.gov/news/releases/2002/ 12/20021212-6.html. Posted on December 12, 2002. This executive order led FEMA to broaden the eligibility for nonprofit organizations to obtain federal disaster assistance. Under the new rules, faith-based organizations receive treatment no different than other types of organizations. As a result, they can do more to help communities respond to disasters and can receive assistance when their property has been damaged by a disaster.

"Executive Order: Improving Disaster Assistance for Victims." The White House, President George W. Bush. Available online. URL: http://www. whitehouse.gov/news/releases/2006/08/20060829-9.html. Posted on August 29, 2006. Responding to complaints about the slow delivery of benefits to disaster victims, President Bush ordered several improvements in disaster assistance programs with this executive order. It requires federal agencies to give prompt and efficient access to disaster assistance and sets up a task force to improve coordination between agencies in delivering assistance.

"FEMA for Kids." FEMA. Available online. URL: http://www.fema.gov/kids. Downloaded in July 2007. This web page introduces children to FEMA, disasters, and preparedness. The introductory information it presents on these topics is clear, to the point, and surprisingly informative for adults.

"FEMA Independent Study Program." Emergency Management Institute. Available online. URL: http://training.fema.gov/EMIWeb/IS/crslist.asp. Downloaded in July 2007. The courses listed on this web page cover the topics and information that emergency personnel need to master. The material is broad, ranging from community hurricane preparedness to radiological response and the incident command system.

"FEMA Shakeup." Online NewsHour, PBS Online. Available online. URL: http://www.pbs.org/newshour/bb/fedagencies/july-dec05/fema_9-09. html. Posted on September 9, 2005. Following replacement of Michael Brown as the head of FEMA, the public television show *News Hour with Jim Lehrer* interviewed a reporter and two former homeland security employees to discuss FEMA, its organization, and the possible changes it faced. The interviews highlight problems such as the appointment of leaders without emergency experience and tensions within the DHS. This web page contains the transcript of the full interviews along with links to related stories and resources.

"Five Years Post 9/11, One Year Post Katrina: The State of America's Readiness: 183-City Survey." Unites States Conference of Mayors. Available online. URL: http://www.usmayors.org/uscm/news/press_releases/documents/disasterpreparednesssurvey_2006. pdf. Posted on July 26, 2006. This report presents statistics from a survey of city officials across the country (though without much comment or interpretation on the statistics). Most cities say they have improved their readiness for a disaster and remain confident of their ability to respond, even without help from FEMA.

"Get Disaster Information." FEMA. Available online. URL: http://www.fema.gov/hazard/index.shtm. Downloaded in July 2007. Designed for potential or actual victims of disasters, this web page is organized by type of disaster: chemical, dam failure, earthquake, fire or wildfire, flood, hazardous materials, heat, hurricane, landslide, nuclear plant emergency, terrorism, thunderstorm, tornado, tsunami, volcano, and winter storm. A click on any one of the topics tells how members of the public can protect themselves from the hazard. With other clicks, readers can find still more information on preparation, response, and recovery from a hazard.

Hogue, Henry B., and Keith Bea. "Federal Emergency Management and Homeland Security Organization: Historical Developments and Legislative Options." CRS Report for Congress. Available online. URL: http://www.mipt.org/GetDoc.asp?id=3052&type=d. Posted April 19, 2006. The background information on FEMA contained in this report is meant to inform Congress about options for changing the agency. Congress has introduced at least nine bills since Hurricane Katrina to reorganize emergency management functions within the DHS. The report's review of how FEMA developed into its current structure can help guide congressional decisions about the agency's future.

"Individuals and Households Fact Sheet." FEMA. Available online. URL: http://www.fema.gov/news/newsrelease.fema?id=5404. Posted on September 30, 2006. This web page outlines the various programs available to individuals and households harmed by a disaster. These programs grant funds for temporary living, repair of housing, replacement of severely damaged housing, and new housing construction. They also cover other needs such as clothing, furnishings, school supplies, cleaning equipment, transportation to work, medical care, and funeral costs.

"National Flood Insurance Program." Wood River Flood Protection. Available online. URL: http://www.woodriver.org/FloodInfo/Insurance/NatlFloodInsurancePgm.htm. Updated on September 16, 2006. The city of Wood River, Illinois, has prepared a thorough and clear summary of the National Flood Insurance Program. It explains how the program works, gives tips on how to cope with a flood, and encourages residents to join the program. Those wanting to know more about the program can also consult the links listed on this web page.

"National Incident Management System." FEMA. Available online. URL: http://www.fema.gov/emergency/nims/index.shtm. Downloaded in July 2007. The National Incident Management System was developed to allow responders from different cities, states, agencies, and levels of government to work together. It promises a unified approach to management of unexpected events. Although the system has not always lived up to its promises, it identifies the government's goals in disaster response. Of the topics covered on the page, the sections on basic principles and frequently asked questions will most aid those unfamiliar with the system.

"National Response Plan." Department of Homeland Security. Available online. URL: http://www.dhs.gov/xprepresp/committees/editorial_0566.shtm. Downloaded in July 2007. The National Response Plan, first released in 2004, "establishes a comprehensive, all-hazards approach to enhance the ability of the United States to manage domestic incidents." The full report can be downloaded from this page, along with a notice of changes and a quick reference guide. The plan did not work well during the response to Katrina but remains the guiding blueprint for response to a major disaster or incident of national significance.

"Principles for Legislation to Improve the Nation's Emergency Management System." National Emergency Management Association. Available online. URL: http://www.nemaweb.org/?1636. Posted in May 2006. This organization offers advice to Congress in considering changes in FEMA and federal emergency management. Although the association supported the move of FEMA to the DHS, it now expresses concern about the weakening of FEMA and the mixing of law enforcement functions with emergency management functions. The document on this web page offers recommendations to strengthen the federal role in emergency response.

"Reporting Disaster Response." Disaster News Network. Available online. URL: http://www.disasternews.net. Downloaded in July 2007. This news service funded by a nonprofit organization tells stories of disaster response and how the public can help survivors. The daily listing of disasters reveals how commonly disasters occur.

Weston, Liz Pulliam. "The Case for National Disaster Insurance." MSN Money. Available online. URL: http://articles.moneycentral.msn.com/Insurance/InsureYourHome/TheCaseForNationalDisasterInsurance.aspx?page=all. Downloaded in July 2007. In response to concerns that property owners do not have adequate coverage for disasters and that insurers do not have the resources to pay the enormous costs caused by many disasters, the author suggests creating a national disaster insurance program. The program would require all citizens to contribute to a pool, with those at highest risk contributing the most; the pool rather than private insurance companies would then pay out benefits. Such proposals have received little support but address a serious problem.

PERSONAL AND SOCIAL ASPECTS OF DISASTER RESPONSE

BOOKS

Auf der Heide, Erik. *Disaster Response: Principles of Preparation and Coordination.* St. Louis, Mo.: C.V. Mosby, 1989. Although dated, this early compilation of knowledge about disaster response still proves helpful. It clearly presents information on planning, the media, first responders, and a variety of other topics.

Benthall, Jonathan. *Disaster Relief and the Media.* London: I. B. Tauris, 1993. The author argues that the media has gained unprecedented power to shape the national and international response to disasters. Relief agencies can use images of suffering presented by the media to raise money but face problems when goals of the media differ from those of getting relief to the neediest. In discussing this dilemma, the study describes how the media, particularly television, portray disasters in the United Kingdom, Europe, and the United States.

Clarke, Lee. *Worst Cases: Terror and Catastrophe in the Popular Imagination.* Chicago: University of Chicago Press, 2006. This book differs from nearly all others on the social aspects of disaster. Rather than examining disasters that have occurred, Clarke asks "What is the worst that can happen?" He argues that thinking about worst cases offers insights into how society should prepare for and respond to disasters. For example, he argues that in preparing for low-probability but high-consequence events such as a terrorist attack, the federal government does too little to prepare for more common natural events that in combination have serious consequences.

Enarson, Elaine, and Betty Hearn Morrow, eds. *The Gendered Terrain of Disaster: Through Women's Eyes.* Westport, Conn.: Praeger, 1998. The articles in this volume challenge images of women as hapless victims of disasters and present case studies of the involvement of women in disaster response. They also describe how gender inequality makes women particularly vulnerable to disasters.

FEMA. *Are You Ready? An In-Depth Guide to Citizen Preparedness.* Washington, D.C.: FEMA Citizen Corps, 2004. Also available online. URL: http://purl.access.gpo.gov/GPO/LPS71068. Downloaded in July 2007. This guide written for the public uses the best available research and knowledge to help individuals and families prepare for a disaster. It encourages people to develop and practice emergency plans and to assemble disaster supplies. Sections of the book describe special needs for each of the major kinds of disasters—natural hazards, technological hazards, and terrorism—in language that is clear and easy to understand.

Fischer, Henry W., Jr. *Response to Disaster: Fact versus Fiction and Its Perpetuation.* Lanham: University Press of New York, 1998. This book by a sociologist disputes claims that disasters lead to widespread panic, selfishness, looting, and psychological shock. It compiles and reviews the evidence that people in fact respond to disasters with altruism, rationality, and legal behavior. Despite the evidence, the media continues to perpetuate myths about disaster behavior. With clear writing and numerous examples, the book makes a good case for its arguments.

Hogan, David E., and Jonathan L Burstein, eds. *Disaster Medicine.* Philadelphia: Lippincott Williams and Wilkins, 2002. This comprehensive volume written by emergency physicians with first-hand disaster experience is best suited for medical personnel. Others can benefit from discussions of the defining characteristics of a disaster, the roles of hospitals and emergency medical services agencies, and the integration of these resources into a coordinated city response.

Hooke, William, and Paul G. Rogers, ed. *Public Health Risks of Disasters: Communication, Infrastructure, and Preparedness.* Washington, D.C.: National Academies Press, 2005. Experts in disaster research and environmental health met at a workshop to consider the health risks of disasters and find common ground in their approaches to the risks. The articles in the volume come from that workshop and suggest ways to increase collaboration and communication among scholars interested in the diverse aspects of disaster preparedness and response.

Mileti, Dennis. *Disasters by Design: A Reassessment of Natural Hazards in the United States.* Washington, D.C.: National Academies Press, 1999. In criticizing the social practices that increase the risk of death and damage from natural hazards—that in a sense are designed to create disasters—this book proposes a new approach. A sustainable approach to disaster mitigation aims to protect the environment and reduce social inequality rather than respond to disasters after they have already done their damage. The book also summarizes a vast amount of research conducted before 1999 on social aspects of natural hazards and disasters.

National Research Council. *Facing Hazards and Disasters: Understanding Human Dimensions.* Washington, D.C.: National Academies Press, 2006. As Katrina and 9/11 make clear, the United States remains vulnerable to a variety of natural, willful, and technological disasters. This volume, written by a distinguished committee of experts, summarizes the social science research on coping with disasters and reducing risk. It gives special attention to how social changes in the population and economy increase the vulnerability to disasters and to disseminating knowledge about disasters to the public.

O'Leary, Margaret, ed. *The First 72 Hours: A Community Approach to Disaster Preparedness.* Lincoln, Neb.: iUniverse, 2004. This volume contains articles that aim to help communities become more resilient to disasters. Noting that communities will receive little help during the first 72 hours, the articles give advice on what communities can do during this short period to respond quickly and effectively to disasters.

Perry, Ronald W., and E. L. Quarantelli, eds. *What Is a Disaster? New Answers to Old Questions.* Philadelphia: Xlibris, 2005. Continuing the examination of issues raised in the 1998 book of the same title (see Quarantelli on page 210), this book presents the answers of several respected scholars to the question in the title and a long essay by Quarantelli on future research needs. Like the previous book, this one raises more questions than it answers.

Platt, Rutherford H. *Disasters and Democracy: The Politics of Extreme Natural Events.* Washington, D.C.: Island Press, 1999. In addressing the political response to natural disasters, this book gives special attention to major disaster declarations, which have increased greatly over time. The author suggests that making federal funds available to areas harmed by a disaster through the disaster declaration process has undesired consequences. By removing the costs of disasters from communities and residents, federal programs may encourage building in high-risk areas and discourage self-protection. Based on his observations and some case studies, the author makes recommendations for an alternative federal disaster policy.

Quarantelli, E. L. ed. *What Is a Disaster" Perspectives on the Question.* London: Routledge, 1998. The debate over what kinds of events should and should not be considered disasters gets a thorough review in this volume. It presents more detail than many readers will want, particularly since it comes to no straightforward conclusion in answering the question in the title. However, it does convey the complexity of the question and topic.

Redlener, Irwin. *Americans at Risk: Why We Are Not Prepared for Megadisasters and What We Can Do.* New York: Knopf, 2006. The theme of the book is that, although the United States is unable to protect itself fully from large-scale disasters, certain changes can improve the safety of the nation's citizens. The author, the founder and director of the National Center for Disaster Preparedness, criticizes political leadership and the federal bureaucracy for its failure in preparedness despite devoting billions of dollars to the task. To illustrate the problems, he presents five scenarios for future natural or human-caused disasters and how the current response system would fail. He then offers a nine-point proposal to improve the system.

Reyes, Gilbert, and Gerard A. Jacobs, eds. *Handbook of International Disaster Psychology.* Westport, Conn.: Praeger, 2006. This volume focuses on the trauma and mental harm faced by disaster survivors and how practitioners can help them. In so doing, the contributors aim to define the new field of disaster psychology and lay out the principles that guide the field. The chapters cover topics such as the rise of international disaster psychology, use of the community psychology model in disaster intervention, and collaboration across cultures. Underlying the scientific discussion is the humanitarian goal of increasing the ability of psychologists to help people in need.

Rosenfeld, Lawrence B., Joanne S. Caye, Ofra Ayalon, and Mooli Lahad. *When Their World Falls Apart: Helping Families and Children Manage the Effects of Disasters.* Washington, D.C.: National Association of Social Workers, 2005. The first part of this book examines the harmful effects of disasters on children, families, and communities; the second part describes intervention strategies to moderate or prevent these harmful effects. The book considers not only how to deal with trauma experienced by victims after a disaster but also what makes for resilience in the face of adversity.

Schneid, Thomas D., and Larry Collins. *Disaster Management and Preparedness*. Boca Raton, Fla.: Lewis Publishers, 2001. This book gives detailed advice to business owners and managers on the risks they face from disasters and how they can deal with them. It emphasizes practical goals such as how businesses can meet government disaster-related requirements for environmental and occupational health and safety.

Spigarelli, Jack A. *Crisis Preparedness Handbook: A Complete Guide to Home Storage and Physical Survival*. Alpine, Utah: Cross-Current Publishing, 2002. With all the attention given to FEMA, federal policy, and the government, it is easy to forget that personal action is the most important form of disaster response. This book describes all aspects of personal preparedness. It is a practical resource for individuals wanting details on what they need to have and do during a disaster.

Stallings, Robert A. *Promoting Risk: Constructing the Earthquake Threat*. Chicago: Aldine de Gruyter, 1995. Although the absence of an earthquake in more than 12 years has led the threat to recede from public attention, the potential remains for tens of thousands of deaths from a major earthquake in populated areas. The author argues that political and economic interests have prevented united efforts to prepare for the problem. The attention given to terrorism and hurricanes should not lead people to minimize the threat of an earthquake.

Tierney, Kathleen J., Michael K. Lindell, and Ronald W. Perry. *Facing the Unexpected: Disaster Preparedness and Response in the United States*. Washington, D.C.: Joseph Henry Press, 2001. This extensive review of the literature on social aspects of disasters predates the 9/11 terrorist attacks and Hurricane Katrina but is filled with insights and information that help in understanding these recent events. The book has chapters on disaster theory, research on preparedness, social behavior during disasters, organizational response, and emergency management policy.

Wallace, Michael, and Lawrence Webber. *The Disaster Recovery Handbook: A Step-by-Step Plan to Ensure Business Continuity and Protect Vital Operations, Facilities, and Assets*. New York: AMACOM American Management Association, 2004. The subtitle of the book summarizes its audience and goals. Businesses wanting to protect themselves from the disruption and lost sales caused by a disaster can consult the book for advice. It discusses how to assess risks, assemble a disaster recovery team, set up an emergency operations center, test and improve recovery plans, and ensure the health and physical safety of employees and customers. Written for nonexperts, the book contains much background information for those new to the field of disaster preparedness and recovery.

Wisner, Ben, Piers Blaikie, Terry Cannon, and Ian Davis. *At Risk: Natural Hazards, People's Vulnerability and Disasters.* New York: Routledge, 2003. This book focuses on the vulnerability of communities to disasters rather than on the physical force of natural hazards. It gives special attention to developing nations where populations are most vulnerable to the death and damage from a disaster (witness the Indian Ocean tsunami in 2004). Written more for scholars than the general public, it includes many specialized terms, models, and theories. But its theme about the need to reduce the vulnerability of populations to disasters is important, and its examples from developing countries are interesting.

Witt, James Lee, and James Morgan. *Stronger in the Broken Places: Nine Lessons for Turning Crisis into Triumph.* New York: Times Book, 2002. The former director of FEMA who received much praise for his leadership, Witt explains the principles that led to his success at FEMA and how they apply to businesses and communities undergoing crises. He offers guidance on preparing for crises, preventing recurring crises, responding with teamwork, and delegating leadership in recovery. Although extending well beyond issues of disaster response, this book gives insight on how federal disaster response should work.

Zebrowski, Ernest, Jr. *Perils of a Restless Planet: Scientific Perspectives on Natural Disasters.* Cambridge: Cambridge University Press, 1997. A science educator and physicist, Zebrowski presents a natural science perspective on disasters and examines questions such as whether natural hazards can be predicted and controlled directly. In addition, he emphasizes social aspects of natural hazards. For example, he criticizes the tendency to view natural hazards as independent of human action: "A swollen river devastates a growing city, and we view the flood as the cause of the devastation. We are not inclined to question whether the presence of the city itself may have caused the flood."

ARTICLES

Elrod, Carrie L., Jessica L. Hamblen, and Fran H. Norris. "Challenges in Implementing Disaster Mental Health Programs: State Program Directors' Perspectives." *Annals of the American Academy of Political and Social Science,* vol. 604, March 2006, pp. 152–170. This study of the effectiveness of state mental health interventions after a disaster finds many challenges to meeting intervention goals. The authors suggest that states need to plan better for mental health needs after disasters.

Gard, Betsy A., and Josef I. Ruzek. "Community Mental Health Response to Crisis." *Journal of Clinical Psychology,* vol. 62, no. 8, August 2006, pp. 1,029–1,041. Community response to a disaster should include efforts to deal with mental health problems. This article reviews recommenda-tions for limiting post-disaster mental health problems and cites the 9/11 and Katrina disasters as examples of how the circumstances of a disaster affect the mental health response needed by victims.

Light, Paul C. "What Citizens Don't Know." *Governing*, vol. 19, no. 1, Oc-tober 2005, p. A1. This article reports on a recent telephone survey of 1,500 Americans. According to the responses, more than two-thirds of the public expect a bombing at a shopping center or grocery store some-where in the United States in the next year. Yet, only 20 percent are fa-miliar with their state or local government's strategy for a terrorist attack, and only 37 percent have a plan for contacting families and friends in the event of a crisis.

Perez-Lugo, Marla. "Media Uses in Disaster Situations: A New Focus on the Impact Phase." *Sociological Inquiry*, vol. 74, no. 2, May 2004, pp. 210–225. As noted in this article, the media are expected to warn people about disasters and provide information on preparation and response. However, the author suggests that media can do more during a disaster to give emotional support, foster a sense of companionship, and help isolated people feel connected to the outside world. Greater attention of the media to these goals can reduce the stress and psychological damage of a disaster on a community, according to the study.

Picou, J. Steven, Brent K. Marshall, and Duane A. Gill. "Disaster, Litiga-tion, and the Corrosive Community." *Social Forces*, vol. 82, no. 4, June 2004, pp. 1,493–1,522. This study of the *Exxon Valdez* oil spill along the Alaska coast suggests that technological or human-caused disasters create added stress for victims through litigation and court deliberations for damages. The authors argue that the slow process of litigation extends psychological damage and insecurity for disaster victims and that alterna-tives are needed to promote quick recovery.

Robson, Katherine. "Are We Ready" *U.S. News & World Report*, vol. 140, no. 16, May 1, 2006, pp. 57–58, 60–62. This report cites the views of ex-perts that the U.S. health-care system is not prepared to deal with a large-scale emergency. Local hospitals in high-risk cities can handle most disasters, but something as widespread as a pandemic or biological terror-ism will overwhelm the nation's resources for health care. Disaster re-sponse policies should focus more on preparing for national catastrophes.

Rodriguez, Havidan, and John Barnshaw. "The Social Construction of Di-sasters: From Heat Waves to Worst-Case Scenarios." *Contemporary Sociol-ogy*, vol. 35, no. 3, May 2006, pp. 218–223. In a review of several recent books on disasters, the authors emphasize that disasters are social as well as natural events and calls for better understanding of social aspects of the topic.

Salholz, Eloise. "Disaster and Denial: Why Do Victims Rebuild in the Same Old Place?" *Newsweek*, vol. 122, July 26, 1993, p. 27. A psychologist quoted in this article says that victims of disasters who stay in place convince themselves that the disaster could not happen again. The common tendency for people and communities in hazard-prone areas to underprepare for the risks they face makes disaster response more difficult and expensive.

Solnit, Rebecca. "The Uses of Disaster." *Harper's*, vol. 311, October 2005, pp. 31–37. The author cites several examples of how the suffering and tragedy caused by a disaster also brought people closer and led to surprising acts of kindness. She argues that disasters bring out the best in people and reveal the interdependence of strangers in everyday life.

Wagner, Cynthia G. "Disaster Planning for the Disabled." *Futurist*, vol. 40, no. 2, March/April 2006, p. 13. Special efforts are needed in disaster response for the disabled. This article describes research to determine how to help the disabled leave public buildings and move through crowds.

———. "Improving Terrorism Preparedness: Emergency Planning—If It's for the People, Shouldn't It Be by the People?" *Futurist*, vol. 40, no. 1, January/February 2006, pp. 6–7. In examining community terrorism response plans, the New York Academy of Medicine found that most plans do not take account of the behavior and psychology of people located in public places. According to this article, the academy and the W. K. Kellogg Foundation are supporting four planning demonstration projects to help communities better plan for and respond to emergencies.

WEB DOCUMENTS

"Assisting Children and Adolescents in Coping with Violence and Disasters." Houston Medical Center. Available online. URL: http://www. houstonmedcenter.com/articles/assisting_children_in_coping_with_violence_and _disasters.php. Downloaded in July 2007. This brief guide defines trauma, (both physical and psychiatric), describes how children respond to trauma, and offers advice on protecting children from trauma during disasters.

"Psychological Research on Disaster Response." APA Online Public Policy Office. Available online. URL: http://www.apa.org/ppo/issues/katrinaresearch.html. Downloaded in July 2007. This web page from the American Psychological Association (APA) summarizes selected research of association members on disaster response. The research studies examine how to promote community solidarity after a disaster, improve coordination and communication during a disaster, and evacuate pets as well as people from a disaster area.

"The Role of Social Science Research in Disaster Preparedness and Response." House Committee on Science. Available online. URL: http://commdocshouse.gov/committees/science/hsy24463.000/hsy24463_0.htm. Posted on November 10, 2005. The testimony of four social scientists with expertise in disaster research explains how their fields of study can help in disaster preparedness and response. The experts present knowledge and research findings on questions such as how individuals perceive risk and respond to warnings, how to foster cooperation and resiliency in the face of disaster, and how to assess the vulnerability of areas to natural and terrorist hazards.

INTERNATIONAL DISASTER RESPONSE

BOOKS

Middleton, Neil, and Phil O'Keefe. *Disaster and Development: The Politics of Humanitarian Aid.* London: Pluto Press, 1998. Based on seven case studies of disasters in nations of Africa and central Asia, the authors suggest that humanitarian aid is influenced by many other factors beside the needs of the victims and the goodwill of the donors. The economic and political goals of high-income donor nations also affect decisions on how to aid developing countries suffering from a disaster.

Organization for Economic Co-operation and Development. *Emerging Risks in the 21st Century: An Agenda for Action.* Geneva: OECD, 2003. Experts on international disasters present their recommendations for dealing with new risks that threaten the world. The volume describes the risks from pandemics, terrorism, technological failure, and natural hazards and suggests ways to assess, prevent, and manage the risks. Policymakers in the United States and other countries around the world can learn from the recommendations for action in the book.

———. *Large Scale Disasters: Lessons Learned.* Geneva: OECD, 2004. This study by a multidisciplinary team reviews the response to and recovery from several famous international disasters, such as the September 11 attacks; Hurricane Andrew; the Kobe, Japan, earthquake; and the Chernobyl nuclear accident. The lessons learned include the obvious—governments must better prepare to minimize the impact of disasters—and the less obvious—governments have to do more to gain the public trust and work with the private sector.

U.S. House of Representatives. *The Tsunami Tragedy: How the U.S. Is Responding and Providing Relief.* Briefing before the Committee on International Relations, House of Representatives, One Hundred Ninth Congress,

First Session, January 26, 2005. Washington, D.C.: U.S. Government Printing Office, 2005. The United States has policies and organizations devoted to international disaster response, and military units stationed outside the United States help with such disasters. This briefing from members of the government and military describe their relief efforts after the Indian Ocean tsunami in December 2004.

ARTICLES

Arnold, Margaret. "Disaster Reconstruction and Risk Management for Poverty Reduction." *Journal of International Affairs*, vol. 59, no. 2, Spring/Summer 2006, pp. 269–279. According to this article about international disaster response, the World Bank has come to recognize that disasters cause both humanitarian and development problems. Disaster reconstruction and risk management should focus on not only getting aid to those harmed by a disaster but also on promoting economic development and reducing poverty.

Chandler, Clay. "A Wave of Corporate Charity." *Fortune*, vol. 151, no. 2, January 24, 2005, pp. 21–22. This article lists large charitable contributions made by U.S. corporations to the Indian Ocean tsunami relief effort.

Continetti, Matthew. "Relief Pitcher." *Weekly Standard*, vol. 10, no. 17, January 17, 2005, pp. 12–15. This article evaluates the performance of Jan Egeland, the UN undersecretary general for humanitarian affairs and chief emergency relief coordinator. As discussed in the article, he received harsh criticism for his claim that high-income nations such as the United States were stingy in their humanitarian donations for disaster relief in the developing world.

"Dazed by Disasters." *Christianity Today*, vol. 50, no. 1, January 2006, pp. 28–29. An editorial in this Christian magazine reviews the coverage of the recent earthquake in Pakistan that killed 73,000 and injured 100,000. After a brief spurt of attention to the disaster, the media and the American public turned its attention to other issues. The result has been inadequate funding and help. The editorial suggests that the U.S. public suffers from compassion fatigue and that the response to international disasters needs more than voluntary donations.

Gillis, Charlie. "Inside the Relief Effort." *Maclean's*, vol. 118, no. 3, January 17, 2005, pp. 18–22. The massive death and destruction of the Indian Ocean tsunami created special problems for the international response teams. This article describes these problems and the efforts to overcome them.

Hicks, Esther K., and Gregory Pappas. "Coordinating Disaster Relief after the South Asia Earthquake." *Society*, vol. 43, no. 5, July/August, 2006, pp. 42–50. This article describes efforts at the United Nations to improve the effectiveness of its disaster response, relief, and recovery. The South Asia earthquake in October 2005 gives the authors a case study to evaluate the new approaches of the United Nations to international disaster response. They argue that reforms have not been entirely successful.

Stone, Richard. "A Race to Beat the Odds." *Science*, vol. 307, January 28, 2005, pp. 502–504. This article describes the efforts of relief workers to prevent disease outbreaks, provide clean water, and supply toilet facilities in Sri Lanka after the Indian Ocean tsunami. The author argues that the efforts have helped, but he sees the need for more funds to build new heath facilities in the country.

Szegedy-Maszak, Marianne. "The Borders of Healing." *U.S. News & World Report*, vol. 138, no. 2, January 17, 2005, pp. 36–37. As part of a special issue on the Indian Ocean tsunami, this article describes the damage to areas worst hit by the disaster and the challenges faced by those involved in relief efforts.

WEB DOCUMENTS

"Disaster Assistance." USAID from the American People. Available online. URL: http://www.usaid.gov/our_work/humanitarian_assistance/disaster_assistance. Updated on July 18, 2006. The U.S. Agency for International Development contains the Office of Foreign Disaster Assistance, the agency responsible for facilitating and coordinating U.S. government emergency assistance overseas. This web page describes the relief efforts of this office after the Indian Ocean tsunami and the 2005 Pakistan earthquake. It also provides statistics and stories on relief efforts and suggests ways for the U.S. public to help with the effort.

"Global Natural Disaster Deaths, 1990–2004." Live Science. Available online. URL: http://www.livescience.com/forcesofnature/disaster_deaths_1990. html. Downloaded in July 2007. The table on this web page summarizes information on international disasters. For each year, it lists the deaths from droughts, earthquakes, heat, floods, landslides, volcanoes, waves/surges, wildfires, and windstorms. The deaths from the 2004 Indian Ocean tsunami dwarf those from other disasters during the period, but earthquakes, heat, and floods typically kill the most people around the world.

"Indian Ocean Tsunami." FirstGov.gov. Available online. URL: http://www.firstgov.gov/Citizen/Topics/Asia_Tsunamis.shtml. Downloaded in July 2007. The U.S. government's official web portal offers information on how to help in the tsunami relief effort, find information on U.S. citizens affected by the disaster, and obtain general information and news. The web page contains links to a wealth of information on the disaster and the international response.

"International Strategy for Disaster Reduction." UN/ISDR. Available online. URL: http://www.unisdr.org/isdrindex.htm. Downloaded in July 2007. The United Nations program described on this web page aims to increase the awareness of the importance of disaster reduction, make disaster reduction a component of sustainable development, and reduce the environmental and human damage of disasters. The web page reviews the program, lists disaster statistics, and includes links to several more specific disaster programs. It reflects the recent attention the United Nations has given to dealing with disasters in low- and middle-income nations.

"Mega Disasters—A Global 'Tipping Point' in Natural Disaster Policy, Planning and Development." Pacific Disaster Center. Available online. URL: http://www.pdc.org/PDCNewsWebArticles/spf/forum.html. Downloaded in July 2007. The summary of a symposium on this web page considers the implications of three recent mega-disasters: the Indian Ocean tsunami, the earthquake and landslides in the Kashmir region of central Asia, and Hurricane Katrina. The symposium participants—officials from the United Nations, international disaster organizations, and nations across the world—view these huge disasters as the result of the unplanned growth of cities, concentration of populations in hazard-prone areas, and overuse of environmental resources.

"Serving the Information Needs of the Humanitarian Relief Community." Relief Web. Available online. URL: http://www.reliefweb.int/rw/dbc.nsf/doc100?OpenForm. Downloaded in July 2007. This web page sponsored by the United Nations Office of Coordination of Humanitarian Affairs lists current emergencies around the world and makes appeals for funding. It also contains policy and issue reports on topics of concern to the international disaster community.

"Tsunami Pictures." Tsunamis.com. Available online. URL: http://www.tsunamis.com/tsunami-pictures.html. Downloaded in July 2007. Although sometimes disturbing, the pictures of death and destruction from the Indian Ocean tsunami illustrate the dangers of international disasters better than words can. The web page also presents information on the tsunami and includes an appeal for help.

CHAPTER 8

ORGANIZATIONS AND AGENCIES

The organizations and agencies listed in this chapter fall into five categories:

- Federal government organizations,
- Selected state and local government organizations,
- International organizations,
- Charitable organizations, and
- Professional and research organizations.

For each organization, the listings include the web site and e-mail. Many organizations do not list their e-mail address but include a Web-based form for submitting questions and comments via the Internet. In these cases, the text notes that e-mail is available via a web form. The listings then include phone numbers (when available), postal addresses, and brief descriptions of the organizations.

FEDERAL GOVERNMENT ORGANIZATIONS

Environmental Protection Agency (EPA)
URL: http://www.epa.gov
E-mail: web form
Phone: (202) 564-4700
Ariel Rios Building
1200 Pennsylvania Avenue, NW
Washington, DC 20460
With a mission to protect human health and the environment, the EPA assesses damage to the environment after a disaster, assists in restoring the environment, and takes the lead in cleanup of hazardous materials.

Federal Emergency Management Agency (FEMA)
URL: http://www.fema.gov
E-mail: FEMAWebmaster@ DHS.gov

Phone: (800) 621-3362
500 C Street, SW
Washington, DC 20472
A unit of the Department of Homeland Security (DHS) since 2003, FEMA leads the efforts to prepare the nation for all hazards and effectively manage federal response and recovery following any national incident; it also initiates mitigation activities, trains first responders, and manages the National Flood Insurance Program.

National Oceanic and Atmospheric Administration (NOAA)
URL: http://www.noaa.gov
E-mail: web form
Phone: (202) 482-6090
14th Street & Constitution Avenue, NW
Room 6217
Washington, DC 20230
NOAA and its units—the National Weather Service and the National Hurricane Center—are responsible for weather and storm forecasts and for declaring storm watches and warnings.

U.S. Agency for International Development (USAID)
URL: http://www.usaid.gov
E-mail: web form
Phone: (202) 712-4810
Ronald Reagan Building
Washington, DC 20523-1000
One component of this agency's goal of helping people overseas is giving assistance to nations, places, and people recovering from a disaster.

U.S. Army Corps of Engineers (ACE)
URL: http://www.usace.army.mil
E-mail: webmaster@usace.army.mil
Phone: (202) 761-0011
441 G Street, NW
Washington, DC 20314-1000
In addition to its military duties, this agency has a mission of planning, designing, building, and operating water resources, flood control structures, and other civil works projects.

U.S. Department of Commerce (DOC)
URL: http://www.commerce.gov
E-mail: webmaster@doc.gov
Phone: (202) 482-2000
1401 Constitution Avenue, NW
Washington, DC 20230
In its goal of fostering commerce, the department provides weather-related information and warnings and helps restore the economy and businesses in areas damaged by disasters.

U.S. Department of Defense (DOD)
URL: http://www.defenselink.mil
E-mail: public@defenselink.mil
Phone: (703) 697-5737
1000 Defense Pentagon
Washington, DC 20301-1000
When directed by the president, the department provides resources and personnel in support of the response to terrorist events, major disasters, and other emergencies.

**U.S. Department of Energy
(DOE)**
URL: http://www.energy.gov
E-mail: The.Secretary@hq.doe.
 gov
Phone: (800) 342-5363
1000 Independence Avenue, SW
Washington, DC 20585
The department helps to protect energy supplies during a disaster and restore energy after a disaster.

**U.S. Department of Health and
 Human Services (HSS)**
URL: http://www.hhs.gov
E-mail: web form
Phone: (877) 696-6775
200 Independence Avenue, SW
Washington, DC 20201
Since disasters create special health and human service needs, this department has a division devoted to disaster and emergency response and gives special attention to bioterrorism, hurricanes, and emergency preparedness.

**U.S. Department of Homeland
 Security (DHS)**
URL: http://www.dhs.gov/
 dhspublic
E-mail: web form
Phone: (202) 282-8000
Washington, DC 20528
This new agency established after the attacks of September 11, 2001, is responsible for securing the nation from terrorism; since this mission includes protecting against and responding to threats and hazards, the department has subsumed FEMA and emergency and disaster management duties.

**U.S. Department of Housing and
 Urban Development (HUD)**
URL: http://www.hud.gov
E-mail: webmanager@hud.gov
Phone: (202) 708-1112
451 7th Street, SW
Washington, DC 20410
This department has the major goal of increasing home affordability and ownership, but after a disaster, it also helps find, supply, and pay for housing for victims.

**U.S. Department of Justice
 (DOJ)**
URL: http://www.usdoj.gov
E-mail: AskDOJ@usdoj.gov
Phone: (202) 514-2000
950 Pennsylvania Avenue, NW
Washington, DC 20530-0001
With a mission to enforce the law and ensure public safety, the department aids law enforcement in responding to disasters, helps prisons and police departments in recovering from a disaster, prosecutes fraudulent receipt of disaster assistance, and investigates terrorist acts and threats.

**U.S. Department of
 Transportation (DOT)**
URL: http://www.dot.gov
E-mail: dot.comments@dot.gov
Phone: (202) 366-4000
400 7th Street, SW
Washington, DC 20590
Before a disaster, the department aids in the evacuation along roads and highways; after a disaster, it contributes to clearing and repairing roads and bridges.

U.S. Geological Survey (USGS)
URL: http://www.usgs.gov
E-mail: web form
Phone: (888) 275-8747
1849 C Street, NW
Washington, DC 20240
With the general goal of providing scientific understanding of natural resource conditions, issues, and problems, this agency has expertise in geography, geology, and water science that helps in predicting and responding to earthquakes, fires, and floods.

STATE AND LOCAL GOVERNMENT ORGANIZATIONS

California Governor's Office of Emergency Services (OEC)
URL: http://www.oes.ca.gov
Phone: (916) 845-8510
3650 Schriever Avenue
Mather, CA 95655
Lead state agency for emergency mitigation, preparation, response, and recovery.

City of New Orleans Office of Emergency Preparedness (OEP)
URL: http://www.cityofno.com/portal.aspx?portal=46
E-mail: webmaster@cityofno.com
Phone: (504) 658-4000
1300 Perdido Street
New Orleans, LA 70112
Has responsibility for the response to natural or human-made disasters and for coordinating the actions needed to protect the lives and property of New Orleans citizens.

Florida Division of Emergency Management (FDEM)
URL: http://www.floridadisaster.org
E-mail: web form
2555 Shumard Oak Boulevard
Tallahassee, FL 32399-2100
Works to ensure that the state is prepared to respond to emergencies, recover from them, and mitigate against their impacts.

Louisiana Governor's Office of Homeland Security and Emergency Preparedness (GOHSEP)
URL: http://www.loep.state.la.us
Phone: (225) 925-7500
7667 Independence Boulevard
Baton Rouge, LA 70806
Leads, coordinates, and supports the emergency management system in order to protect lives and prevent the loss of property of state residents from all hazards.

New York City Office of Emergency Management (OEM)
URL: http://www.nyc.gov/html/oem
E-mail: web form
Phone: (718) 422-4800
11 Water Street
Brooklyn, NY 11201

Works to mitigate, plan, and prepare for emergencies, educate the public about preparedness, and coordinate emergency response and recovery efforts.

**New York State Emergency
  Management Office (SEMO)**
URL: http://www.semo.state.ny.us
E-mail: postmaster@semo.state.
  ny.us
Phone: (518) 292-2301
1220 Washington Avenue
Building 22, Suite 101
Albany, NY 12226-2251
Responsible for coordinating all activities necessary to protect New York State's communities from natural, technological, and human-made disasters and other emergencies.

**San Francisco Office of
  Emergency Services and
  Homeland Security (OES/HS)**
URL: http://www.sfgov.org/site/
  oes
E-mail: web form
Phone: (415) 558-2700
1011 Turk Street
San Francisco, CA 94102
Protects the City and County of San Francisco from the threat or effects of natural, human-made, or technological disasters.

**Texas Governor's Division of
  Emergency Management
  (GDEM)**
URL: http://www.txdps.state.
  tx.us/dem
E-mail: saa@txdps.state.tx.us
Phone: (512) 424-2138
P.O. Box 4087
Austin, TX 78773-0220
Carries out a comprehensive, all-hazard emergency management program for the state.

INTERNATIONAL ORGANIZATIONS

**Center for International
  Disaster Information (CIDI)**
URL: http://www.cidi.org
E-mail: cidi@cidi.org
Phone: (703) 276-1914
The center handles public inquires related to international emergencies, particularly about making donations to international disaster relief organizations.

**International Federation of
  Red Cross and Red Crescent
  Societies (IFRC)**
URL: http://www.ifrc.org

E-mail: web form
Phone: (4122) 730-4222
P.O. Box 372
CH-1211 Geneva 19
Switzerland
The world's largest humanitarian assistance organization carries out relief operations for victims of disasters and promotes health and development throughout the world.

**United Nations Environment
  Programme (UNEP)**
URL: http://www.grid.unep.ch
E-mail: infogrid@grid.unep.ch

Phone: (4122) 917-8294
International Environment House
11 Chemin des Anémones
1219 Châtelaine
Switzerland
With a focus on assessing environmental risks and informing the nations of the world about them, this organization gathers information on human vulnerability to natural disasters.

United Nations Office for the
    Coordination of Humanitarian
    Affairs (OCHA)
URL: http://ochaonline.un.org
E-mail: ochany@un.org
Phone: (212) 963-1234
United Nations S-3600
New York, NY 10017

Under the leadership of the Emergency Relief Coordinator, this UN office coordinates humanitarian response to emergencies and disasters.

World Bank
URL: http://www.worldbank.org
E-mail: pic@worldbank.org
Phone: (202) 473-1000
1818 H Street, NW
Washington, DC 20433
With a mission to fight world poverty, the World Bank provides assistance to prepare for and recover from disasters, a major source of human and economic loss in developing countries.

CHARITABLE ORGANIZATIONS

Adventist Development and
    Relief Agency (ADRA)
    International
URL: http://www.adra.org
Phone: (800) 424-2372
12501 Old Columbia Pike
Silver Spring, MD 20904
The humanitarian agency of the Seventh-day Adventist Church sponsors an emergency management initiative to provide aid to disaster survivors.

American Red Cross
URL: http://www.redcross.org
E-mail: web form
Phone: (202) 303-4498
2025 E Street, NW

Washington, DC 20006
Although not a government agency, the American Red Cross has congressional authority to provide disaster services, and it works closely with government agencies in disaster response.

Catholic Charities USA
URL: http://www.
    catholiccharitiesusa.org
E-mail: web form
Phone: (703) 549-1390
1731 King Street
Alexandria, VA 22314
This charitable social service agency of the Catholic Church treats disaster response as one of its major mis-

sions and typically coordinates activities of and disburses funds to local Catholic Charities.

Christian Disaster Response International
URL: http://www.cdresponse. org
Phone: (863) 967-4357
200 Avenue K, SE
Winter Haven, FL 33880
An interdenominational organization that provides disaster assistance through local churches and agencies.

Christian Reformed World Relief Committee (CRWRC)
URL: http://www.crwrc.org
Phone: (616) 241-1691
2850 Kalamazoo Avenue, SE
Grand Rapids, MI 49560
Through its programs for Disaster Response Services and International Relief, this committee of the Christian Reformed Church responds to natural and human-made disasters with food, medicine, shelter, and other supplies.

Church World Service Emergency Response Program (CWSERP)
URL: http://www.cwserp.org
Phone: (212) 870-3151
475 Riverside Drive
Suite 700
New York, NY 10115
This relief and development agency of the 36 denominations of the National Churches of Christ helps local churches and agencies respond to disasters and emergencies.

Disaster Psychiatry Outreach (DPO)
URL: http://www.disasterpsych. org
E-mail: info@disasterpsych.org
Phone: (212) 598-9995
50 Broad Street, #1714
New York, NY 10004
A nonprofit volunteer organization of psychiatrists committed to providing high-quality mental health services after a disaster.

Habitat for Humanity
URL: http://www.habitat.org
E-mail: publicinfo@habitat.org
Phone: (229) 924-6935
121 Habitat Street
Americus, GA 31709-3498
This nonprofit, ecumenical Christian organization builds and rebuilds housing for families in need and has devoted much effort to areas damaged by disasters.

Humane Society of the United States (HSUS)
URL: http://www.hsus.org
E-mail: web form
Phone: (202) 452-1100
2100 L Street, NW
Washington, DC 20037
This organization devoted to the protection of animals has a program to assist animals and owners when disasters strike.

Islamic Relief Worldwide
URL: http://www.islamic-relief. com
E-mail: HQ@islamic-relief.org. uk
Phone: (0121) 605-5555

19 Rea Street South
Birmingham B5 6LB
United Kingdom
An international charity that responds to disasters and emergencies, regardless of race, religion, and gender of the victims, and has a goal of alleviating suffering of the world's poor.

Lutheran Disaster Response (LDR)
URL: http://www.ldr.org
Phone: (800) 638-3522
8765 West Higgins Road
Chicago, IL 60631
After a domestic disaster, this Lutheran social ministry agency provides emotional and spiritual care, hardship grants, and help in longterm recovery to victims of all faiths and creeds.

Mennonite Disaster Service (MDS)
URL: http://www.mds.
mennonite.net
E-mail: mdsus@mds.mennonite.
net
Phone: (717) 859-2210
1018 Main Street
Akron , PA 17501
This church organization focuses on cleanup, repair, and rebuilding after a disaster, but it also aims to help people regain faith and wholeness after a disaster.

National Voluntary Organizations Active in Disaster (NVOAD)
URL: http://www.nvoad.org
Phone: (703) 339-5596

P.O. Box 151973
Alexandria, VA 22315
NVOAD coordinates efforts of voluntary organizations across the country in responding to disasters and by so doing encourages cooperation across organizations during a crisis.

Nazarene Disaster Response (NDR)
URL: http://www.ncm.org/min_
ndr.aspx
E-mail: ncm@nazarene.org
Phone: (877) 626-4145
6401 The Paseo
Kansas City, MO 64131-1213
This organization associated with the Church of the Nazarene consists of a network of disaster volunteers assisted by trained leaders that responds to natural and humanmade disasters.

Presbyterian Disaster Assistance (PDA)
URL: http://www.pcusa.org/pda
E-mail: pda@pcusa.org
Phone: (888) 728-7228, ext. 5839
100 Witherspoon Street
Louisville, KY 40202
This organization manages volunteer teams that work on long-term recovery with church partners in disaster-impacted communities.

Salvation Army
URL: http://www.
salvationarmyusa.org
E-mail: NHQ_Webmaster@usn.
salvationarmy.org
Phone: (703) 684-5500

615 Slaters Lane
P.O. Box 269
Alexandria, VA 22313
Although focused on a variety of charitable activities, this well-known religious organization has since 1900 devoted much effort to disaster relief.

United Methodist Committee on Relief (UMCOR)
URL: http://gbgm-umc.org/umcor
E-mail: umcor@gbgm-umc.org
Phone: (800) 554-8583
475 Riverside Drive
Room 330
New York, NY 10115
This organization helps nationally and internationally in disaster relief by providing supplies and personnel.

United Way
URL: http://national.unitedway.org/hs06
E-mail: web form
701 North Fairfax Street
Alexandria, VA 22314
This well-known charitable organization includes disaster response as one of its major goals.

World Relief
URL: http://www.wr.org
E-mail: worldrelief@wr.org
Phone: (443) 451-1900
7 East Baltimore Street
Baltimore, MD 21202
Works with evangelical churches to obtain and send relief supplies and assistance to areas harmed by natural and human-caused disasters.

PROFESSIONAL AND RESEARCH ORGANIZATIONS

American Disaster Reserve
URL: http://www.disasterreserve.us
E-mail: headquarters@disasterreserve.us
3355 North Academy Boulevard, #232
Colorado Springs, CO 80917-5103
A civilian nonsectarian organization composed of volunteer professional disasters responders.

Center for Preparedness and Training, Inc. (CPTI)
URL: http://www.cpti.us

E-mail: contact@cpti.us
Phone: (303) 880-8908
P.O. Box 351057
Westminster, CO 80035-1057
This company offers help to businesses in managing risk, assessing vulnerabilities, preparing for emergencies, and training employees.

Center for Public Health and Disaster Relief, University of California at Los Angeles (CPHD)
URL: http://www.cphd.ucla.edu
E-mail: cphdr@ucla.edu
Phone: (310) 794-0864

1145 Gayley Avenue
Suite 304
Los Angeles, CA 90024
The center promotes interdisciplinary efforts to reduce the health impacts of natural and human-generated disasters that occur nationally and internationally.

Disaster Management Center, University of Wisconsin (UW-DMC)
URL: http://dmc.engr.wisc.edu
E-mail: dmc@epd.engr.wisc.edu
Phone: (800) 462-0876
Department of Engineering
  Professional Development
432 North Lake Street
Madison, WI 53706
The center offers a comprehensive professional development program in disaster management as a way to help improve the emergency management performance of nongovernmental organizations, local and national governments, and international organizations.

Disaster Preparedness and Emergency Response Association (DERA)
URL: http://www.disasters.org
E-mail: DERA@disasters.org
Phone: (352) 447-5691
P.O. Box 797
Longmont, CO 80502
DERA offers resources, professional support, leadership opportunities and extensive networking for members and is actively involved in providing critical emergency assistance.

Disaster Research Center (DRC)
URL: http://www.udel.edu/DRC
E-mail: drc-mail@udel.edu
Phone: (302) 831-6618
87 East Main Street
Newark, DE 19716-2581
The center conducts field and survey research on group, organizational, and community preparation for, response to, and recovery from natural and technological disasters and other community-wide crises.

First Responder Institute
URL: http://www.firstresponder.org
Phone: (301) 421-0096
15312 Spencerville Court
Suite 100
Burtonsville, MD 20866
Dedicated to improving first-responder readiness and performance, this nonprofit organization designs education and training programs.

Hazard Reduction and Recovery Center, Texas A&M University (HRRC)
URL: http://archone.tamu.edu/hrrc
E-mail: hrrc@archmail.tamu.edu
Phone: (979) 845-7813
TAMU MS 3137
College Station, TX 77843-3137
The center engages in research on hazard mitigation, preparedness, response, and recovery and provides access to hazards information for homeowners, professionals, business investors, and academics.

Institute for Crisis, Disaster, and Risk Management, The George Washington University (ICDRM)
URL: http://www.gwu.edu/~icdrm
E-mail: icdrm@gwu.edu
Phone: (202) 994-6736
1776 G Street, NW
Suite 110
Washington, D.C. 20052
The institute teaches courses, creates knowledge through research, and disseminates information in the areas of crisis, disaster, and risk management.

International Association of Emergency Managers (IAEM)
URL: http://www.iaem.com
E-mail: web form
Phone: (703) 538-1795
201 Park Washington Court
Falls Church, VA 22046-4527
With the goal of saving lives and protecting property during emergencies and disasters, this organization provides information, networking, and professional opportunities to members of the emergency management profession.

James Lee Witt Associates
URL: http://www.wittassociates.com
E-mail: info@wittassociates.com
Phone: (202) 585-0780
701 13th Street, NW
Suite 850
Washington, DC 20005
An emergency management consulting firm headed by the former

director of FEMA, it offers information and links to state emergency and homeland security services on its web page.

National Association for Search and Rescue (NASAR)
URL: http://www.nasar.org
E-mail: info@nasar.org
Phone: (703) 222-6277
Seeks to save lives through emergency response and rescue operations and consists of members interested in all aspects of search and rescue.

National Association of Emergency Medical Technicians (NAEMT)
URL: http://www.naemt.org
E-mail: info@naemt.org
Phone: (601) 924-7744
P.O. Box 1400
Clinton, MS 39060-1400
Represents and serves emergency medical services personnel, a key group in disaster response, through advocacy, educational programs, and research.

National Center for Disaster Preparedness, Columbia University (NCDP)
URL: http://www.ncdp.mailman.columbia.edu
Phone: (212) 342-5161
722 West 168th Street
10th Floor
New York, NY 10032
This interdisciplinary teaching and research program focuses on the nation's capacity to prevent and

respond to terrorism and major disasters.

National Emergency Management Association (NEMA)
URL: http://www.nemaweb.org
E-mail: nemaadmin@csg.org
Phone: (859) 244-8000
P.O. Box 11910
Lexington, KY 40578
With state directors of emergency services as its core, this organization provides information and networking opportunities for its members and promotes effective emergency management across the nation.

Natural Hazards Center
URL: http://www.colorado.edu/hazards
E-mail: hazctr@colorado.edu
Phone: (303) 492-6818
482 UCB
University of Colorado
Boulder, CO 80309-0482

Using an all-hazards and interdisciplinary framework, the center aims to advance and communicate knowledge on hazards mitigation and disaster preparedness, response, and recovery.

Oak Ridge National Laboratory Emergency Management Center (EMC)
URL: http://emc.ornl.gov
Phone: (865) 576-2716
P.O. Box 2008 MS6206
Oak Ridge, TN 37831-6206
The center conducts research and assists in developing emergency plans for government agencies such as the Department of Energy, FEMA, and the Army Corps of Engineers.

PART III

APPENDICES

APPENDIX A

---

30 TIPS FOR EMERGENCY PREPAREDNESS

This document from the Department of Homeland Security advises on how to prepare for an emergency, a key for effective response. Updated September 18, 2006.

Here are 30 tips to help you and your family become better prepared for an emergency.

Preparedness Tip #1

Take a moment to imagine that there is an emergency, like a fire in your home, and you need to leave quickly. What are the best escape routes from your home? Find at least two ways out of each room. Now, write it down—you've got the beginning of a plan.

Preparedness Tip #2

Pick a place to meet after a disaster. Designate two meeting places. Choose one right outside your home, in case of a sudden household emergency, such as a fire. The second place you choose needs to be outside your neighborhood, in the event that it is not safe to stay near or return to your home.

Preparedness Tip #3

Choose an emergency contact person outside your area because it may be easier to call long distance than locally after a local/regional disaster. Take a minute now to call or e-mail an out-of-town friend or family member to ask him or her to be your family's designated contact in the event of an emergency. Be sure to share the contact's phone number with everyone in the family. During an emergency, you can call your contact who can share with other family members where you are; how you are doing; and how to get in contact with you.

Preparedness Tip #4

Complete an emergency contact card and make copies for each member of your family to carry with them. Be sure to include an out-of-town contact on your contact card. It may be easier to reach someone out of town if local phone lines are out of service or overloaded. You should also have at least one traditionally wired landline phone, as cordless or cellular phones may not work in an emergency. Visit www.redcross.org or www.ready.gov for sample emergency contact cards.

Preparedness Tip #5

Dogs may be man's best friend, but due to health regulations, most emergency shelters cannot house animals. Find out in advance how to care for your pets and working animals when disaster strikes. Pets should not be left behind, but could be taken to a veterinary office, family member's home or animal shelter during an emergency. Also be sure to store extra food and water for pets. For more information, visit the Animal Safety section on www.redcross.org or visit the Humane Society Web site at www.hsus.org.

Preparedness Tip #6

Go through your calendar now, and put a reminder on it—every six months—to review your plan, update numbers, and check supplies to be sure nothing has expired, spoiled, or changed. Also remember to practice your tornado, fire escape or other disaster plans.

Preparedness Tip #7

Check your child's school Web site or call the school office to request a copy of the school's emergency plan. Keep a copy at home and work or other places where you spend a lot of your time and make sure the school's plan is incorporated into your family's emergency plan. Also, learn about the disaster plans at your workplace or other places where you and your family spend time.

Preparedness Tip #8

Teach your children how and when to call 9-1-1 or your local Emergency Medical Services number for help. Post these and other emergency telephone numbers by telephones.

Preparedness Tip #9

Practice. Conduct fire drills and practice evacuating your home twice a year. Drive your planned evacuation route and plot alternate routes on a map in case main roads are blocked or gridlocked. Practice earthquake and tornado drills at home, school and work. Commit a weekend to update telephone numbers, emergency supplies and review your plan with everyone.

Preparedness Tip #10

A community working together during an emergency makes sense.

- Talk to your neighbors about how you can work together during an emergency.
- Find out if anyone has specialized equipment like a power generator, or expertise such as medical knowledge, that might help in a crisis.
- Decide who will check on elderly or disabled neighbors.
- Make back-up plans for children in case you can't get home in an emergency.

Sharing plans and communicating in advance is a good strategy.

Preparedness Tip #11

What if disaster strikes while you're at work? Do you know the emergency preparedness plan for your workplace? While many companies have been more alert and pro-active in preparing for disasters of all types since the September 11, 2001 attacks, a national survey indicates that many employees still don't know what their workplace plan is for major or minor disasters. If you don't know yours, make a point to ask. Know multiple ways to exit your building, participate in workplace evacuation drills, and consider keeping some emergency supplies at the office. Visit www.ready.gov and click on Ready Business for more information about business preparedness.

Preparedness Tip #12

You should keep enough supplies in your home to meet the needs of you and your family for at least three days. Build an emergency supply kit to take with you in an evacuation. The basics to stock in your portable kit include: water, food, battery-powered radio and flashlight with extra batteries, first aid supplies, change of clothing, blanket or sleeping bag, wrench or pliers, whistle, dust mask, plastic sheeting and duct tape, trash bags, map, a manual can opener for canned food and special items for infants, elderly, the sick or people with disabilities. Keep these items in an easy to carry container such as a covered trash container, a large backpack, or a duffle bag.

Disaster Response

Preparedness Tip #13

Preparing for emergencies needn't be expensive if you're thinking ahead and buying small quantities at a time. Make a list of some foods that:

- Have a long shelf-life and will not spoil (non-perishable).
- You and your family like.
- Do not require cooking.
- Can be easily stored.
- Have a low salt content as salty foods will make you more thirsty.

Keep the list in your purse or wallet and pick up a few items each time you're shopping and/or see a sale until you have built up a well-stocked supply that can sustain each member of your family for at least three days following an emergency.

Preparedness Tip #14

Take a minute to check your family's first aid kit, and note any depleted items—then, add them to your shopping list. Don't have a first aid kit? Add that to the list or build a kit yourself. Just add the following items to your shopping list and assemble a first aid kit. Consider creating a kit for each vehicle as well:

First Aid Kits—Assemble a first aid kit for your home and one for each car.
- (20) adhesive bandages, various sizes
- (1) 5" x 9" sterile dressing
- (1) conforming roller gauze bandage
- (2) triangular bandages
- (2) 3 × 3 sterile gauze pads
- (2) 4 × 4 sterile gauze pads
- (1) roll 3" cohesive bandage
- (2) germicidal hand wipes or waterless alcohol-based hand sanitizer
- (6) antiseptic wipes
- (2) pair large medical grade non-latex gloves
- Adhesive tape, 2" width
- Anti-bacterial ointment
- Cold pack
- Scissors (small, personal)

- Tweezers
- CPR breathing barrier, such as a face shield
- First aid manual

Non-Prescription and Prescription Drugs
- Aspirin or non-aspirin pain reliever
- Anti-diarrhea medication
- Antacid (for stomach upset)
- Syrup of Ipecac (use to induce vomiting if advised by the Poison Control Center)
- Laxative
- Activated charcoal (use if advised by the Poison Control Center)
- Prescription drugs, as recommended by your physician, and copies of the prescriptions in case they need to be replaced

For more information about first aid kits, visit www.redcross.org.

Preparedness Tip #15

Keep at least a three-day supply of water per person. Store a minimum of one gallon of water per person per day (two quarts for drinking, two quarts for food preparation and sanitation). Store water in plastic containers such as soft drink bottles. Avoid using containers that will decompose or break, such as milk cartons or glass bottles. A normally active person needs to drink at least two quarts of water each day. Hot environments and strenuous activity can double that amount. Children, nursing mothers, and people who are sick will also need more.

Preparedness Tip #16

One of the easiest ways you can prepare for emergencies is to keep some supplies readily available. Every kit is unique and can be tailored to meet the specific needs of your family, but below is a general list of supplies you may want to consider:

Tools and Supplies (Essential Items are Marked with an Asterisk *)
- Mess kits, or paper cups, plates, and plastic utensils
- Emergency preparedness manual and a copy of your disaster plan, including your emergency contacts list

- Battery-operated radio and extra batteries*
- Flashlight and extra batteries*
- Cash or traveler's checks, change*
- Non-electric can opener, utility knife*
- Fire extinguisher: small ABC type stored near where fires are likely to occur such as a kitchen, or near a fireplace. It should not be kept in the disaster supplies kit.
- Tube tent
- Duct tape*
- Compass
- Matches in a waterproof container
- Aluminum foil
- Plastic storage containers
- Signal flare
- Paper, pencil*
- Needles, thread
- Medicine dropper
- Shut-off wrench or pliers, to turn off household gas and water
- Whistle*
- Plastic sheeting*
- Map of the area (for locating shelters and evacuation routes)

Preparedness Tip #17

Also include items for sanitation in your emergency supply kit. Consider the following:

Sanitation (Essential Items are Marked with an Asterisk *)
- Toilet paper, towelettes*
- Soap, liquid detergent*
- Feminine supplies*
- Personal hygiene items*
- Plastic garbage bags, ties (for personal sanitation uses)*
- Plastic bucket with tight lid

- Disinfectant
- Household chlorine bleach

Preparedness Tip #18

Include at least one complete change of clothing and footwear per person in your emergency supply kit. We suggest long pants and long sleeves for additional protection after a disaster.

Clothing and Bedding (Essential Items are Marked with an Asterisk *)
- Sturdy shoes or work boots*
- Rain gear*
- Blankets or sleeping bags*
- Hat and gloves
- Thermal underwear
- Sunglasses

Preparedness Tip #19

You should also keep a smaller version of your emergency supply kit in your vehicle, in case you are commuting or traveling when disaster strikes.

Emergency Kit For Your Vehicle
- Bottled water and non-perishable high energy foods, such as granola bars, raisins and peanut butter
- Flashlight and extra batteries
- Blanket
- Booster cables
- Fire extinguisher (5 lb., A-B-C type)
- First aid kit and manual
- Maps
- Shovel
- Tire repair kit and pump
- Flares or other emergency marking devices

Preparedness Tip #20

Teach children how to dial 9-1-1 in an emergency. Review emergency action steps with all family members:

- Check the scene and the victim
- Call 9-1-1 or your local emergency number posted by the telephone
- Care for the victim

Help your children learn more about emergencies. Download this preparedness coloring book or visit Red Cross' "Masters of Disaster."

Preparedness Tip #21

Read the information on your city, county and/or state government Web sites as well as the "Be Prepared" section of www.redcross.org or Ready.gov and print emergency preparedness information. Be sure to keep a copy with your disaster supplies kit. It can provide telephone numbers, addresses and other information you need when electronic connections are not available options for obtaining the information.

Preparedness Tip #22

When water is of questionable purity, it is easiest to use bottled water for drinking and cooking if it is available. When it's not available, it is important to know how to treat contaminated water. In addition to having a bad odor and taste, water from questionable sources may be contaminated by a variety of microorganisms, including, bacteria and parasites that cause diseases such as dysentery, cholera, typhoid, and hepatitis. All water of uncertain purity should be treated before use. Use one or a combination of these treatments:

- Filter: Filter the water using a piece of cloth or coffee filter to remove solid particles.
- Boil: Bring it to a rolling boil for about one full minute. Cool it and pour it back and forth between two clean containers to improve its taste before drinking it.
- Chlorinate:
  - Add 16 drops (1/8 teaspoon) of liquid chlorine bleach per gallon of water. Stir to mix. Sodium hypochlorite of the concentration of 5.25% to 6% should be the only active ingredient in the bleach. There should not be any added soap or fragrances. A major bleach manufacturer has

also added Sodium Hydroxide as an active ingredient, which they state does not pose a health risk for water treatment.

- Let stand 30 minutes.
- If it smells of chlorine, you can use it. If it does not smell of chlorine, add 16 more drops (1/8 teaspoon) of chlorine bleach per gallon of water, let stand 30 minutes, and smell it again. If it smells of chlorine, you can use it. If it does not smell of chlorine, discard it and find another source of water.

Flood water can also be contaminated by toxic chemicals. Do NOT try to treat flood water.

Preparedness Tip #23

In some emergencies you may be required to turn off your utilities. To prepare for this type of event:

- Locate the electric, gas and water shut-off valves.
- Keep necessary tools near gas and water shut-off valves
- Teach adult family members how to turn off utilities.

If you turn off the gas, a professional must turn it back on. Do not attempt to do this yourself.

Preparedness Tip #24

Understand that during an emergency you may be asked to "shelter-in-place" or evacuate. Plan for both possibilities and be prepared to listen to instructions from your local emergency management officials. Visit Ready. gov and www.redcross.org/preparedness for more information on sheltering-in-place.

Preparedness Tip #25

A disaster can cause significant financial loss. Your apartment or home may be severely damaged or destroyed. You may be forced to live in temporary housing. Income may be cut off or significantly reduced. Important financial records could be destroyed. Take the time now to assess your situation and ask questions.

To help you, consider using the Emergency Financial First Aid Kit (EFFAK), a tool developed by Operation Hope, FEMA and Citizen Corps or contact your local Red Cross chapter for *Disasters and Financial Planning: A Guide for Preparedness.*

Preparedness Tip #26

Learn if earthquakes are a risk in your area by contacting your local emergency management office, local American Red Cross chapter, or state geological survey or department of natural resources. Information about earthquake risk is also available from the U.S. Geological Survey National Seismic Hazards project.

Preparedness Tip #27

Floods are among the most frequent and costly natural disasters in terms of human hardship and economic loss. As much as 90 percent of the damage related to all natural disasters (excluding draught) is caused by floods and associated debris flow. Most communities in the United States can experience some kind of flooding. Melting snow can combine with rain in the winter and early spring; severe thunderstorms can bring heavy rain in the spring or summer; or hurricanes can bring intense rainfall to coastal and inland states in the summer and fall. Regardless of how a flood occurs, the rule for being safe is simple: head for higher ground and stay away from floodwater. Even a shallow depth of fast-moving floodwater produces more force than most people imagine. You can protect yourself by being prepared and having time to act. Local radio or television stations or a NOAA Weather Radio are the best sources of information in a flood situation.

Preparedness Tip #28

When there is concern about a potential exposure to a chemical or other airborne hazard, local officials may advise you to "shelter-in-place" and "seal the room." This is different from taking shelter on the lowest level of your home in case of a natural disaster like a tornado. If you believe the air may be badly contaminated or if you are instructed by local officials, follow the instructions below to create a temporary barrier between you and the contaminated air outside.

To shelter-in-place and seal-the-room:
• Close and lock all windows and exterior doors.
• Turn off all fans, heating and air conditioning systems.
• Close the fireplace damper.
• Get your disaster supplies kit and turn on your battery-powered radio.

- Go to an interior room that is above ground level and without windows, if possible. In the case of a chemical threat, an above-ground location is preferable because some chemicals are heavier than air, and may seep into basements even if the windows are closed.
- If directed by local authorities on the radio, use duct tape to seal all cracks around the door and any vents into the room. Tape plastic sheeting, such as heavy-duty plastic garbage bags, over any windows.
- Listen to your radio or television for further instructions. Local officials will tell you when you can leave the room in which you are sheltering, or they may call for evacuation in specific areas at greatest risk in your community

Preparedness Tip #29

If there is an explosion:
- Take shelter against your desk or a sturdy table.
- Exit the building immediately.
- Do not use elevators.
- Check for fire and other hazards.
- Take your emergency supply kit if time allows.

If there is a fire:
- Exit the building immediately.
- If there is smoke, crawl under the smoke to the nearest exit and use a cloth, if possible, to cover your nose and mouth.
- Use the back of your hand to feel the upper, lower, and middle parts of closed doors.
- If the door is not hot, brace yourself against it and open slowly.
- If the door is hot, do not open it. Look for another way out.
- Do not use elevators.
- If your clothes catch on fire, stop-drop-and-roll to put out the fire. Do not run.
- If you are at home, go to your previously designated outside meeting place.
- Account for your family members and carefully supervise small children.
- GET OUT and STAY OUT. Never go back into a burning building.
- Call 9-1-1 or your local emergency number.

Disaster Response

Unlike an explosion, a biological attack may or may not be immediately obvious. Most likely local health care workers will report a pattern of unusual illness or a wave of sick people seeking medical attention. The best source of information will be radio or television reports. Understand that some biological agents, such as anthrax, do not cause contagious diseases. Others, like the smallpox virus, can result in diseases you can catch from other people. In the event of a biological attack, public health officials may not immediately be able to provide information on what you should do. It will take time to determine exactly what the illness is, how it should be treated, and who may have been exposed. You should watch TV, listen to the radio, or check the Internet for official news including the following:

- Are you in the group or area authorities believe may have been exposed?
- What are the signs and symptoms of the disease?
- Are medications or vaccines being distributed?
- Where? Who should get them and how?
- Where should you seek emergency medical care if you become sick?

During a declared biological emergency:
- If a family member becomes sick, it is important to be suspicious.
- Do not assume, however, that you should go to a hospital emergency room or that any illness is the result of the biological attack. Symptoms of many common illnesses may overlap.
- Use common sense, practice good hygiene and cleanliness to avoid spreading germs, and seek medical advice.
- Consider if you are in the group or area authorities believe to be in danger.
- If your symptoms match those described and you are in the group considered at risk, immediately seek emergency medical attention.

If you are potentially exposed:
- Follow instructions of doctors and other public health officials.
- If the disease is contagious expect to receive medical evaluation and treatment. You may be advised to stay away from others or even deliberately quarantined.
- For non-contagious diseases, expect to receive medical evaluation and treatment.

Appendix A

If you become aware of an unusual and suspicious substance nearby:

- Quickly get away.

- Protect yourself. Cover your mouth and nose with layers of fabric that can filter the air but still allow breathing. Examples include two to three layers of cotton such as a t-shirt, handkerchief or towel. Otherwise, several layers of tissue or paper towels may help.

- Wash with soap and water.

- Contact authorities.

- Watch TV, listen to the radio, or check the Internet for official news and information including what the signs and symptoms of the disease are, if medications or vaccinations are being distributed and where you should seek medical attention if you become sick. If you become sick seek emergency medical attention.

Source: Department of Homeland Security. Available online. URL: http://www.dhs. gov/xcitizens/editorial_0711.shtm.

APPENDIX B

DISASTER ASSISTANCE AVAILABLE FROM FEMA

The Federal Emergency Management Agency (FEMA) summarizes in simple and clear terms the benefits it makes available to victims of disasters. This material also describes conditions of eligibility. Updated on August 16, 2006.

HOUSING NEEDS

- **Temporary Housing** (a place to live for a limited period of time): Money is available to rent a different place to live, or a government provided housing unit when rental properties are not available.

- **Repair:** Money is available to homeowners to repair damage from the disaster to their primary residence that is not covered by insurance. The goal is to make the damaged home safe, sanitary, and functional.

- **Replacement:** Money is available to homeowners to replace their home destroyed in the disaster that is not covered by insurance. The goal is to help the homeowner with the cost of replacing their destroyed home.

- **Permanent Housing Construction:** Direct assistance or money for the construction of a home. This type of help occurs only in insular areas or remote locations specified by FEMA, where no other type of housing assistance is possible.

WHAT SPECIFIC ITEMS ARE COVERED BY "HOUSING NEEDS" ASSISTANCE?

"Housing Needs"assistance is assistance from FEMA that may be used to repair any of the following:

- Structural parts of your home (foundation, outside walls, roof).
- Windows, doors, floors, walls, ceilings, cabinetry.
- Septic or sewage system.
- Well or other water system.
- Heating, ventilating, and air conditioning system.
- Utilities (electrical, plumbing, and gas systems).
- Entrance and exit ways from your home, including privately owned access roads.
- Blocking, leveling, and anchoring of a mobile home and reconnecting or resetting its sewer, water, electrical, fuel lines, and tanks.

DO I QUALIFY FOR "HOUSING NEEDS" ASSISTANCE?

To receive money or help for "Housing Needs" that are the result of a disaster, all of the following must be true:

- You have losses in an area that has been declared a disaster by the president.
- You have filed for insurance benefits and the damage to your property is not covered by your insurance or your insurance settlement is insufficient to meet your losses.
- You or someone who lives with you is a citizen of the United States, a non-citizen national, or a qualified alien.
- The home in the disaster area is where you usually live and where you were living at the time of the disaster.
- You are not able to live in your home now, you cannot get to your home due to the disaster, or your home requires repairs because of damage from the disaster.

You may not be eligible for "Housing Needs" assistance if:
- You have other, adequate rent-free housing that you can use (for example, rental property that is not occupied).
- Your home that was damaged is your secondary or vacation residence.
- Your expenses resulted only from leaving your home as a precaution and you were able to return to your home immediately after the incident.
- You have refused assistance from your insurance provider(s).

- Your only losses are business losses (including farm business other than the farmhouse and self-employment) or items not covered by this program.
- The damaged home where you live is located in a designated flood hazard area and your community is not participating in the National Flood Insurance Program. In this case, the flood damage to your home would not be covered, but you may qualify for rental assistance or items not covered by flood insurance, such as water wells, septic systems, medical, dental, or funeral expenses.

OTHER THAN HOUSING NEEDS

Money is available for necessary expenses and serious needs caused by the disaster. This includes:

- Disaster-related medical and dental costs.
- Disaster-related funeral and burial cost.
- Clothing; household items (room furnishings, appliances); tools (specialized or protective clothing and equipment) required for your job; necessary educational materials (computers, school books, supplies).
- Fuels for primary heat source (heating oil, gas, firewood).
- Clean-up items (wet/dry vacuum, air purifier, dehumidifier).
- Disaster damaged vehicle.
- Moving and storage expenses related to the disaster (moving and storing property to avoid additional disaster damage while disaster-related repairs are being made to the home).
- Other necessary expenses or serious needs as determined by FEMA.
- Other expenses that are authorized by law.

DO I QUALIFY FOR "OTHER THAN HOUSING NEEDS" ASSISTANCE?

To receive money for "Other than Housing Needs" that are the result of a disaster, all the following must be true:

- You have losses in an area that has been declared a disaster area by the President.
- You have filed for insurance benefits and the damage to your property is not covered by your insurance or your insurance settlement is insufficient to meet your losses.

- You or someone who lives with you is a citizen of the United States, a non-citizen national, or a qualified alien.
- You have necessary expenses or serious needs because of the disaster.
- You have accepted assistance from all other sources for which you are eligible, such as insurance proceeds or Small Business Administration disaster loans.

CRISIS COUNSELING

The Crisis Counseling Assistance and Training Program (CCP), authorized by §416 of the Stafford Act, is designed to provide supplemental funding to States for short-term crisis counseling services to people affected in Presidentially declared disasters. There are two separate portions of the CCP that can be funded: immediate services and regular services. A State may request either or both types of funding.

The **immediate services** program is intended to enable the State or local agency to respond to the immediate mental health needs with screening, diagnostic, and counseling techniques, as well as outreach services such as public information and community networking.

The **regular services** program is designed to provide up to nine months of crisis counseling, community outreach, and consultation and education services to people affected by a Presidentially declared disaster. Funding for this program is separate from the immediate services grant.

To be eligible for crisis counseling services funded by this program, the person must be a resident of the designated area or must have been located in the area at the time the disaster occurred. The person must also have a mental health problem which was caused by or aggravated by the disaster or its aftermath, or he or she must benefit from services provided by the program.

DISASTER UNEMPLOYMENT ASSISTANCE

The Disaster Unemployment Assistance (DUA) program provides unemployment benefits and re-employment services to individuals who have become unemployed because of major disasters. Benefits begin with the date the individual was unemployed due to the disaster incident and can extend up to 26 weeks after the Presidential declaration date. These benefits are made available to individuals not covered by other unemployment compensation programs, such as self-employed, farmers, migrant and seasonal workers, and those who have insufficient quarters to qualify for other unemployment compensation.

All unemployed individuals must register with the State's employment services office before they can receive DUA benefits. However, although most States have a provision that an individual must be able and available to accept employment opportunities comparable to the employment the individual held before the disaster, not all States require an individual to search for work.

LEGAL SERVICES

When the President declares a disaster, FEMA/EPR, through an agreement with the Young Lawyers Division of the American Bar Association, provides free legal assistance to disaster victims. Legal advice is limited to cases that will not produce a fee (i.e., these attorneys work without payment). Cases that may generate a fee are turned over to the local lawyer referral service.

The assistance that participating lawyers provide typically includes:

- Assistance with insurance claims (life, medical, property, etc.)
- Counseling on landlord/tenant problems
- Assisting in consumer protection matters, remedies, and procedures
- Replacement of wills and other important legal documents destroyed in a major disaster.
- Disaster legal services are provided to low-income individuals who, prior to or because of the disaster, are unable to secure legal services adequate to meet their needs as a consequence of a major disaster.

SPECIAL TAX CONSIDERATIONS

Taxpayers who have sustained a casualty loss from a declared disaster may deduct that loss on the federal income tax return for the year in which the casualty actually occurred, or elect to deduct the loss on the tax return for the preceding tax year. In order to deduct a casualty loss, the amount of the loss must exceed 10 percent of the adjusted gross income for the tax year by at least $100. If the loss was sustained from a federally declared disaster, the taxpayer may choose which of those two tax years provides the better tax advantage.

The Internal Revenue Service (IRS) can expedite refunds due to taxpayers in a federally declared disaster area. An expedited refund can be a relatively quick source of cash, does not need to be repaid, and does not need an Individual Assistance declaration. It is available to any taxpayer in a federally declared disaster area.

Source: FEMA. Available online. URL:http://www.fema.gov/assistance/process/additional.shtm#2.

APPENDIX C

SELECTIONS FROM THE ROBERT T. STAFFORD DISASTER RELIEF AND EMERGENCY ASSISTANCE ACT (PUBLIC LAW 93-288) AS AMENDED

The Stafford Act sets disaster law and policy, which the Department of Homeland Security (DHS) and the Federal Emergency Management Agency (FEMA) implement. Although the full law is too long to present here, Subchapter IV reproduced below covers key sections on assistance for disaster victims.

UNITED STATES CODE TITLE 42. THE PUBLIC HEALTH AND WELFARE CHAPTER 68. DISASTER RELIEF

Subchapter IV—Major Disaster Assistance Programs

---

§ 5170. PROCEDURE FOR DECLARATION {SEC. 401}

All requests for a declaration by the President that a major disaster exists shall be made by the Governor of the affected State. Such a request shall be based on a finding that the disaster is of such severity and magnitude that effective response is beyond the capabilities of the State and the affected local governments and that Federal assistance is necessary. As part of such request, and as a prerequisite to major disaster assistance under this Act, the Governor shall take appropriate response action under State law and direct execution of the State's emergency plan. The Governor shall furnish information on the nature and amount of State and local resources which have been or will be committed to alleviating the results of the disaster, and shall certify that, for the current disaster, State and local government obligations and expenditures (of which State commitments must be a significant proportion) will comply with all applicable cost-sharing requirements of this Act. Based on the request of a Governor under this section, the President may declare under this Act that a major disaster or emergency exists.

§ 5170A. GENERAL FEDERAL ASSISTANCE {SEC. 402}

In any major disaster, the President may—

1. direct any Federal agency, with or without reimbursement, to utilize its authorities and the resources granted to it under Federal law (including personnel, equipment, supplies, facilities, and managerial, technical, and advisory services) in support of State and local assistance efforts;
2. coordinate all disaster relief assistance (including voluntary assistance) provided by Federal agencies, private organizations, and State and local governments;
3. provide technical and advisory assistance to affected State and local governments for—
   A. the performance of essential community services;
   B. issuance of warnings of risks and hazards;
   C. public health and safety information, including dissemination of such information;
   D. provision of health and safety measures; and
   E. management, control, and reduction of immediate threats to public health and safety; and
4. assist State and local governments in the distribution of medicine, food, and other consumable supplies, and emergency assistance.

§ 5170B. ESSENTIAL ASSISTANCE {SEC. 403}

a. In general
Federal agencies may on the direction of the President, provide assistance essential to meeting immediate threats to life and property resulting from a major disaster, as follows:
1. Federal resources, generally
Utilizing, lending, or donating to State and local governments Federal equipment, supplies, facilities, personnel, and other resources, other

than the extension of credit, for use or distribution by such governments in accordance with the purposes of this Act.

2. Medicine, food, and other consumables
Distributing or rendering through State and local governments, the American National Red Cross, the Salvation Army, the Mennonite Disaster Service, and other relief and disaster assistance organizations medicine, food, and other consumable supplies, and other services and assistance to disaster victims.

3. Work and services to save lives and protect property
Performing on public or private lands or waters any work or services essential to saving lives and protecting and preserving property or public health and safety, including—
   A. debris removal;
   B. search and rescue, emergency medical care, emergency mass care, emergency shelter, and provision of food, water, medicine, and other essential needs, including movement of supplies or persons;
   C. clearance of roads and construction of temporary bridges necessary to the performance of emergency tasks and essential community services;
   D. provision of temporary facilities for schools and other essential community services;
   E. demolition of unsafe structures which endanger the public;
   F. warning of further risks and hazards;
   G. dissemination of public info rmation and assistance regarding health and safety measures;
   H. provision of technical advice to State and local governments on disaster management and control; and
   I. reduction of immediate threats to life, property, and public health and safety.

4. Contributions
Making contributions to State or local governments or owners or operators of private nonprofit facilities for the purpose of carrying out the provisions of this subsection.

b. Federal share
The Federal share of assistance under this section shall be not less than 75 percent of the eligible cost of such assistance.

c. Utilization of DOD [Department of Defense] resources
1. General rule
During the immediate aftermath of an incident which may ultimately qualify for assistance under this title or title V of this Act [42 U.S.C 5170 et seq. or 5191 et seq.], the Governor of the State in

which such incident occurred may request the President to direct the Secretary of Defense to utilize the resources of the Department of Defense for the purpose of performing on public and private lands any emergency work which is made necessary by such incident and which is essential for the preservation of life and property. If the President determines that such work is essential for the preservation of life and property, the President shall grant such request to the extent the President determines practicable. Such emergency work may only be carried out for a period not to exceed 10 days.

2. Rules applicable to debris removal
   Any removal of debris and wreckage carried out under this subsection shall be subject to section 5173(b) of this title, relating to unconditional authorization and indemnification for debris removal.

3. Expenditures out of disaster relief funds
   The cost of any assistance provided pursuant to this subsection shall be reimbursed out of funds made available to carry out this Act.

4. Federal share
   The Federal share of assistance under this subsection shall be not less than 75 percent.

5. Guidelines
   Not later than 180 days after the date of the enactment of the Disaster Relief and Emergency Assistance Amendments of 1988 [enacted Nov. 23, 1988], the President shall issue guidelines for carrying out this subsection. Such guidelines shall consider any likely effect assistance under this subsection will have on the availability of other forms of assistance under this Act.

6. Definitions
   For purposes of this section—
   A. Department of Defense
      The term "Department of Defense" has the meaning the term "department" has under section 101 of title 10.
   B. Emergency work
      The term "emergency work" includes clearance and removal of debris and wreckage and temporary restoration of essential public facilities and services.

§ 5170C. HAZARD MITIGATION {SEC. 404}

a. In General.
The President may contribute up to 75 percent of the cost of hazard mitigation measures which the President has determined are cost-effective and which substantially reduce the risk of future damage, hardship,

loss, or suffering in any area affected by a major disaster. Such measures shall be identified following the evaluation of natural hazards under section 5165 of this title and shall be subject to approval by the President. Subject to section 5165 of this title, the total of contributions under this section for a major disaster shall not exceed 7.5 percent of the estimated aggregate amount of grants to be made (less any associated administrative costs) under this Act with respect to the major disaster.

b. Property acquisition and relocation assistance.—

  1. General authority. In providing hazard mitigation assistance under this section in connection with flooding, the Director of the Federal Emergency Management Agency may provide property acquisition and relocation assistance for projects that meet the requirements of paragraph (2).

  2. Terms and conditions.

  An acquisition or relocation project shall be eligible to receive assistance pursuant to paragraph (1) only if—

    A. the applicant for the assistance is otherwise eligible to receive assistance under the hazard mitigation grant program established under subsection (a); and

    B. on or after the date of enactment of this subsection [enacted Dec. 3, 1993], the applicant for the assistance enters into an agreement with the Director that provides assurances that—

      i. any property acquired, accepted, or from which a structure will be removed pursuant to the project will be dedicated and maintained in perpetuity for a use that is compatible with open space, recreational, or wetlands management practices;

      ii. no new structure will be erected on property acquired, accepted or from which a structure was removed under the acquisition or relocation program other than—

        I. a public facility that is open on all sides and functionally related to a designated open space;

        II. a rest room; or

        III. a structure that the Director approves in writing before the commencement of the construction of the structure; and

      iii. after receipt of the assistance, with respect to any property acquired, accepted or from which a structure was removed under the acquisition or relocation program—

        I. no subsequent application for additional disaster assistance for any purpose will be made by the recipient to any Federal entity; and

        II. no assistance referred to in subclause (I) will be provided to the applicant by any Federal source.

3. Statutory construction

Nothing in this subsection is intended to alter or otherwise affect an agreement for an acquisition or relocation project carried out pursuant to this section that was in effect on the day before the date of enactment of this subsection [enacted Dec. 3, 1993].

c. Program Administration by States.—

1. In general.—A State desiring to administer the hazard mitigation grant program established by this section with respect to hazard mitigation assistance in the State may submit to the President an application for the delegation of the authority to administer the program.

2. Criteria.—The President, in consultation and coordination with States and local governments, shall establish criteria for the approval of applications submitted under paragraph (1). The criteria shall include, at a minimum—

   A. the demonstrated ability of the State to manage the grant program under this section;

   B. there being in effect an approved mitigation plan under section 5165 of this title; and

   C. a demonstrated commitment to mitigation activities.

3. Approval.—The President shall approve an application submitted under paragraph (1) that meets the criteria established under paragraph (2).

4. Withdrawal of approval.—If, after approving an application of a State submitted under paragraph (1), the President determines that the State is not administering the hazard mitigation grant program established by this section in a manner satisfactory to the President, the President shall withdraw the approval.

5. Audits.—The President shall provide for periodic audits of the hazard mitigation grant programs administered by States under this subsection.

§ 5171. FEDERAL FACILITIES {SEC. 405}

a. Repair, reconstruction, restoration or replacement of United States facilities

The President may authorize any Federal agency to repair, reconstruct, restore, or replace any facility owned by the United States and under the jurisdiction of such agency which is damaged or destroyed by any major disaster if he determines that such repair, reconstruction, restoration, or replacement is of such importance and urgency that it cannot reasonably be deferred pending the enactment of specific authorizing legislation or the making of an appropriation for such purposes, or the obtaining of congressional committee approval.

b. Availability of funds appropriated to agency for repair, reconstruction, restoration, or replacement of agency facilities

In order to carry out the provisions of this section, such repair, reconstruction, restoration, or replacement may be begun notwithstanding a lack or an insufficiency of funds appropriated for such purpose, where such lack or insufficiency can be remedied by the transfer, in accordance with law, of funds appropriated to that agency for another purpose.

c. Steps for mitigation of hazards

In implementing this section, Federal agencies shall evaluate the natural hazards to which these facilities are exposed and shall take appropriate action to mitigate such hazards, including safe land-use and construction practices, in accordance with standards prescribed by the President.

§ 5172. REPAIR, RESTORATION, AND REPLACEMENT OF DAMAGED FACILITIES {SEC. 406}

a. Contributions.—

1. In general.—The President may make contributions—
   A. to a State or local government for the repair, restoration, reconstruction, or replacement of a public facility damaged or destroyed by a major disaster and for associated expenses incurred by the government; and
   B. subject to paragraph (3), to a person that owns or operates a private nonprofit facility damaged or destroyed by a major disaster for the repair, restoration, reconstruction, or replacement of the facility and for associated expenses incurred by the person.

2. Associated expenses.—For the purposes of this section, associated expenses shall include—
   A. the costs of mobilizing and employing the National Guard for performance of eligible work;
   B. the costs of using prison labor to perform eligible work, including wages actually paid, transportation to a worksite, and extraordinary costs of guards, food, and lodging; and
   C. base and overtime wages for the employees and extra hires of a State, local government, or person described in paragraph (1) that perform eligible work, plus fringe benefits on such wages to the extent that such benefits were being paid before the major disaster.

3. Conditions for assistance to private nonprofit facilities.—
   A. In general.—The President may make contributions to a private nonprofit facility under paragraph (1)(B) only if—
      i. the facility provides critical services (as defined by the President) in the event of a major disaster; or

      ii. the owner or operator of the facility—
- I. has applied for a disaster loan under section 7(b) of the Small Business Act (15 U.S.C. 636(b)); and
- II. (aa) has been determined to be ineligible for such a loan; or (bb) has obtained such a loan in the maximum amount for which the Small Business Administration determines the facility is eligible.

  B. Definition of critical services.—In this paragraph, the term "critical services" includes power, water (including water provided by an irrigation organization or facility), sewer, wastewater treatment, communications, and emergency medical care.

4. Notification to Congress.—Before making any contribution under this section in an amount greater than $20,000,000, the President shall notify—
- A. the Committee on Environment and Public Works of the Senate;
- B. the Committee on Transportation and Infrastructure of the House of Representatives;
- C. the Committee on Appropriations of the Senate; and
- D. the Committee on Appropriations of the House of Representatives.

b. Federal Share.—

1. Minimum federal share.—Except as provided in paragraph (2), the Federal share of assistance under this section shall be not less than 75 percent of the eligible cost of repair, restoration, reconstruction, or replacement carried out under this section.

2. Reduced federal share.—The President shall promulgate regulations to reduce the Federal share of assistance under this section to not less than 25 percent in the case of the repair, restoration, reconstruction, or replacement of any eligible public facility or private nonprofit facility following an event associated with a major disaster—
- A. that has been damaged, on more than one occasion within the preceding 10-year period, by the same type of event; and
- B. the owner of which has failed to implement appropriate mitigation measures to address the hazard that caused the damage to the facility.

c. Large In-Lieu Contributions.—

1. For public facilities.—
- A. In general.—In any case in which a State or local government determines that the public welfare would not best be served by repairing, restoring, reconstructing, or replacing any public facility owned or controlled by the State or local government, the State or local government may elect to receive, in lieu of a contribution under subsection (a)(1)(A), a contribution in an amount equal to 75

percent of the Federal share of the Federal estimate of the cost of repairing, restoring, reconstructing, or replacing the facility and of management expenses.

B. Areas with unstable soil.—In any case in which a State or local government determines that the public welfare would not best be served by repairing, restoring, reconstructing, or replacing any public facility owned or controlled by the State or local government because soil instability in the disaster area makes repair, restoration, reconstruction, or replacement infeasible, the State or local government may elect to receive, in lieu of a contribution under subsection (a)(1)(A), a contribution in an amount equal to 90 percent of the Federal share of the Federal estimate of the cost of repairing, restoring, reconstructing, or replacing the facility and of management expenses.

C. Use of funds.—Funds contributed to a State or local government under this paragraph may be used—

   i. to repair, restore, or expand other selected public facilities;

   ii. to construct new facilities; or

   iii. to fund hazard mitigation measures that the State or local government determines to be necessary to meet a need for governmental services and functions in the area affected by the major disaster.

D. Limitations.—Funds made available to a State or local government under this paragraph may not be used for—

   i. any public facility located in a regulatory floodway (as defined in section 59.1 of title 44, Code of Federal Regulations (or a successor regulation)); or

   ii. any uninsured public facility located in a special flood hazard area identified by the Director of the Federal Emergency Management Agency under the National Flood Insurance Act of 1968 (42 U.S.C. 4001 et seq.).

2. For private nonprofit facilities.—

A. In general.—In any case in which a person that owns or operates a private nonprofit facility determines that the public welfare would not best be served by repairing, restoring, reconstructing, or replacing the facility, the person may elect to receive, in lieu of a contribution under subsection (a)(1)(B), a contribution in an amount equal to 75 percent of the Federal share of the Federal estimate of the cost of repairing, restoring, reconstructing, or replacing the facility and of management expenses.

B. Use of funds.—Funds contributed to a person under this paragraph may be used—

i. to repair, restore, or expand other selected private nonprofit facilities owned or operated by the person;

ii. to construct new private nonprofit facilities to be owned or operated by the person; or

iii. to fund hazard mitigation measures that the person determines to be necessary to meet a need for the person's services and functions in the area affected by the major disaster.

C. Limitations.—Funds made available to a person under this paragraph may not be used for—

i. any private nonprofit facility located in a regulatory floodway (as defined in section 59.1 of title 44, Code of Federal Regulations (or a successor regulation)); or

ii. any uninsured private nonprofit facility located in a special flood hazard area identified by the Director of the Federal Emergency Management Agency under the National Flood Insurance Act of 1968 (42 U.S.C. 4001 et seq.).

d. Flood insurance

1. Reduction of Federal assistance

If a public facility or private nonprofit facility located in a special flood hazard area identified for more than 1 year by the Director pursuant to the National Flood Insurance Act of 1968 (42 U.S.C. 4001 et seq.) is damaged or destroyed, after the 180th day following the date of the enactment of the Disaster Relief and Emergency Assistance Amendments of 1988 [enacted Nov. 23, 1988], by flooding in a major disaster and such facility is not covered on the date of such flooding by flood insurance, the Federal assistance which would otherwise be available under this section with respect to repair, restoration, reconstruction, and replacement of such facility and associated expenses shall be reduced in accordance with paragraph (2).

2. Amount of reduction

The amount of a reduction in Federal assistance under this section with respect to a facility shall be the lesser of—

A. the value of such facility on the date of the flood damage or destruction, or

B. the maximum amount of insurance proceeds which would have been payable with respect to such facility if such facility had been covered by flood insurance under the National Flood Insurance Act of 1968 on such date.

3. Exception

Paragraphs (1) and (2) shall not apply to a private nonprofit facility which is not covered by flood insurance solely because of the local government's failure to participate in the flood insurance program established by the National Flood Insurance Act.

4. Dissemination of information

The President shall disseminate information regarding the reduction in Federal assistance provided for by this subsection to State and local governments and the owners and operators of private nonprofit facilities who may be affected by such a reduction.

e. Eligible Cost.—

1. Determination.—

A. In general.—For the purposes of this section, the President shall estimate the eligible cost of repairing, restoring, reconstructing, or replacing a public facility or private nonprofit facility—

i. (i) on the basis of the design of the facility as the facility existed immediately before the major disaster; and

ii. in conformity with codes, specifications, and standards (including floodplain management and hazard mitigation criteria required by the President or under the Coastal Barrier Resources Act (16 U.S.C. 3501 et seq.)) applicable at the time at which the disaster occurred.

B. Cost estimation procedures.—

i. In general.—Subject to paragraph (2), the President shall use the cost estimation procedures established under paragraph (3) to determine the eligible cost under this subsection.

ii. Applicability.—The procedures specified in this paragraph and paragraph (2) shall apply only to projects the eligible cost of which is equal to or greater than the amount specified in section 5189 of this title.—

2. Modification of eligible cost.—

A. Actual cost greater than ceiling percentage of estimated cost.—In any case in which the actual cost of repairing, restoring, reconstructing, or replacing a facility under this section is greater than the ceiling percentage established under paragraph (3) of the cost estimated under paragraph (1), the President may determine that the eligible cost includes a portion of the actual cost of the repair, restoration, reconstruction, or replacement that exceeds the cost estimated under paragraph (1).

B. Actual cost less than estimated cost.—

i. Greater than or equal to floor percentage of estimated cost.—In any case in which the actual cost of repairing, restoring, reconstructing, or replacing a facility under this section is less than 100 percent of the cost estimated under paragraph (1), but is greater than or equal to the floor percentage established under paragraph (3) of the cost estimated under paragraph (1), the State or local government or person receiving funds under this section shall use the excess funds to carry out cost-effective activities that reduce the risk of future damage, hardship, or suffering from a major disaster.

   ii. Less than floor percentage of estimated cost.—In any case in which the actual cost of repairing, restoring, reconstructing, or replacing a facility under this section is less than the floor percentage established under paragraph (3) of the cost estimated under paragraph (1), the State or local government or person receiving assistance under this section shall reimburse the President in the amount of the difference.

  C. No effect on appeals process.—Nothing in this paragraph affects any right of appeal under section 5189a of this title.

3. Expert panel.—

  A. Establishment.—Not later than 18 months after the date of the enactment of this paragraph [enacted Oct. 30, 2000], the President, acting through the Director of the Federal Emergency Management Agency, shall establish an expert panel, which shall include representatives from the construction industry and State and local government.

  B. Duties.—The expert panel shall develop recommendations concerning—

   i. procedures for estimating the cost of repairing, restoring, reconstructing, or replacing a facility consistent with industry practices; and

   ii. the ceiling and floor percentages referred to in paragraph (2).

  C. Regulations.—Taking into account the recommendations of the expert panel under subparagraph (B), the President shall promulgate regulations that establish—

   i. cost estimation procedures described in subparagraph (B)(i); and

   ii. the ceiling and floor percentages referred to in paragraph (2).

  D. Review by President.—Not later than 2 years after the date of promulgation of regulations under subparagraph (C) and periodically thereafter, the President shall review the cost estimation procedures and the ceiling and floor percentages established under this paragraph.

  E. Report to Congress.—Not later than 1 year after the date of promulgation of regulations under subparagraph (C), 3 years after that date, and at the end of each 2-year period thereafter, the expert panel shall submit to Congress a report on the appropriateness of the cost estimation procedures.

4. Special rule.—In any case in which the facility being repaired, restored, reconstructed, or replaced under this section was under con-

struction on the date of the major disaster, the cost of repairing, restoring, reconstructing, or replacing the facility shall include, for the purposes of this section, only those costs that, under the contract for the construction, are the owner's responsibility and not the contractor's responsibility.

§ 5173. DEBRIS REMOVAL {SEC. 407}

a. Authorization for use of Federal assistance and grants to State or local government
The President, whenever he determines it to be in the public interest, is authorized—
1. through the use of Federal departments, agencies, and instrumentalities, to clear debris and wreckage resulting from a major disaster from publicly and privately owned lands and waters; and
2. to make grants to any State or local government or owner or operator of a private non-profit facility for the purpose of removing debris or wreckage resulting from a major disaster from publicly or privately owned lands and waters.
b. State or local government authorization; indemnification of Federal government No authority under this section shall be exercised unless the affected State or local government shall first arrange an unconditional authorization for removal of such debris or wreckage from public and private property, and, in the case of removal of debris or wreckage from private property, shall first agree to indemnify the Federal Government against any claim arising from such removal.
c. Rules relating to large lots
The President shall issue rules which provide for recognition of differences existing among urban, suburban, and rural lands in implementation of this section so as to facilitate adequate removal of debris and wreckage from large lots.
d. Federal share
The Federal share of assistance under this section shall be not less than 75 percent of the eligible cost of debris and wreckage removal carried out under this section.

§ 5174. FEDERAL ASSISTANCE TO INDIVIDUALS AND HOUSEHOLDS {SEC. 408}

a. In General.—
1. Provision of assistance.—In accordance with this section, the President, in consultation with the Governor of a State, may provide financial as-

sistance, and, if necessary, direct services, to individuals and households in the State who, as a direct result of a major disaster, have necessary expenses and serious needs in cases in which the individuals and households are unable to meet such expenses or needs through other means.

2. Relationship to other assistance.—Under paragraph (1), an individual or household shall not be denied assistance under paragraph (1), (3), or (4) of subsection (c) solely on the basis that the individual or household has not applied for or received any loan or other financial assistance from the Small Business Administration or any other Federal agency.

b. Housing Assistance.—

1. Eligibility.—The President may provide financial or other assistance under this section to individuals and households to respond to the disaster-related housing needs of individuals and households who are displaced from their predisaster primary residences or whose predisaster primary residences are rendered uninhabitable as a result of damage caused by a major disaster.

2. Determination of appropriate types of assistance.—

A. In general.—The President shall determine appropriate types of housing assistance to be provided under this section to individuals and households described in subsection (a)(1) based on considerations of cost effectiveness, convenience to the individuals and households, and such other factors as the President may consider appropriate.

B. Multiple types of assistance.—One or more types of housing assistance may be made available under this section, based on the suitability and availability of the types of assistance, to meet the needs of individuals and households in the particular disaster situation.

c. Types of Housing Assistance.—

1. Temporary housing.—

A. Financial assistance.—

i. In general.—The President may provide financial assistance to individuals or households to rent alternate housing accommodations, existing rental units, manufactured housing, recreational vehicles, or other readily fabricated dwellings.

ii. Amount.—The amount of assistance under clause (i) shall be based on the fair market rent for the accommodation provided plus the cost of any transportation, utility hookups, or unit installation not provided directly by the President.

B. Direct assistance.—

i. In general.—The President may provide temporary housing units, acquired by purchase or lease, directly to individuals or households who, because of a lack of available housing resources, would be unable to make use of the assistance provided under subparagraph (A).

  ii. Period of assistance.—The President may not provide direct assistance under clause (i) with respect to a major disaster after the end of the 18-month period beginning on the date of the declaration of the major disaster by the President, except that the President may extend that period if the President determines that due to extraordinary circumstances an extension would be in the public interest.

  iii. Collection of rental charges.—After the end of the 18-month period referred to in clause (ii), the President may charge fair market rent for each temporary housing unit provided.

2. Repairs.
  A. In general.—The President may provide financial assistance for—
    i. the repair of owner-occupied private residences, utilities, and residential infrastructure (such as a private access route) damaged by a major disaster to a safe and sanitary living or functioning condition; and
    ii. eligible hazard mitigation measures that reduce the likelihood of future damage to such residences, utilities, or infrastructure.
  B. Relationship to other assistance.—A recipient of assistance provided under this paragraph shall not be required to show that the assistance can be met through other means, except insurance proceeds.
  C. Maximum amount of assistance.—The amount of assistance provided to a household under this paragraph shall not exceed $5,000, as adjusted annually to reflect changes in the Consumer Price Index for All Urban Consumers published by the Department of Labor.

3. Replacement.—
  A. In general.—The President may provide financial assistance for the replacement of owner-occupied private residences damaged by a major disaster.
  B. Maximum amount of assistance.—The amount of assistance provided to a household under this paragraph shall not exceed $10,000, as adjusted annually to reflect changes in the Consumer Price Index for All Urban Consumers published by the Department of Labor.
  C. Applicability of flood insurance requirement.—With respect to assistance provided under this paragraph, the President may not waive any provision of Federal law requiring the purchase of flood insurance as a condition of the receipt of Federal disaster assistance.

4. Permanent housing construction.—The President may provide financial assistance or direct assistance to individuals or households to construct permanent housing in insular areas outside the continental United States and in other remote locations in cases in which—

    A. no alternative housing resources are available; and

    B. the types of temporary housing assistance described in paragraph (1) are unavailable, infeasible, or not cost-effective.

d. Terms and Conditions Relating to Housing Assistance.—

  1. Sites.—

    A. In general.—Any readily fabricated dwelling provided under this section shall, whenever practicable, be located on a site that—

      i. is complete with utilities; and

      ii. is provided by the State or local government, by the owner of the site, or by the occupant who was displaced by the major disaster.

    B. Sites provided by the president.—A readily fabricated dwelling may be located on a site provided by the President if the President determines that such a site would be more economical or accessible.

  2. Disposal of units.—

    A. Sale to occupants.—

      i. In general.—Notwithstanding any other provision of law, a temporary housing unit purchased under this section by the President for the purpose of housing disaster victims may be sold directly to the individual or household who is occupying the unit if the individual or household lacks permanent housing.

      ii. Sale price.—A sale of a temporary housing unit under clause (i) shall be at a price that is fair and equitable.

      iii. Deposit of proceeds.—

      Notwithstanding any other provision of law, the proceeds of a sale under clause (i) shall be deposited in the appropriate Disaster Relief Fund account.

      iv. Hazard and flood insurance.—A sale of a temporary housing unit under clause (i) shall be made on the condition that the individual or household purchasing the housing unit agrees to obtain and maintain hazard and flood insurance on the housing unit.

      v. Use of GSA services.—The President may use the services of the General Services Administration to accomplish a sale under clause (i).

    B. Other methods of disposal.—If not disposed of under subparagraph (A), a temporary housing unit purchased under this section by the President for the purpose of housing disaster victims—

      i. may be sold to any person; or

ii. may be sold, transferred, donated, or otherwise made available directly to a State or other governmental entity or to a voluntary organization for the sole purpose of providing temporary housing to disaster victims in major disasters and emergencies if, as a condition of the sale, transfer, or donation, the State, other governmental agency, or voluntary organization agrees—

    I. to comply with the nondiscrimination provisions of section 5151 of this title; and

    II. to obtain and maintain hazard and flood insurance on the housing unit.

e. Financial Assistance To Address Other Needs.—

1. Medical, dental, and funeral expenses.—The President, in consultation with the Governor of a State, may provide financial assistance under this section to an individual or household in the State who is adversely affected by a major disaster to meet disaster-related medical, dental, and funeral expenses.

2. Personal property, transportation, and other expenses.—The President, in consultation with the Governor of a State, may provide financial assistance under this section to an individual or household described in paragraph (1) to address personal property, transportation, and other necessary expenses or serious needs resulting from the major disaster.

f. State Role.—

1. Financial assistance to address other needs.—

A. Grant to state.—Subject to subsection (g), a Governor may request a grant from the President to provide financial assistance to individuals and households in the State under subsection (e).

B. Administrative costs.—A State that receives a grant under subparagraph (A) may expend not more than 5 percent of the amount of the grant for the administrative costs of providing financial assistance to individuals and households in the State under subsection (e).

2. Access to records.—In providing assistance to individuals and households under this section, the President shall provide for the substantial and ongoing involvement of the States in which the individuals and households are located, including by providing to the States access to the electronic records of individuals and households receiving assistance under this section in order for the States to make available any additional State and local assistance to the individuals and households.

g. Cost Sharing.—

1. Federal share.—Except as provided in paragraph (2), the Federal share of the costs eligible to be paid using assistance provided under this section shall be 100 percent.

2. Financial assistance to address other needs.—In the case of financial assistance provided under subsection (e)—
   A. the Federal share shall be 75 percent; and
   B. the non-Federal share shall be paid from funds made available by the State.
h. Maximum Amount of Assistance.—
   1. In general.—No individual or household shall receive financial assistance greater than $25,000 under this section with respect to a single major disaster.
   2. Adjustment of limit.—The limit established under paragraph (1) shall be adjusted annually to reflect changes in the Consumer Price Index for All Urban Consumers published by the Department of Labor.
   (i) Rules and Regulations.—The President shall prescribe rules and regulations to carry out this section, including criteria, standards, and procedures for determining eligibility for assistance.

§ 5177. UNEMPLOYMENT ASSISTANCE {SEC. 410}

a. Benefit assistance
   The President is authorized to provide to any individual unemployed as a result of a major disaster such benefit assistance as he deems appropriate while such individual is unemployed for the weeks of such unemployment with respect to which the individual is not entitled to any other unemployment compensation (as that term is defined in section 85(b) of the Internal Revenue Code of 1986 or waiting period credit. Such assistance as the President shall provide shall be available to an individual as long as the individual's unemployment caused by the major disaster continues or until the individual is reemployed in a suitable position, but no longer than 26 weeks after the major disaster is declared. Such assistance for a week of unemployment shall not exceed the maximum weekly amount authorized under the unemployment compensation law of the State in which the disaster occurred. The President is directed to provide such assistance through agreements with States which, in his judgment, have an adequate system for administering such assistance through existing State agencies.
b. Reemployment assistance
   1. State assistance
      A State shall provide, without reimbursement from any funds provided under this Act, reemployment assistance services under any other law administered by the State to individuals receiving benefits under this section.
   2. Federal assistance

The President may provide reemployment assistance services under other laws to individuals who are unemployed as a result of a major disaster and who reside in a State which does not provide such services.

§ 5179. FOOD COUPONS AND DISTRIBUTION {SEC. 412}

a. Persons eligible; terms and conditions
Whenever the President determines that, as a result of a major disaster, low-income households are unable to purchase adequate amounts of nutritious food, he is authorized, under such terms and conditions as he may prescribe, to distribute through the Secretary of Agriculture or other appropriate agencies coupon allotments to such households pursuant to the provisions of the Food Stamp Act of 1964 (P.L. 91-671; 84 Stat. 2048) [7 U.S.C. 2011 et seq.] and to make surplus commodities available pursuant to the provisions of this Act.

b. Duration of assistance; factors considered
The President, through the Secretary of Agriculture or other appropriate agencies, is authorized to continue to make such coupon allotments and surplus commodities available to such households for so long as he determines necessary, taking into consideration such factors as he deems appropriate, including the consequences of the major disaster on the earning power of the households, to which assistance is made available under this section.

c. Food Stamp Act [7 U.S.C. §§ 2011 et seq.] provisions unaffected.
Nothing in this section shall be construed as amending or otherwise changing the provisions of the Food Stamp Act of 1964 except as they relate to the availability of food stamps in an area affected by a major disaster.

§ 5180. FOOD COMMODITIES {SEC. 413}

a. Emergency mass feeding
The President is authorized and directed to assure that adequate stocks of food will be ready and conveniently available for emergency mass feeding or distribution in any area of the United States which suffers a major disaster or emergency.

b. Funds for purchase of food commodities
The Secretary of Agriculture shall utilize funds appropriated under section 612c of title 7, to purchase food commodities necessary to provide

adequate supplies for use in any area of the United States in the event of a major disaster or emergency in such area.

§ 5181. RELOCATION ASSISTANCE {SEC. 414}

Notwithstanding any other provision of law, no person otherwise eligible for any kind of replacement housing payment under the Uniform Relocation Assistance and Real Property Acquisition Policies Act of 1970 (P.L. 91-646) shall be denied such eligibility as a result of his being unable, because of a major disaster as determined by the President, to meet the occupancy requirements set by such Act.

§ 5182. LEGAL SERVICES {SEC. 415}

Whenever the President determines that low-income individuals are unable to secure legal services adequate to meet their needs as a consequence of a major disaster, consistent with the goals of the programs authorized by this Act, the President shall assure that such programs are conducted with the advice and assistance of appropriate Federal agencies and State and local bar associations.

§ 5183. CRISIS COUNSELING ASSISTANCE AND TRAINING {SEC. 416}

The President is authorized to provide professional counseling services, including financial assistance to State or local agencies or private mental health organizations to provide such services or training of disaster workers, to victims of major disasters in order to relieve mental health problems caused or aggravated by such major disaster or its aftermath.

§ 5184. COMMUNITY DISASTER LOANS {SEC. 417}

a. In General.—The President is authorized to make loans to any local government which may suffer a substantial loss of tax and other revenues as a result of a major disaster, and has demonstrated a need for financial assistance in order to perform its governmental functions.

b. Amount.—The amount of any such loan shall be based on need, shall not exceed 25 per centum of the annual operating budget of that local government for the fiscal year in which the major disaster occurs, and shall not exceed $5,000,000.

c. Repayment.—

1. Cancellation.—Repayment of all or any part of such loan to the extent that revenues of the local government during the three full fiscal year

period following the major disaster are insufficient to meet the operating budget of the local government, including additional disaster-related expenses of a municipal operation character shall be cancelled.

2. Condition on continuing eligibility.—A local government shall not be eligible for further assistance under this section during any period in which the local government is in arrears with respect to a required repayment of a loan under this section.

d. Effect on Other Assistance.—Any loans made under this section shall not reduce or otherwise affect any grants or other assistance under this Act.

§ 5185. EMERGENCY COMMUNICATIONS {SEC. 418}

The President is authorized during, or in anticipation of an emergency or major disaster to establish temporary communications systems and to make such communications available to State and local government officials and other persons as he deems appropriate.

§ 5186. EMERGENCY PUBLIC TRANSPORTATION {SEC. 419}

The President is authorized to provide temporary public transportation service in an area affected by a major disaster to meet emergency needs and to provide transportation to governmental offices, supply centers, stores, post offices, schools, major employment centers, and such other places as may be necessary in order to enable the community to resume its normal pattern of life as soon as possible.

§ 5187. FIRE MANAGEMENT ASSISTANCE. {SEC. 420}

a. In General.—The President is authorized to provide assistance, including grants, equipment, supplies, and personnel, to any State or local government for the mitigation, management, and control of any fire on public or private forest land or grassland that threatens such destruction as would constitute a major disaster.

b. Coordination With State and Tribal Departments of Forestry.—In providing assistance under this section, the President shall coordinate with State and tribal departments of forestry.

c. Essential Assistance.—In providing assistance under this section, the President may use the authority provided under section 5170b of this title.

d. Rules and Regulations.—The President shall prescribe such rules and regulations as are necessary to carry out this section.

§ 5188. Timber sale contracts {Sec. 421}

a. Cost-sharing arrangement

Where an existing timber sale contract between the Secretary of Agriculture or the Secretary of the Interior and a timber purchaser does not provide relief from major physical change not due to negligence of the purchaser prior to approval of construction of any section of specified road or of any other specified development facility and, as a result of a major disaster, a major physical change results in additional construction work in connection with such road or facility by such purchaser with an estimated cost, as determined by the appropriate Secretary, (1) of more than $ 1,000 for sales under one million board feet, (2) of more than $1 per thousand board feet for sales of one to three million board feet, or (3) of more than $3,000 for sales over three million board feet, such increased construction cost shall be borne by the United States.

b. Cancellation of authority

If the appropriate Secretary determines that damages are so great that restoration, reconstruction, or construction is not practical under the cost-sharing arrangement authorized by subsection (a) of this section, he may allow cancellation of a contract entered into by his Department notwithstanding contrary provisions therein.

c. Public notice of sale

The Secretary of Agriculture is authorized to reduce to seven days the minimum period of advance public notice required by section 476 of title 16, in connection with the sale of timber from national forests, whenever the Secretary determines that (1) the sale of such timber will assist in the construction of any area of a State damaged by a major disaster, (2) the sale of such timber will assist in sustaining the economy of such area, or (3) the sale of such timber is necessary to salvage the value of timber damaged in such major disaster or to protect undamaged timber.

d. State grants for removal of damaged timber; reimbursement of expenses limited to salvage value of removed timber.

The President, when he determines it to be in the public interest, is authorized to make grants to any State or local government for the purpose of removing from privately owned lands timber damaged as a result of a major disaster, and such State or local government is authorized upon application, to make payments out of such grants to any person for reimbursement of expenses actually incurred by such person in the removal of damaged timber, not to exceed the amount that such expenses exceed the salvage value of such timber.

Appendix C

§ 5189. SIMPLIFIED PROCEDURES {SEC. 422}

If the Federal estimate of the cost of—

1. repairing, restoring, reconstructing, or replacing under section 5172 of this title any damaged or destroyed public facility or private nonprofit facility,
2. emergency assistance under section 5170b or 5192 of this title, or
3. debris removed under section 5173 of this title, is less than $35,000, the President (on application of the State or local government or the owner or operator of the private nonprofit facility) may make the contribution to such State or local government or owner or operator under section 5170b, 5172, 5173 or 5192 of this title, as the case may be, on the basis of such Federal estimate. Such $35,000 amount shall be adjusted annually to reflect changes in the Consumer Price Index for All Urban Consumers published by the Department of Labor.

§ 5189A. APPEALS OF ASSISTANCE DECISIONS {SEC. 423}

a. Right of appeal

Any decision regarding eligibility for, from, or amount of assistance under this title [42 U.S.C. 5170 et seq.] may be appealed within 60 days after the date on which the applicant for such assistance is notified of the award or denial of award of such assistance.

b. Period for decision

A decision regarding an appeal under subsection (a) shall be rendered within 90 days after the date on which the Federal official designated to administer such appeals receives notice of such appeal.

c. Rules

The President shall issue rules which provide for the fair and impartial consideration of appeals under this section.

§ 5189B. DATE OF ELIGIBILITY; EXPENSES INCURRED BEFORE DATE OF DISASTER {SEC. 424}

Eligibility for Federal assistance under this title shall begin on the date of the occurrence of the event which results in a declaration by the President that a major disaster exists; except that reasonable expenses which are incurred in anticipation of and immediately preceding such event may be eligible for Federal assistance under this Act.

APPENDIX D

FEMA ORGANIZATIONAL CHART

The organizational arrangements of FEMA, depicted as of January 23, 2006, follow changes initiated by Department of Homeland Security Michael Chertoff in 2005. As a unit of the Department of Homeland Security (DHS), FEMA has three mains divisions that cover the functions of disaster response, mitigation, has recovery. Preparedness functions previously delegated to FEMA are now part of a separate preparedness directorate in the DHS. FEMA also contains numerous offices relating to policy and planning, administration, and regional operations.

Source: Hogue, Henry B., and Keith Bea. "Federal Emergency Management and Homeland Security Organization: Hostorical Developments and Legislative Options." CRS Report for Congress. Available online. URL://http://www.mipt.org/getDoc.asp?id=3052&type=d. Posted April 19, 2006.

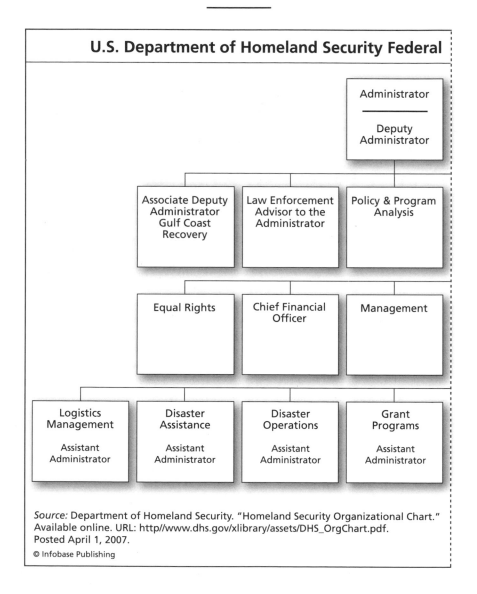

U.S. Department of Homeland Security Federal

Administrator

Deputy Administrator

Associate Deputy Administrator Gulf Coast Recovery

Law Enforcement Advisor to the Administrator

Policy & Program Analysis

Equal Rights

Chief Financial Officer

Management

Logistics Management

Assistant Administrator

Disaster Assistance

Assistant Administrator

Disaster Operations

Assistant Administrator

Grant Programs

Assistant Administrator

Source: Department of Homeland Security. "Homeland Security Organizational Chart." Available online. URL: http//www.dhs.gov/xlibrary/assets/DHS_OrgChart.pdf. Posted April 1, 2007.

© Infobase Publishing

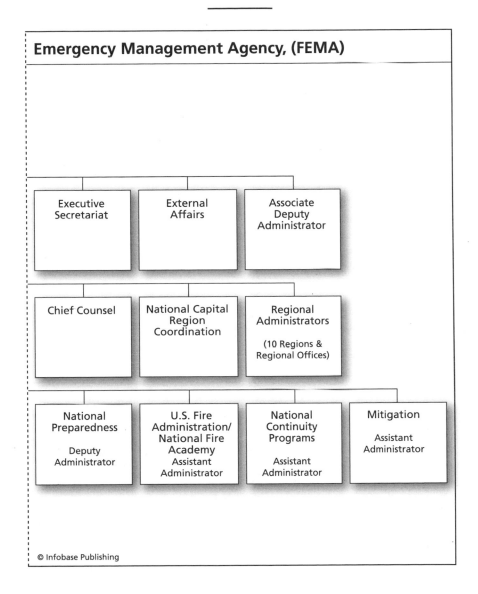

Emergency Management Agency, (FEMA)

| Executive Secretariat | External Affairs | Associate Deputy Administrator |

| Chief Counsel | National Capital Region Coordination | Regional Administrators

(10 Regions & Regional Offices) |

| National Preparedness

Deputy Administrator | U.S. Fire Administration/ National Fire Academy Assistant Administrator | National Continuity Programs

Assistant Administrator | Mitigation

Assistant Administrator |

© Infobase Publishing

279

INDEX

Locators in **boldface** indicate main topics. Locators followed by *c* indicate chronology entries. Locators followed by *b* indicate biographical entries. Locators followed by *g* indicate glossary entries.

Index

Index

Index

Index

Index

Index

Index

Index